J.D. FERGUSSON

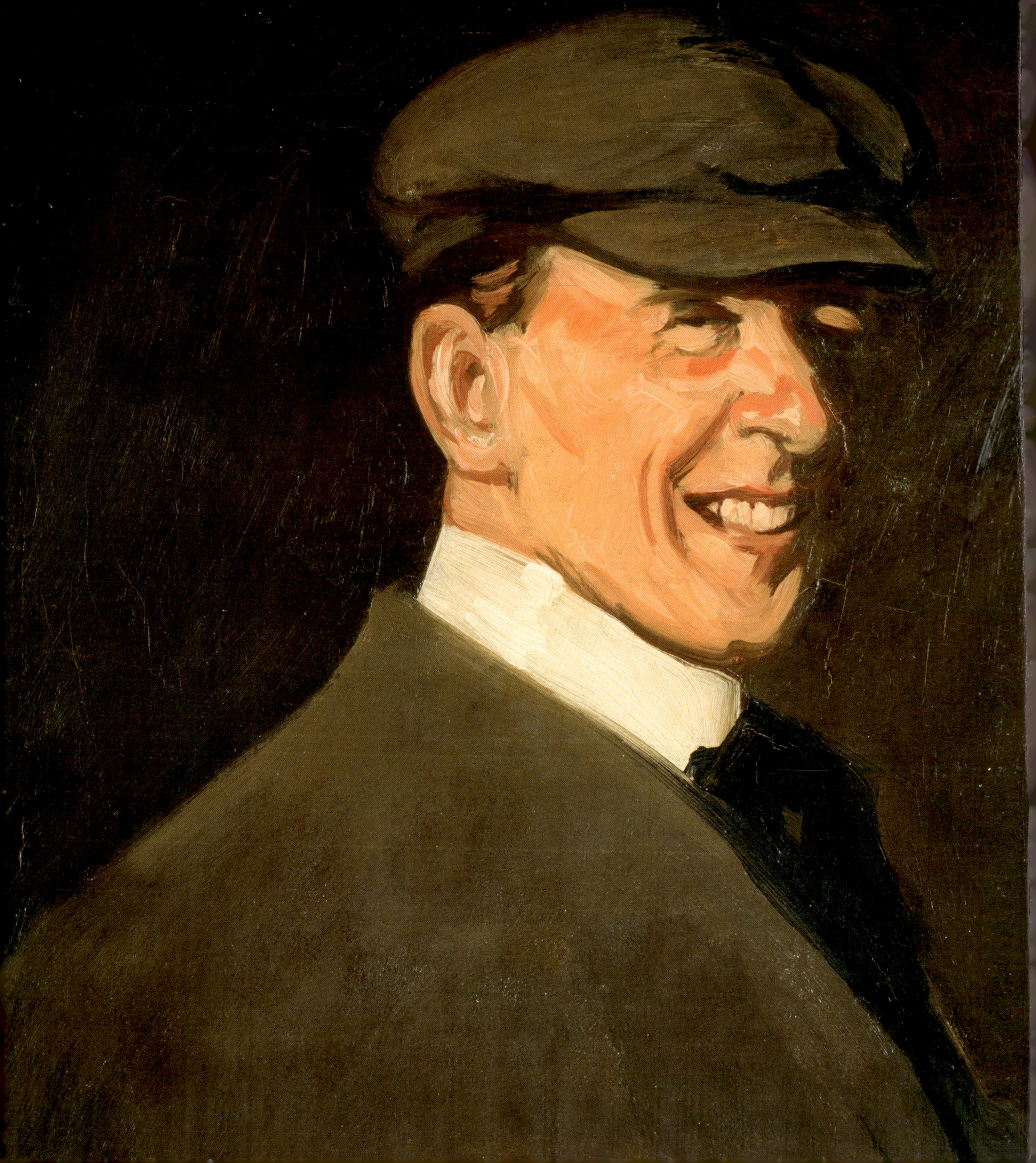

J.D. FERGUSSON

Alice Strang, Elizabeth Cumming and Sheila McGregor

National Galleries of Scotland
Edinburgh 2013

Published by the Trustees of the National Galleries of Scotland to accompany the exhibition, *J.D. Fergusson*, held at the Scottish National Gallery of Modern Art, Edinburgh, from 7 December 2013 until 15 June 2014.

Tour of selected works to Pallant House Gallery, Chichester, from 5 July until 19 October 2014.

A partnership between the National Galleries of Scotland, Edinburgh and The Fergusson Gallery, Perth & Kinross Council

Exhibition curated by Alice Strang
Research by Rachel Smith, Doughty Hanson Assistant Curator

ISBN 978-1-906270-62-9

Designed and typeset in Arnhem by Dalrymple
Printed on Perigord 150gsm by die Keure, Belgium

Front cover: detail from *Le Manteau Chinois* [64]
Back cover: detail from *Bathing Boxes and Tents at St. Palais* [51]
Frontispiece: detail from *Self-portrait* [18]

This exhibition has been made possible with the assistance of the Scottish Government Indemnity Scheme provided by Scottish Government.

The proceeds from the sale of this book go towards supporting the National Galleries of Scotland. For a complete list of current publications, please write to NGS Publishing, Scottish National Gallery of Modern Art, 75 Belford Road, Edinburgh EH4 3DR, or visit our website: www.nationalgalleries.org

National Galleries of Scotland is a charity registered in Scotland (no.SC003728)

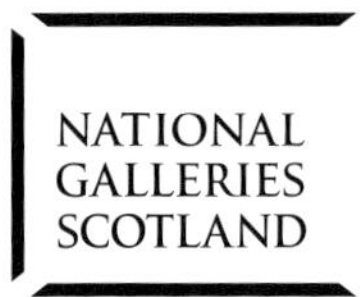

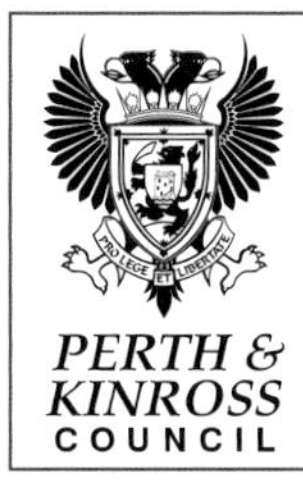

CONTENTS

SPONSOR'S FOREWORD

Dickson Minto W.S., established in 1985, is a leading multinational practice law firm providing corporate and commercial legal services to national and international clients. With offices in London and Edinburgh, the firm is committed to delivering the highest standard of service to all clients whether small, medium or large, private or public. We also have a high regard for the visual arts and are delighted to be sponsoring the exhibition *J.D. Fergusson*, following upon our first two sponsorships with the National Galleries of Scotland of the exhibitions *F.C.B. Cadell* and *S.J. Peploe*. Of the group of artists known as the Scottish Colourists, Fergusson had the most international career, assimilating and developing in particular initiatives in French painting and having a significant involvement in Anglo-American art circles.

We are pleased to be associated with this very important retrospective of the artist by the National Galleries of Scotland, the first major retrospective of Fergusson's work to be mounted for forty years. We know that this exhibition will give enormous pleasure to every visitor and are delighted to have had the opportunity to support another outstanding exhibition at the Galleries. We look forward to extending our relationship with the National Galleries of Scotland for many years to come.

DIRECTORS' FOREWORD

This book accompanies the first major exhibition of the work of J.D. Fergusson to be mounted by the National Galleries of Scotland. It concludes our *Scottish Colourist Series* devoted to the work of F.C.B. Cadell (2011), S.J. Peploe (2012) and J.D. Fergusson (2013). Along with G.L. Hunter, these four artists are widely known as the Scottish Colourists.

Following Fergusson's death in 1961, his partner Margaret Morris established the J.D. Fergusson Art Foundation. The works and archive for which they were responsible now form the core of the collection of The Fergusson Gallery, which opened in Perth in 1992. We are delighted to be working in partnership with Perth & Kinross Council, who run the gallery and who are the major lenders to the exhibition. We would like to thank Jenny Kinnear, Maria Devaney and their colleagues for their contribution to this project.

We are grateful to all the lenders to the exhibition. The University of Stirling have lent seven paintings given to them by Morris and the Fergusson Foundation in 1968. The J.D. Fergusson Art Foundation, Edinburgh Decorative & Fine Arts Society, Tayside Decorative & Fine Arts Society and Iain More have given conservation grants. Our thanks are also due to those who have negotiated loans on our behalf and who have helped with our research. We have enjoyed contact with those who knew 'Fergus and Meg', who have shared their memories with us. An anonymous donation of thirty-one exhibition catalogues relating to Fergusson's career has made a tremendous difference to our archive.

Alice Strang, Senior Curator at the Scottish National Gallery of Modern Art, has curated the complete *Scottish Colourist Series*, with her customary passion and professionalism. Shortly before his untimely death, Nigel Doughty agreed to fund a post to support our Peploe project, through the British private equity firm which he co-founded. Doughty Hanson & Co. has since generously agreed to extend this funding to help deliver the Fergusson project. Rachel Smith has thus ably assisted Alice and we would like to thank all of their colleagues who have also been involved. Alice, Elizabeth Cumming and Sheila McGregor have written essays for this publication.

We are delighted that selected paintings and sculptures will tour to Pallant House Gallery, Chichester. It has been a pleasure working on this with Gregory Perry, Simon Martin and their colleagues.

Finally, we would like to offer a special thank you to Bruce Minto for his encouragement and enthusiasm for our work. We are thrilled that Dickson Minto W.S. have generously agreed to continue their patronage of the National Galleries of Scotland by supporting the Fergusson project. This means that, in a gesture of outstanding corporate philanthropy, they have sponsored the entire *Scottish Colourist Series*.

SIR JOHN LEIGHTON
Director-General, National Galleries of Scotland

SIMON GROOM
Director, Scottish National Gallery of Modern Art

PREFACE

Perth & Kinross Council is delighted to be a partner in the J.D. Fergusson project with the National Galleries of Scotland. It is wholly fitting that, just over fifty years since his death, Fergusson's key place in the history of early modern British art is being reasserted with this catalogue and exhibitions in two Scottish cities; one in Edinburgh, the place of his birth, and one in the locale of his ancestral home, Perthshire.

What set Fergusson apart from the other Scottish Colourists was his sustained contact with France and the sheer length of his prolific career which began in Paris in the 1890s, at a critical moment in the development of the Modern Movement. In 1909, his place as a pioneer of European Modernism was acknowledged in Paris when he was elected a *sociétaire* of the Salon d'Automne. Fergusson commented: 'To me, considering myself a revolutionary, this was a very great honour – and being based on the Glasgow School, it had the effect of confirming my feeling of independence, the greatest thing in the world, not merely in art but in everything.'

By referring back to the Glasgow School, Fergusson placed his own achievement within the vigorous, distinct tradition of art in Scotland, underpinned by thinking and intellect, painterly approach and an international outlook. Later, he became a major contributor to debates about the 'Scottishness' of Scottish art and cultural identity. Increasingly he saw its source, stretching back through the Scottish Enlightenment to where his ancestral roots lay, in Celtic culture. Both his parents were from Highland Perthshire as his father came from Logierait near Pitlochry and his mother from Moulin, a few miles further north. Although by the time he was born his family had moved to Leith, Fergusson believed it was his Celtic ancestry that fuelled his creativity, as he searched for his heritage and identity. He subsequently cited his interest in Celtic themes and design as beginning as far back as his developmental years in Paris around 1910–13.

Returning to Scotland in 1939 with his partner, Margaret Morris, after prolonged stays in France and England, Fergusson also felt this Celtic consciousness was the touchstone for a new, radical Scottish art. Settling in Glasgow brought him into contact with Scottish intellectuals such as Hugh MacDiarmid and the publisher William MacLellan, who also looked to Celtic spirit for a cultural vision of renewal. Fergusson continued to engage with this debate, and to champion independent artists in Scotland until his death in 1961.

Fergusson's place as one of the leading figures of Celtic Modernism is the key theme of the partnership exhibition in Perth at The Fergusson Gallery, titled *J.D. Fergusson: Picture of a Celt*. The Fergusson Gallery has been home to the largest and most comprehensive collection of Fergusson's work since it opened in 1992. The collection includes just short of 4,000 examples of his artwork (paintings in oil and watercolour, drawings, sculpture and sketchbooks) representing all phases of his career, plus a substantial archive which includes correspondence, photographs, exhibition catalogues, journals and press cuttings. A collection of personalia such as his art materials and library help complete the picture, offering an unusually in-depth window into one artist's life and career.

The collection was gifted to Perth & Kinross, along with the copyright of all of Fergusson's work, by the J.D. Fergusson Art Foundation which had been established by Margaret Morris in 1963. Its primary aim was to secure a permanent home for the substantial collection, with space to show Fergusson's artwork alongside that of other progressive artists of Scottish descent. This aim was realised with the opening of The Fergusson Gallery and then, three years later, when they set up the J.D. Fergusson Arts Award Trust. The Trust provides encouragement and support to Scottish artists by way of an annual award, which alternates each year between a travel bursary and financial assistance for development of new work along with an exhibition opportunity at The Fergusson Gallery.

Perth & Kinross Council acknowledges the Foundation's valuable and ongoing support towards realising the potential of Fergusson's rich artistic legacy, which is now officially designated a Recognised Collection of National Significance to Scotland. With regard to this partnership project, the Council would like to thank them for their generous grant for conservation which has made it possible to include several of Fergusson's large key works in the National Galleries of Scotland show. Similarly, it would like to acknowledge the financial assistance given by Tayside Decorative & Fine Arts Society in this respect.

Perth & Kinross Council is very pleased to have the opportunity to work with the National Galleries of Scotland to reaffirm Fergusson's place as a leader of international art and is proud to lend paintings, sculpture and archival material to their major retrospective exhibition. Together, the exhibitions in Edinburgh and Perth offer an insight into a man of great creativity and far-sighted vision who, without doubt, possessed the necessary qualities for modern painting which he identified in *Modern Scottish Painting* (1943): 'vision, imagination, independence of spirit, rhythm, colour sense, courage, invention and creative power'.

JENNY KINNEAR
Curator, The Fergusson Gallery, Perth & Kinross Council

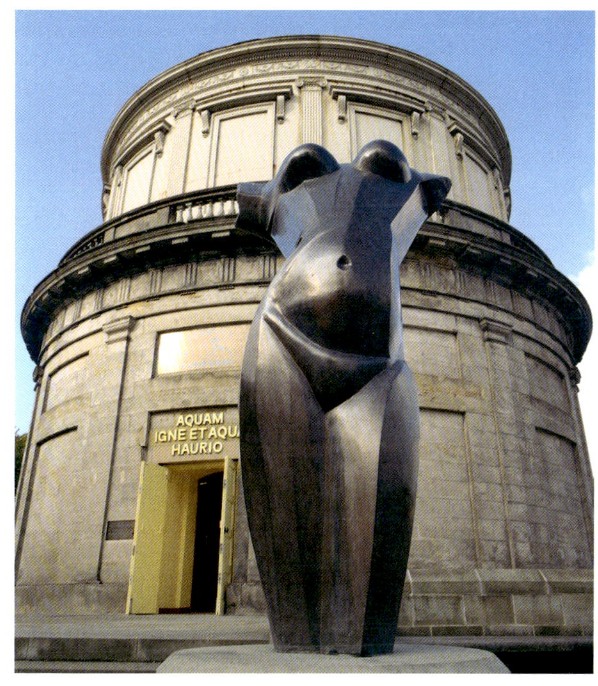

[1] The Fergusson Gallery, Perth

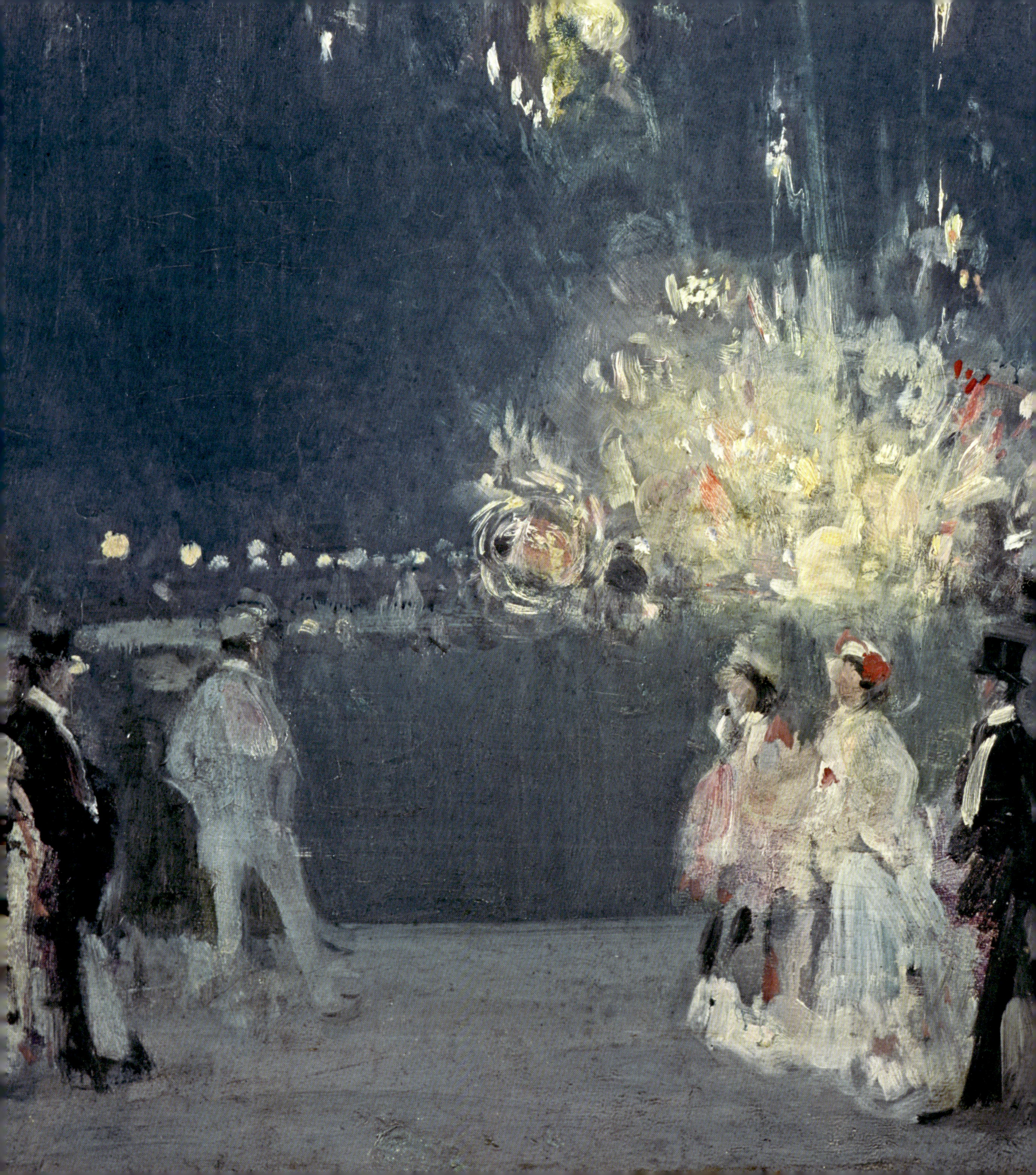

1 · Introduction: Fergusson and the Scottish Colourists

ALICE STRANG

J.D. FERGUSSON (1874–1961) was proud to be a Scot, despite spending the majority of his career in France and England. In 1943 he explained: 'I ... decided to persist in being what I considered an artist, and a Scots artist, and the art atmosphere and the painting I was surrounded by in Scotland, in my opinion, were not Scots at all.'[1] A love of colour and its skilful manipulation is apparent throughout Fergusson's work; of equal importance was his use of rhythmic line. The classification of him as a 'Scottish Colourist' is therefore not incorrect, but it is not entirely accurate.

The other artists most commonly known as 'the Scottish Colourists' are Francis Campbell Boileau Cadell (1883–1937), George Leslie Hunter (1877–1931) and Samuel John Peploe (1871–1935). All four spent time in France, particularly in Paris, and had an early awareness of developments in French painting from Manet and the Impressionists to Cézanne. They also shared a love of brilliant colour, taken in part from Fauve artists like Matisse and Derain. Fergusson outlived the others by some thirty years and exhibited with them on only three occasions whilst they were all alive.[2] He and Peploe were usually singled out as the leaders of the group, with the critic P.G. Konody stating in *The Times* 'Mr Fergusson is the most stimulating and intriguing of this group of modern Scotsmen.'[3]

The artists never formed an official association with each other; rather their work was displayed together for commercial reasons. The term 'Scottish Colourists' was not coined until an exhibition of that name held at T. & R. Annan & Sons in Glasgow in 1948, to which Fergusson lent four paintings.[4] T.J. Honeyman's influential book of 1950, *Three Scottish Colourists*, omitted Fergusson, reflecting the taste of Ion Harrison, on whose collection the book was based.[5]

[2] Detail from *Dieppe, 14 July 1905: Night,* 1905 [23]

Of the four, Fergusson first became friends with Peploe. They are thought to have met at the studio club run by Joseph Simpson in Edinburgh in about 1900.[6] Both men had begun sending to the annual exhibitions of the Royal Scottish Academy (RSA), Royal Glasgow Institute (RGI) and Society of Scottish Artists (SSA), but neither had yet had a solo exhibition. From 1904 they spent the summers painting together in France before Fergusson decided to settle in Paris in 1907. Peploe joined him there in 1910 and they spent two years experiencing at first hand the birth of modern art. Peploe returned to Edinburgh in 1912 and never again lived in the same country as Fergusson. They remained close, however, and in 1945 Fergusson declared 'it was, I think, one of the best friendships that has ever been between two painters'.[7]

It is thought that Fergusson met Hunter in Paris by 1906, before the latter met Peploe or Cadell.[8] Both were self-taught and despite Hunter's nomadic lifestyle and Fergusson's bases in Paris and London, they stayed in contact, not least through their mutual friendship with Peploe. In 1922 Hunter explained that he, Fergusson and Peploe hoped to arrange 'some lectures in Glasgow on modern art to colour this winter – [Roger] Fry if one can get him, etc. .... Fergusson proposed that Scotland takes its place as foremost in culture as in war.'[9] Hunter summed up Fergusson as 'a most likeable chap, determined yet sympathetic'.[10]

Fergusson was the least close to Cadell, who was nine years his junior. They both registered at the Académie Julian in Paris in 1898 but it is unlikely that they met at that point. They probably became aware of each other through Peploe, whom Cadell knew by 1909 when they had solo exhibitions at The Scottish Gallery in Edinburgh. Indeed, in 1936, Cadell told Ion Harrison that he had not seen Fergusson since 1909.[11]

Fergusson could be claimed by any of the groups of creative people with whom he was involved throughout his life, from the 'Rhythmists' of Paris before the First World War, to the New Scottish Group of Glasgow of the 1940s and 1950s. He was the most intellectual and political of the Scottish Colourists, becoming involved with various journals including *Rhythm* (1911–12) and *Scottish Art and Letters* (1944–50) as Art Editor and writer; his book *Modern Scottish Painting* was published in 1943.[12] Throughout his life, Fergusson made tremendous efforts to help other artists and to promote modern art.

Fergusson was the most international of the Scottish Colourists, exhibiting outside Scotland from early in his career.[13] His first solo exhibition was in London in 1905. Fergusson left Edinburgh in 1907 and did not settle in Scotland again until 1939. Living in Paris between 1907 and 1913, London between 1914 and 1929 and returning to Paris from 1929 until 1939 before settling in Glasgow, meant that Fergusson was involved with the European art world in a way in which his Colourist colleagues were not.

Of the four, Fergusson was the only one whose personal partner was also of historical significance. After they met in 1913, Fergusson's career became inextricable from that of the dance pioneer Margaret Morris (1891–1980); his interest in dance expanded to costume and set design for her, and her pupils provided an endless supply of models. The female form was by far Fergusson's preferred genre, in contrast to the other Colourists who favoured the still life and the landscape. He was the only one of them to work in three dimensions and his sculpture, particularly of the period of about 1918 to 1922, is an important, if little-known aspect of his oeuvre.

Due to his longevity, Fergusson became involved with the next generation of artists. He has the most obvious legacy of the Colourists, not least in the encouragement he gave to artists such as Donald Bain (1904–1979) and Pat Douthwaite (1939–2002). Thanks to Morris's indefatigable efforts on his behalf following Fergusson's death, a gallery dedicated to his work opened in Perth in 1992. The foundation established in his name in 1963 continues to support up-and-coming artists.

NOTE: *Fergusson usually signed his works and often dated them, although sometimes years after their creation and somewhat unreliably; where evidence for dates has been found they are given, otherwise approximate dates have been suggested. Scant information exists about his sculptures, so approximate dates are provided where definite ones are unknown; cast sculptures are referred to as bronze unless they have been specifically identified as brass. Dimensions are in centimetres, height before width, before depth.*

[3] J.D. Fergusson in his Paris studio, *c.*1910

The Fergusson Gallery, Perth & Kinross Council

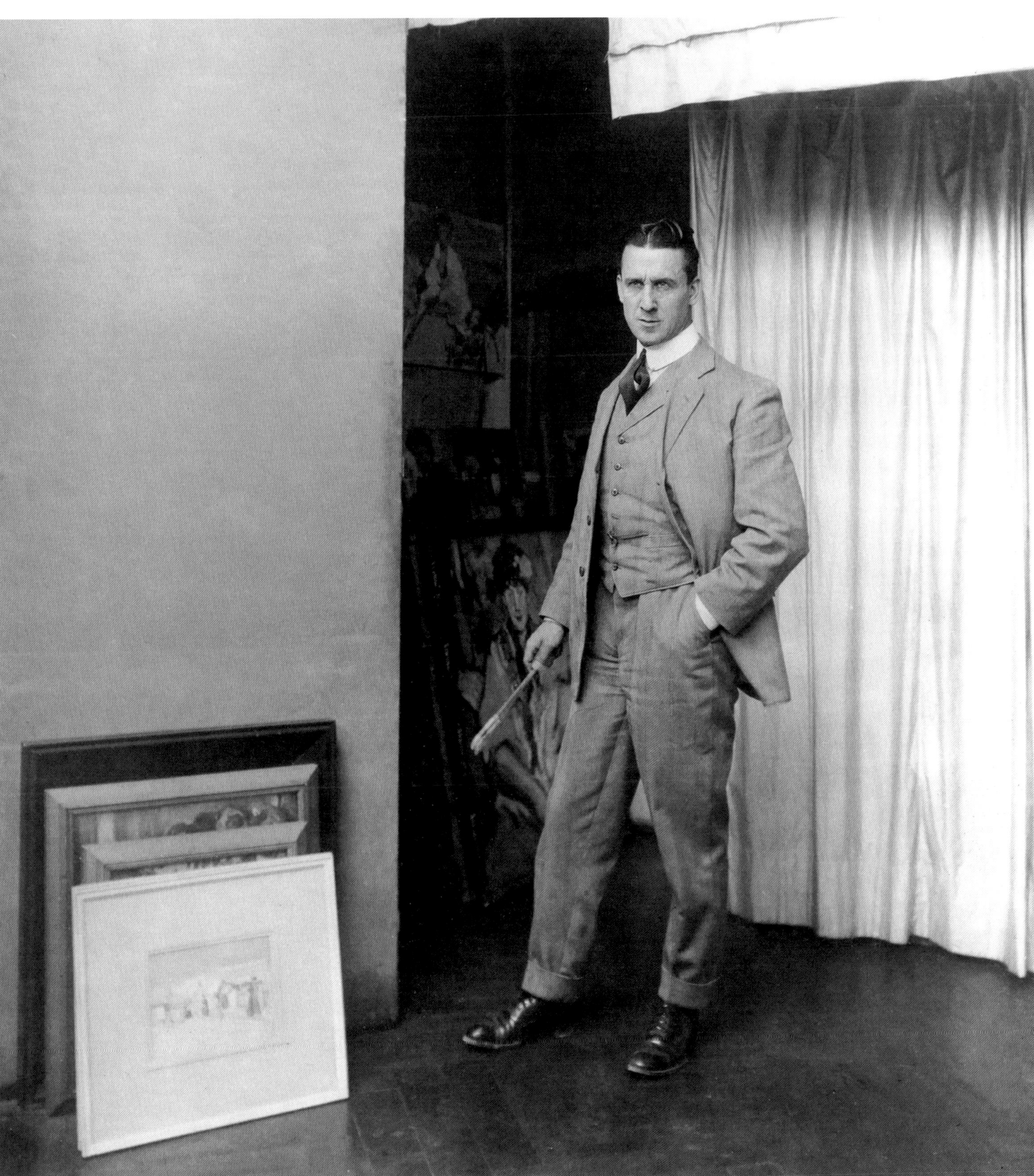

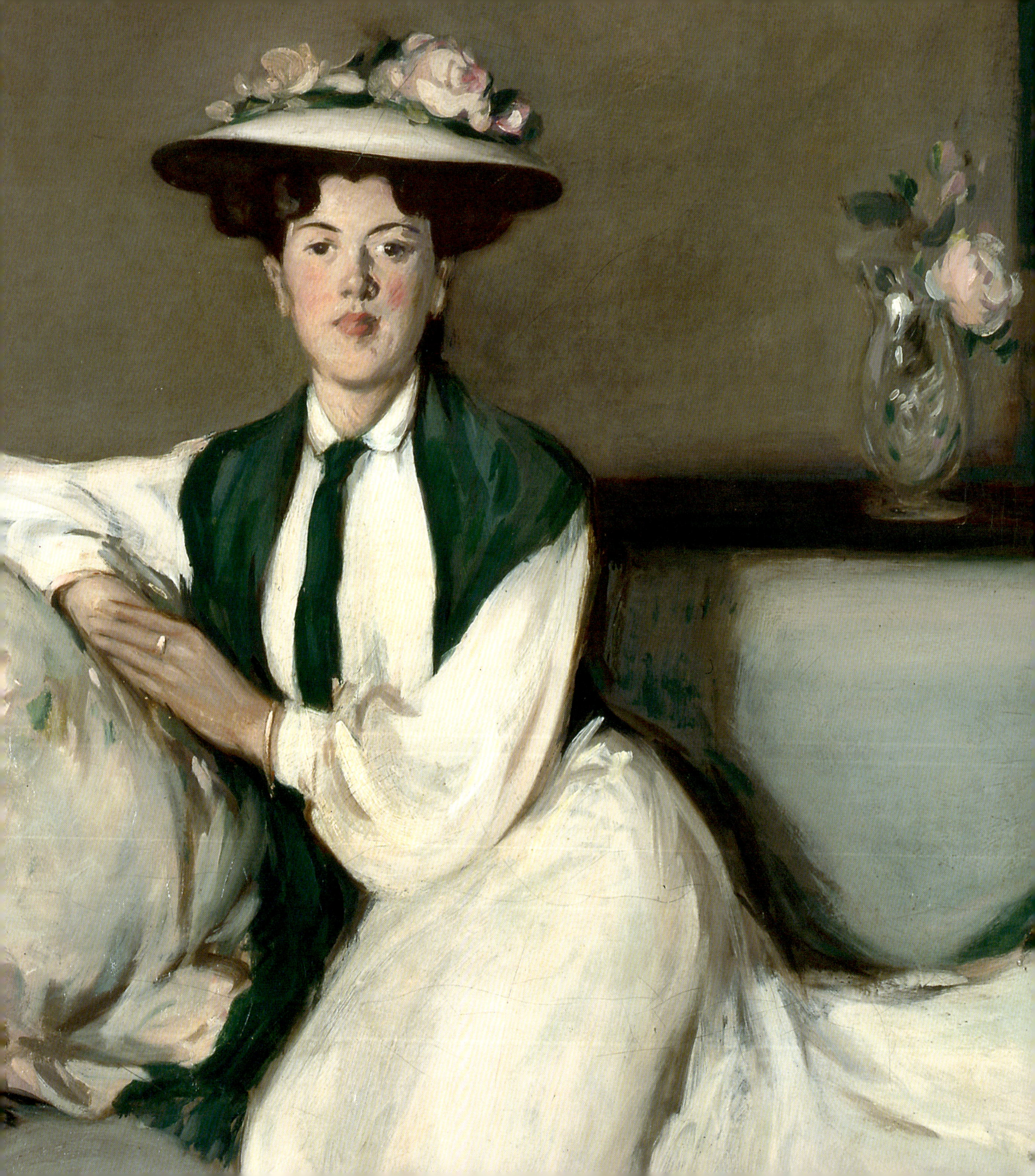

2 · 'Trying for truth, for reality; through light': A Life of J.D. Fergusson

ALICE STRANG

IN 1905 JOHN DUNCAN FERGUSSON stated that the artist is 'trying for truth, for reality; through light'.[1] This ethos informed his international career, which lasted for over sixty years. Fergusson was essentially self-taught, was opposed to 'the establishment' and developed a profound sense of his Scottishness whilst living in France and London. His belief in the importance of art was conveyed through membership of artist groups, exhibitions, discussion and publications; he did much to encourage other artists, especially following his move to Glasgow in 1939. From 1913, Fergusson's involvement with the work of his partner, the dance pioneer Margaret Morris, meant that he was immersed in many branches of the creative arts.[2] Indeed Morris, her Margaret Morris Movement (MMM) technique and her pupils informed much of Fergusson's output, and the female form as subject matter dominates his oeuvre.[3] Fergusson made his name in Paris between 1907 and 1913 when he occupied a unique position amongst British artists during the birth of modern Western art. It is on the originality of the work he made then that Fergusson's reputation continues to rest, and it is this that earned him the description of 'the doyen of modern Scottish painting' following his death in 1961.[4]

LEITH AND EDINBURGH

Fergusson was born on 9 March 1874 at 7 Crown Street, Leith, near Edinburgh. His father, John Ferguson [sic] (1839–1906) [7], was born in Logierait in Perthshire. In 1870 he married Christina Fergusson (b.1845) [6], who came from Moulin in the same county.[5] Both of his parents spoke Gaelic and Fergusson's Highland ancestry had more influence on his life than his father's profession as a wine and spirit merchant. Fergusson was the eldest of four children; his birth was followed by that of Elizabeth in 1877, Christina in 1880 and Robert in 1882. Perhaps due to his unorthodox lifestyle, Fergusson later became estranged from his relatives.[6]

After attending the Royal High School in Edinburgh and Blair Lodge near Linlithgow, Fergusson claimed that he began to study Medicine at Edinburgh University. No records exist to prove this, but he did meet John MacMillan Marshall, whilst sketching in a university Anatomy class, and painted his portrait.[7] Fergusson's artistic ability was encouraged by his mother from an early age, but it was not until the late 1890s that he gained his father's support. As Fergusson recalled, 'he said, "Well, John, I'll give you some money and you can do what you like with it." So I went every year in May to Paris, and made the money last as long as possible, walked everywhere and never took a bus.'[8] Having spurned the classical training available at the Trustees School of Art in Edinburgh, Fergusson attended the French capital's more informal Académie Colarossi, where one could work from the model, and the Académie Julian, where he signed in for a session on 11 April 1898.[9] Further travels took him to Morocco in 1899 and to Spain in 1901.

Fergusson exhibited his work for the first time at the RGI annual exhibition of 1897. By 1902 he had taken on his first studio, at 16 Picardy Place, Edinburgh. He paid an annual rent of £12 for it, presumably from his income as owner of the Cathedral Hotel at 71 Cockburn Street, next door to his father's spirit merchant business.[10] During this period he was a familiar figure in Princes Street Gardens [8], where he painted swiftly and spontaneously in the French *plein-air* manner, on small panels, as can be seen in *Bank of Scotland from Princes Street Gardens* [22].

When Fergusson met S.J. Peploe in about 1900, it is clear that the two established an immediate rapport.

[4] Detail from *The White Dress: Portrait of Jean*, 1904 [21]

This, and the influence that the elder Peploe had on Fergusson, is evident from the similarities between the self-portraits which the friends painted around this time [18, 5]. Peploe's interest in seventeenth-century Dutch old masters such as Frans Hals (*c.*1580/85–1666) and Rembrandt van Rijn (1606–1669) can be seen, whilst both men admired the paintings of the French nineteenth-century artist Édouard Manet (1832–1883). Fergusson's work was originally known as *Man Laughing*, perhaps in reference to Peploe's portrait of the Edinburgh tramp Tom Morris of the early 1900s.[11] The accomplishment of *The Silk Hat* [19] explains why the critic Frank Rutter recalled how 'the personal force of his portraits first thrilled us amid the rather staid surroundings of the RBA exhibitions'.[12]

This Dutch influence gave way to Edwardian elegance and opulence in Fergusson's contemporary depictions of women, most significantly in paintings of Jean Maconochie (1880–1945) [20, 21]. A member of Fergusson's social circle in Leith and his partner for a time from about 1902, Jean [9] was typical of the independent women who rose above social mores, to whom Fergusson was attracted.[13] The influence of Hals is still apparent in *Jean Maconochie* [20], which shows Fergusson's emerging interest in women's millinery. The life-size *The White Dress: Portrait of Jean* [21] is a *tour de force* image of stylish and confident femininity, which was to become a defining characteristic of Fergusson's oeuvre. In it, his confidence in entering the territory of more established artists such as John Singer Sargent (1856–1925) and John Lavery (1856–1941) is remarkable.

From 1904 Fergusson and Peploe embarked on summer painting trips to France, to destinations including Berneval, Étaples and Paris-Plage (now Le Touquet) [52]. Fergusson painted the magnificent *Dieppe, 14 July 1905: Night* [23], in a manner reminiscent of James Abbott McNeill Whistler (1834–1903), following a visit to the coastal town in Normandy; Peploe appears as the figure in grey to the left. Peploe's influence is also felt in the still lifes which Fergusson painted during this period, such as *Jonquils and Silver* [24] and *Carnations and Narcissus* [25]. Moreover, they also show a shared interest in Diego Velázquez (1599–1660), whose work Fergusson would have seen whilst in Spain in 1901. Whereas Peploe was to become most celebrated for his endeavours in this genre, Fergusson only returned to it occasionally during his career.

Fergusson exhibited in London for the first time in 1901, when he showed at the RBA. Four years later, he had his first solo exhibition, at the Baillie Gallery in the English capital. For the next eighteen years his professional focus was on London and Paris; he did not have a solo exhibition in Scotland until 1923.[14] An increasing interest in developments in contemporary art in Paris and parallel frustration with the conservatism of the art world in Scotland, an inheritance following his father's death in 1906, and the start of his relationship with the painter Anne Estelle Rice (1877–1959) [10] in Paris-Plage in 1907, culminated in Fergusson's decision to move to Paris later that year. He was not to live in Scotland again until 1939.

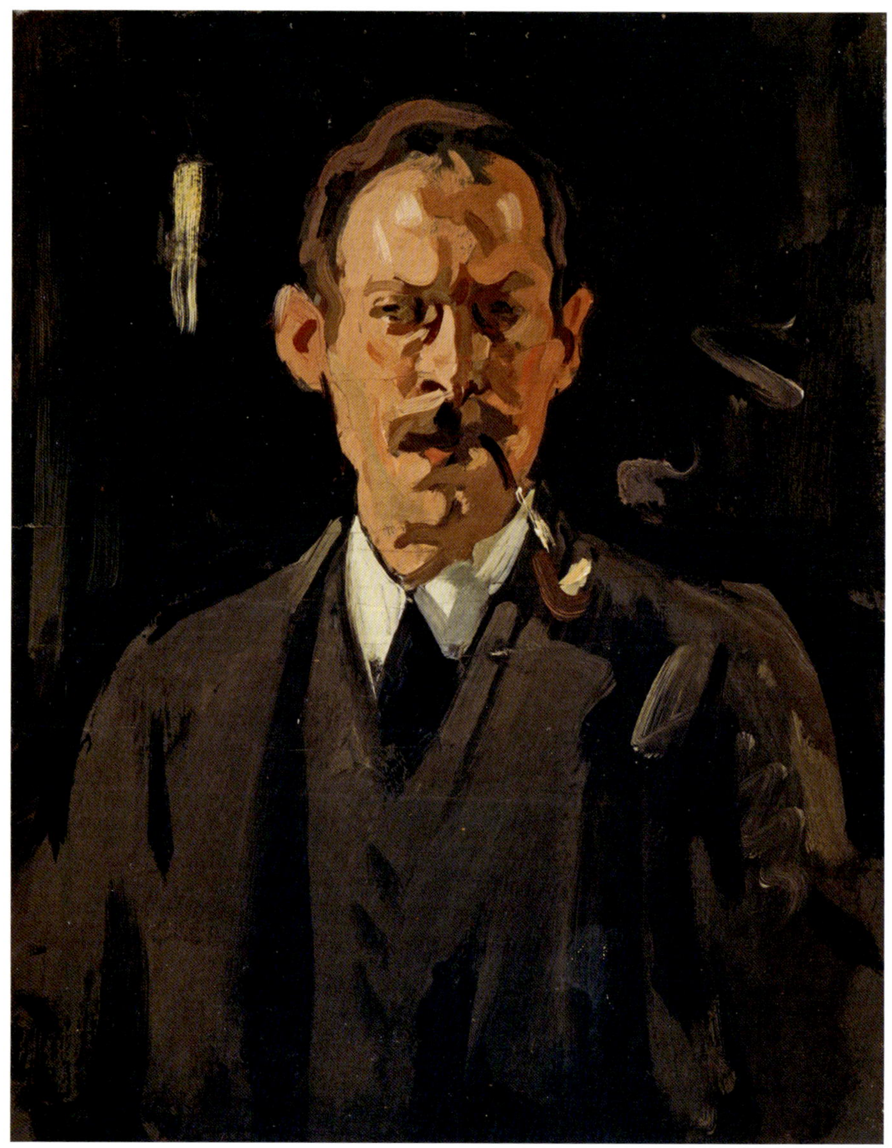

[5] S. J. Peploe
Self Portrait, *c.*1900
Oil on canvas, 50.8 × 40.6
Scottish National Portrait Gallery, Edinburgh, presented by John Thorburn, 1947

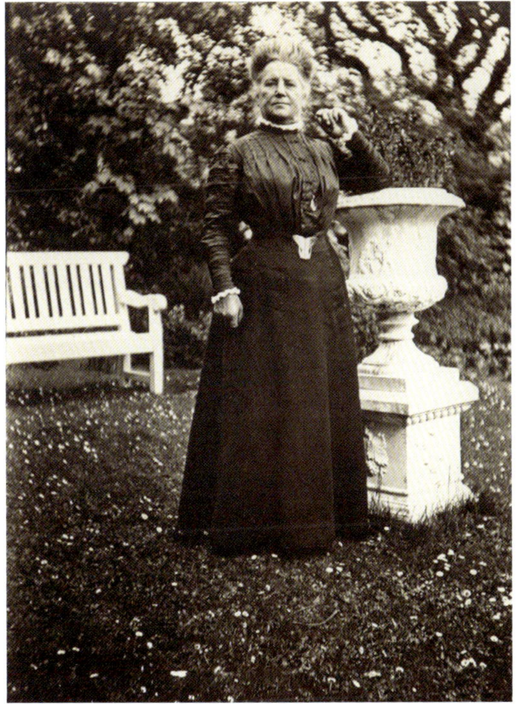

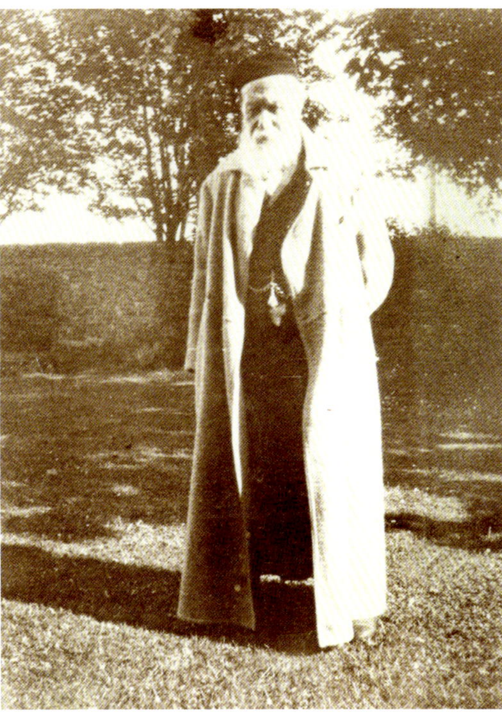

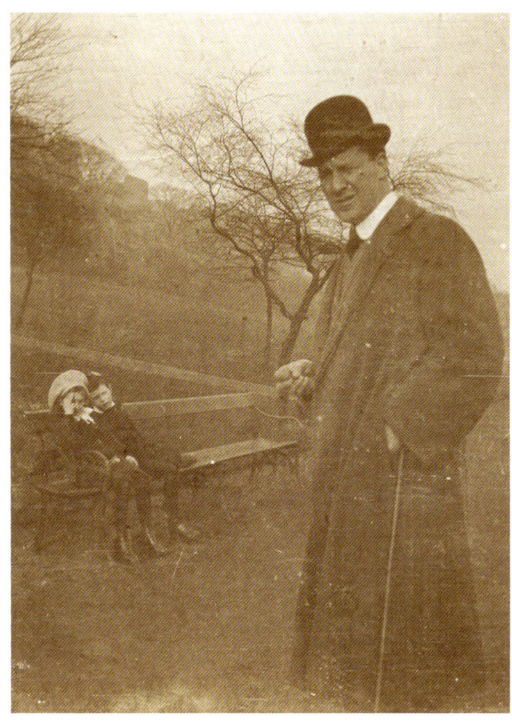

[6] Christina Fergusson, the artist's mother, date unknown
The Fergusson Gallery, Perth & Kinross Council

[7] John Ferguson, the artist's father, date unknown
The Fergusson Gallery, Perth & Kinross Council

[8] J. D. Fergusson in Princes Street Gardens, Edinburgh, late 1890s/ early 1900s
The Fergusson Gallery, Perth & Kinross Council

PARIS

Fergusson declared 'Paris is simply a place of freedom'.[15] He rented a studio first at 18 boulevard Edgar Quinet and later at 83 rue Notre-Dame-des-Champs in Montparnasse, the renowned artists' quarter [3].[16] Fergusson immersed himself in the artistic and social life of the French capital, where 'he was exposed to a tornado of new influences ... till he gradually evolved a new style of his own'.[17] The searing colour and unrefined technique of the Fauves, or 'wild beasts', including Henri Matisse (1869–1954), André Derain (1880–1954) and Kees van Dongen (1877–1968), was of great interest to Fergusson. The dramatic effect this first-hand experience of avant-garde art had on his work can be seen in his *Self-portrait* of 1907 [26]. A lighter palette, the flattening and outlining of form and the oblique composition make it a startling contrast to his earlier portrayal of himself [18].

Mere months after settling in Paris, Fergusson was included in the progressive Salon d'Automne annual exhibition. Just two years later he was elected one of its *sociétaires*, in recognition of his contribution to the modern movement. This was exemplified in paintings such as the life-sized *The Red Shawl* [27], which encompasses the bold colour, striking evocation of feminine beauty and combination of a female figure with decorative background which informed much of his future work. The sitter was the American writer Elizabeth Dryden (d. 1932), who moved to Paris with Rice in 1905. Fergusson came into contact with many important French artists, including Antoine Bourdelle (1861–1929), Auguste Chabaud (1882–1955), Othon Friesz (1879–1949), Jules Pascin (1885–1930) and Pablo Picasso (1881–1973). However, his most significant friendship was with André Dunoyer de Segonzac (1884–1974), whom he met as a result of teaching at the Académie de la Palette.

A change in personal circumstances also contributed to the development of Fergusson's work. The art critic Frank Rutter recalled:

> *In order that he might see better and more clearly he gave up smoking. 'When I used to smoke', he told me, 'I saw things like this,' and he waved his hand about vaguely and languidly; 'now', he continued, 'I see things like this,' and he stabbed the air rapidly with his finger. To keep his palette pure and bright he lived in a white studio, all white walls and white furniture. Here, as he explained, not only every note of colour in his sitter had its full value, but he knew if his painting, when finished, looked clean and true against his own white walls, it would look right anywhere else.*[18]

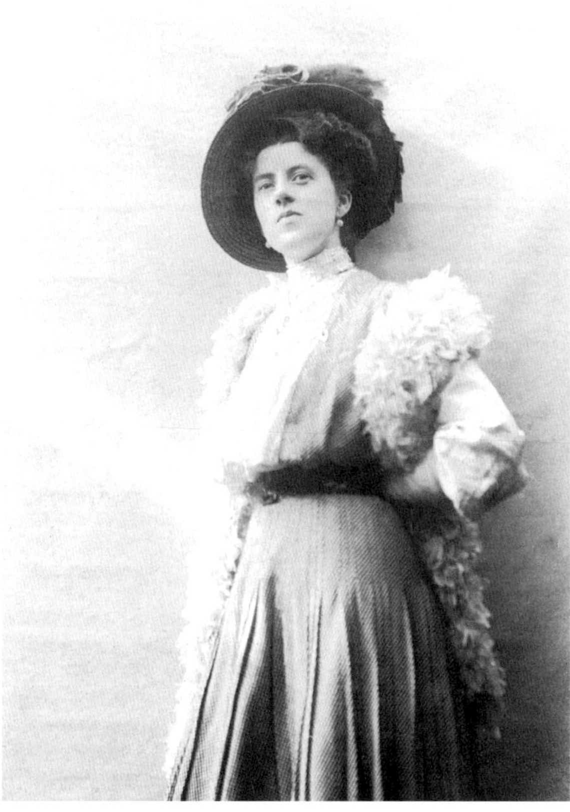

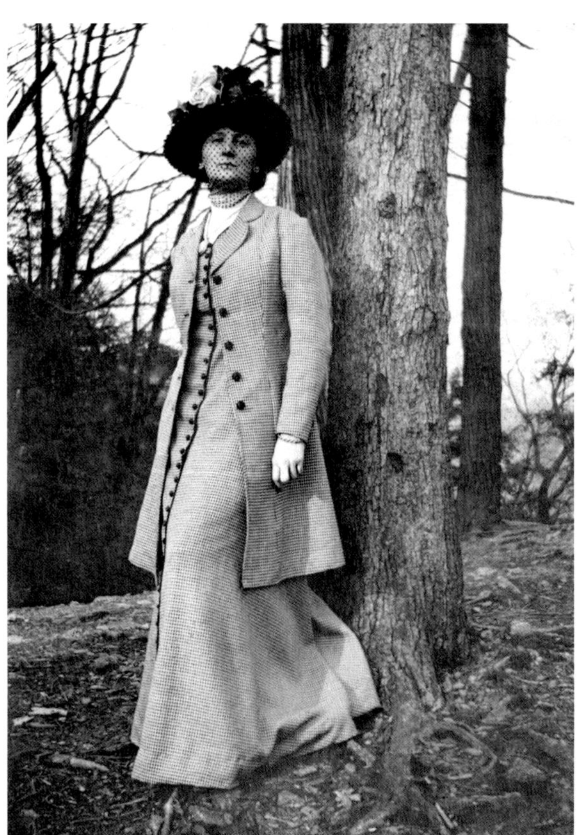

[9] Jean Maconochie, *c.*1904

The Fergusson Gallery, Perth & Kinross Council

[10] Anne Estelle Rice, *c.*1910

The Fergusson Gallery, Perth & Kinross Council

Fergusson lived a frugal lifestyle, as his 1912 accounts book reveals; entries for sundries including kippers, chops, rice pudding and marmalade resulted in a bill of 17 francs 3 centimes between 19 and 23 March.[19] He augmented his income with part-time teaching, some commercial work and the occasional sale of drawings and paintings.

With Rice, Fergusson became a central figure in a now celebrated group of Anglo-American artists including Jo Davidson (1883–1952), Jessica Dismorr (1885–1939), Jessie M. King (1875–1949), E.A. Taylor (1874–1951), Marguerite Thompson (1887–1968) and William Zorach (1887–1966). In 1910, they were joined by Peploe, whom Fergusson persuaded to move to Paris with his wife Margaret and their son Willy [11]. Now it was Fergusson's turn to influence his friend with his knowledge of the latest developments in French art. Paintings made whilst the two were in Royan on the Atlantic coast in 1910 show Peploe getting to grips with an approach of which Fergusson was already a master [51, 47].

As Fergusson recalled:

> *We were a very happy group … we used to meet round the corner table at Boudet's restaurant … When we couldn't pay we did our signed and dated portraits on the back of the bill … We were all very excited with the Russian ballet when it came to Paris. [Léon] Bakst was a Sociétaire of the Salon d'Automne and used all the ideas of modern painting for his décor. [Sergei] Diaghilev made a triumph, surely even greater than he had hoped for. No wonder S.J. [sic] said these were some of the greatest nights of his life. They were the greatest nights in anyone's life.*[20]

The achievements of this circle are most obvious in the journal *Rhythm*, of which Fergusson was founding Art Editor from summer 1911 to November 1912, and through the exhibition of their work held at the Stafford Gallery in London in October 1912. Fergusson's painting *Rhythm* [66] epitomises this short-lived but important movement and is one of his masterpieces.

Indeed, *Rhythm* comes from a series of nudes made in *c.*1910–13 which are amongst the most original paintings in British art of the period and which reached their triumphant conclusion in *Les Eus* [68]. The series includes *Voiles indiennes* [29] and *Torse de Femme* [28] which were shown in Fergusson's solo exhibition at the Stafford Gallery in March 1912 [12]. Having

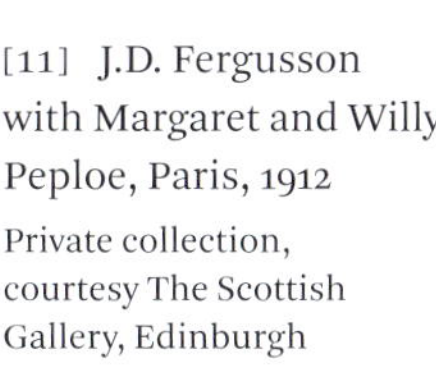

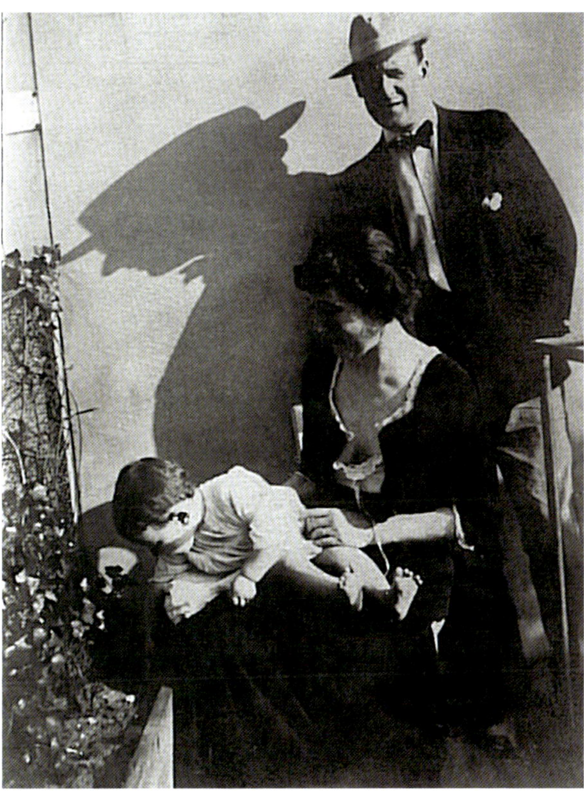

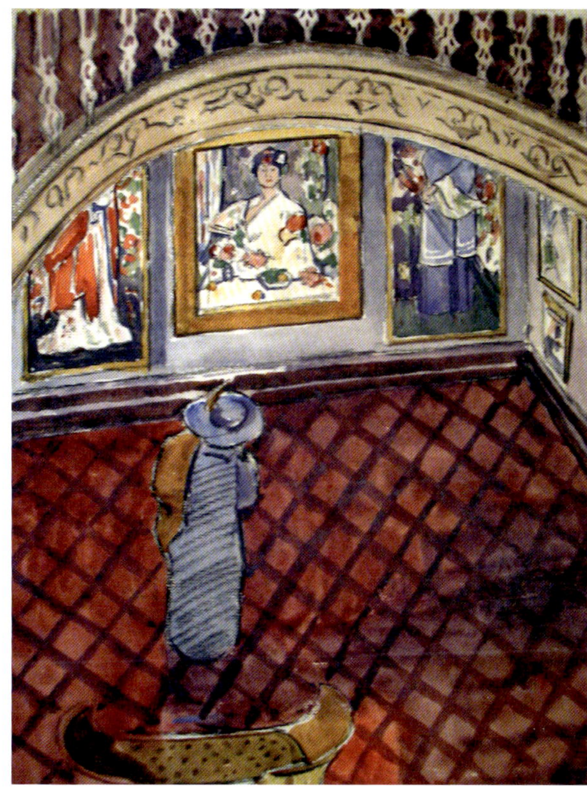

[11] J.D. Fergusson with Margaret and Willy Peploe, Paris, 1912
Private collection, courtesy The Scottish Gallery, Edinburgh

[12] Douglas Fox Pitt
The Stafford Gallery, 1912
Tate, London
This shows a view of J.D. Fergusson's solo exhibition at the Stafford Gallery in London in 1912. *The Red Shawl* [27], *La Dame aux Oranges* and *Le Manteau Chinois* [64] can be seen.

previously painted friends and lovers, Fergusson decided to paint professional models as anonymous nudes. The self-possession and exoticism of the half-dressed figure in *Voiles indiennes* owes much to Matisse. *Torse de femme* is an extraordinarily confrontational image, not only in subject matter, but also in composition, design, colour and technique. It relates to Kees van Dongen, but in its extremeness is akin to contemporary German Expressionism. Fergusson's work was included in important group exhibitions in London whilst he lived in Paris, increasing his profile in the United Kingdom. In 1911 Rutter declared 'we may justly indulge the highest hopes for his future, the future of an artist who has already won what is best worth having, namely, the attention and respect of his most highly gifted contemporaries'.[21]

In 1913, Fergusson met Margaret Morris [13], with whom he began a personal and professional relationship which lasted until his death. Morris had come to Paris with her dance troupe and recalled: 'Armed with an introduction, I presented myself at his studio at about four in the afternoon. The door was opened a few inches and a dripping black head appeared and said – "I mean to say ... I'm in my bath, can you come back in half an hour?"'[22] Her personal dynamism, sensual physicality and dance technique were in absolute sympathy with Fergusson's interests.

By September 1913 Morris had returned to London, where she had established a dance school in 1910. With the end of his relationship with Anne Estelle Rice, Peploe's return to Edinburgh in 1912 and the scheduling of the demolition of his studio, it is not surprising that, despite the position he had achieved within progressive Parisian circles, Fergusson felt: 'I had grown tired of the north of France; I wanted more sun, more colour; I wanted to go south, to Cassis.'[23] Aged forty, he found a modest house on the then little-known Cap d'Antibes, where Morris joined him for Christmas 1913 and during the summer of 1914. Twenty years later Fergusson captured the idyllic time they spent there in *Summer, 1914* [39]. Morris simply stated, 'the wonder of the summer at the Cap d'Antibes passes all description ... I remember standing on the tiny balcony and saying to myself – nothing can ever be as perfect as this.'[24] However, it was whilst there that the couple learnt of the outbreak of the First World War. Morris returned to London straight away, followed not long afterwards by Fergusson. Yet such was their love of the region around Antibes that they returned many summers until a final visit in 1960.

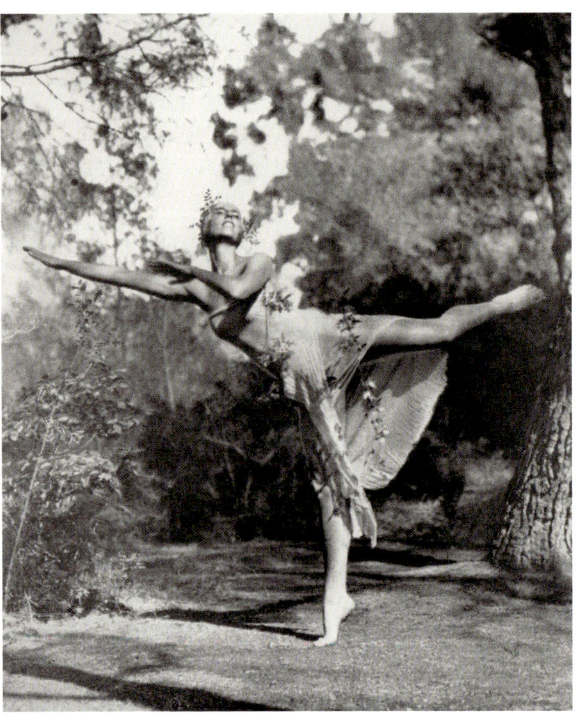

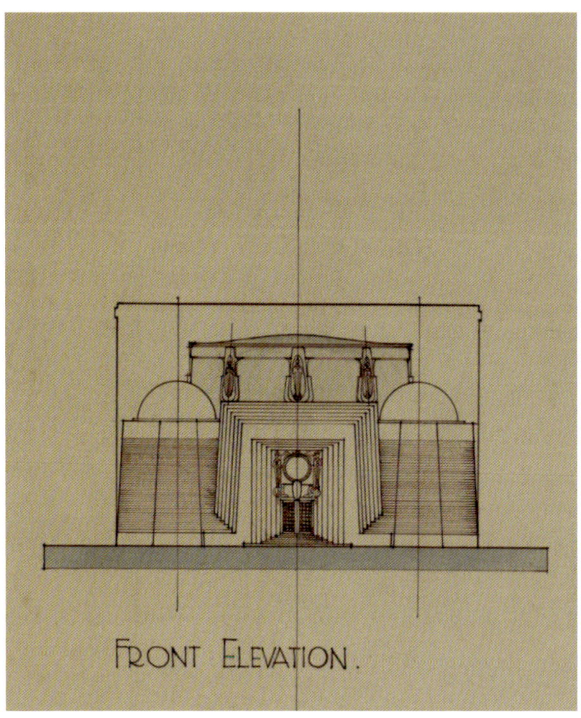

[13] Fred Daniels
Margaret Morris performing her 'Pastorale', *c.*1925
The Fergusson Gallery, Perth & Kinross Council / Fred Daniels Estate

[14] Charles Rennie Mackintosh
Design for proposed theatre in Chelsea, for Margaret Morris: plans 1920, detail of front elevation, 1920
Hunterian Art Gallery, University of Glasgow

LONDON

Through the Margaret Morris Club, which ran alongside her dance school and theatre, Fergusson immediately came into contact with the London avant-garde. Situated on the corner of the King's Road and Glebe Place in Chelsea, the club met three times a month for performance, discussion and socialising. It was within easy walking distance of 14 Redcliffe Road, where Fergusson took lodgings. His *Rhythm* journal co-founder, John Middleton Murry, moved to no.47 in 1917 and the following year Fergusson was a witness at his marriage to the writer Katherine Mansfield (1888–1923). Also in 1918, Fergusson took on a studio at nearby 15 Callow Street.

A vast array of culturally minded people attended the Margaret Morris Club. Prominent visitors included the artists Percy Wyndham Lewis (1882–1957), Augustus John (1878–1961) and Frank Dobson (1886–1963), the poets and writers Edith and Sacheverell Sitwell and Ezra Pound, and the musicians Eugène Goossens, Constant Lambert and Arnold Bax. Morris made the architect-artist-designer Charles Rennie Mackintosh (1868–1928), whom she called 'Toshie', an honorary member with his wife Margaret Macdonald (1865–1933).[25] The two couples became close and in 1920 Mackintosh designed a theatre for Morris, which did not come to fruition due to lack of funds [14].[26] With Fergusson, Mackintosh sat on the Management Committee of the London Salon of the Independants [sic] and became involved with the Arts League of Service, which intended to promote democratic exhibitions and 'to further all forms of Art' respectively.[27]

Little work by Fergusson survives from the war years. He contributed greatly to Morris's activities, not least in terms of set and costume design, and participated in the teaching of painting to her pupils over the next four decades. Mackintosh lamented to his wife: 'It is a pity Meg is tied to London otherwise Fergie could be anywhere and paint quite as well if not better (and at the same time have a better life) than he can in Callow Street.'[28] However, two series of paintings made in 1916, of female heads and of landscapes based on sketches made during an extended visit to his mother in Edinburgh, prove that Fergusson maintained his own practice. *A Lowland Church* [31] shows the late eighteenth-century Lasswade Parish Church, which was demolished in 1955, and reveals Fergusson's interest in the work of Paul Cézanne (1839–1906). The model for *Simplicity* [30] was the MMM dancer and teacher Kathleen Dillon (1898–1990), whom Fergusson described as 'a very good looking, charming and intelligent girl – naturally I wanted to paint her'.[29]

Fergusson and Morris made scant reference to the world wars through which they lived. According to Elizabeth Dryden, Fergusson described patriotism as 'the most over-rated of vices'.[30] Morris explained that he attempted (unsuccessfully) to be commissioned as a War Artist in the Navy as he disliked the khaki colour of the Army's uniform.[31] However, in July 1918 Fergusson was granted permission by the Admiralty 'to go to Portsmouth to gather impressions for painting a picture'.[32] Shortly after his arrival he reported 'the workmen are always reporting me to the police and watching me suspiciously' as he worked in the docks.[33] Once back in London, Fergusson created a series of paintings, including *Damaged Destroyer* [32] and *Portsmouth Docks* [33], which are as distinct in style as they are in subject matter within his oeuvre, as he experimented with a personal interpretation of Vorticism. The completion of the paintings coincided with the end of the war and none were acquired for official purposes until 1975.[34]

In 1908 Fergusson made his first sculpture, a self-portrait, encouraged by his friend the American sculptor Jo Davidson. The years approximately 1918 to 1922 mark the peak of his activity in this field, which Sheila McGregor argues is linked to a parallel development in MMM.[35] Experiments in terracotta in 1909 and clay in Antibes in 1913 led to direct carving in stone whilst in Edinburgh during the war [94, 95]; carving wood [99, 100] and plaster, which he sometimes cast and coloured, followed. Works were also cast in brass and bronze as funds permitted. *Philosophy* [34] and *Standing Female Nude* [35] are thought to date from 1919 and *c.*1920 respectively. However, scant information exists about Fergusson's sculpture, such as conception and casting dates and edition sizes, whether lifetime or posthumous. *Philosophy*, also known as *Meg with Dove*, shows Fergusson's interest in orientalism. *Standing Female Nude* is a powerful depiction of feminine physicality, similar to the lost *Patient Woman*. Sculptures were included in many of Fergusson's exhibitions between 1912 and 1948; the latest known example is *Magnolia* of *c.*1955.[36]

Fergusson's sculpture owes more to artists working in Paris before the First World War, such as Constantin Brancusi (1876–1957), Alexander Archipenko (1887–1964) and Jacob Epstein (1880–1959), than to the British sculptors he encountered later in London, including Frank Dobson (1888–1963) and Maurice Lambert (1901–1964). Fergusson was one of many artists of his generation who worked in three dimensions in such a manner, with similar influences and without formal training. Nonetheless within a British context his endeavours in three dimensions are extremely unusual. As Jonathan Blackwood has argued, 'Fergusson deserves to be considered amongst the ranks of interesting experimental sculptors who worked in vernacular modernism in London in the 1920s'.[37]

In 1922 and 1928 Fergusson made motoring tours of the Scottish Highlands with his friend the businessman and writer John Ressich (1878–1937). He was so inspired by the first trip that Morris stated: 'there is little to say about the next six months, because Fergus was literally painting every minute he was not sleeping or eating' [101, 102].[38] Fergusson exhibited the startling results in his first solo exhibition in Scotland, held at The Scottish Gallery in Edinburgh and La Société des Beaux-Arts in Glasgow in 1923. Duncan Macmillan has argued that 'distinctly Cubist in style, they were truly "modern" Scottish landscapes'.[39]

In some respects, this decade can be considered the most successful of Fergusson's career. *Head of a Girl*, 1917, became the first of his works to enter a public collection when it was given by the Contemporary Art Society to the Corporation of Glasgow for display in Kelvingrove Art Gallery.[40] Thanks to the efforts of the Glasgow-based dealer Alexander Reid (1854–1928) and his son A.J. McNeill Reid (1893–1972), Fergusson's work was shown with that of F.C.B. Cadell, G.L. Hunter and S.J. Peploe in exhibitions held in Paris in 1924 and in London in 1925. In the catalogue preface for the latter, the artist Walter Sickert (1860–1942) commented of Fergusson's contribution: 'it is thus that we might expect a race with knees of granite to express itself'.[41]

Jo Davidson helped bring about the first of three exhibitions of Fergusson's work to be held in America between 1926 and 1929. Mounted at the progressive Whitney Studio in New York, it received positive reviews – with the *New York Herald Tribune* asserting that 'he paints big subjects with a true grasp upon their substance and scale' – and resulted in the sale of five works.[42] With Ressich, Fergusson attended the opening of a solo exhibition in 1928 at the C.W. Kraushaar Art Galleries, also in New York. It toured to the Chester Johnson Gallery, Chicago, and resulted in the sale of three paintings, earning him $1,307.88.[43] *S.S. Transylvania Souvenir* [36] is named after the ship Fergusson sailed on to America and depicts Morris beside his sculpture *Female Nude* of *c.*1920 and in front of the pink box in which he is said to have kept his contraceptives.[44] Following the merger of the Reids' business, La Société des Beaux-Arts in Glasgow, with the Lefèvre Gallery in London, Fergusson had solo shows in London and Glasgow in 1928. However, Fergusson's insistence on the value of his work led McNeill Reid to write to him:

> *I am afraid that I cannot cheer you up very much with the results of your exhibition, as the only sale up to date is one watercolour at 15 guineas. Generally speaking the public have not been very enthusiastic and I have had to face a great deal of criticism. This I expected and was prepared for, but I have also had to contend with the difficulty of your prices … we have gone into the question of prices so often, that I need not repeat my arguments and I merely ask if in this particular case you can give me any reduction.*[45]

Fergusson later explained his stance to the writer Eric de Banzie, who noted: 'His attitude was that, in the Whistlerian phrase, "a lifetime of experience" had to be paid for fairly,' and quoted Fergusson as declaring: 'I'd rather never sell any than descend in my own sense of integrity'.[46]

In the meantime, Fergusson and Morris were spending increasing amounts of time in France. For example, Morris held her Summer Schools in Dinard in 1920, Pourville in 1921 and Antibes in 1923.[47] She and her pupils dancing outdoors, sunbathing and swimming in the sea inspired Fergusson to make numerous sketches and watercolours, which he later worked up into paintings in his studio, exemplifying the couple's creative collaboration. In 1929, Fergusson finally left London for good and moved to Paris: Morris commuted between London and Paris, living out of a suitcase. Fergusson found a studio in the rue Gazan, near the Parc Montsouris, but moved to 6 square Henri Delormel two years later.

RETURN TO PARIS

The new decade began triumphantly with the purchase of *Déesse de la Rivière* for the French national collection.[48] It was acquired from the exhibition *Les Peintres Ecossais* held at the Galeries Georges Petit in Paris in March 1931, along with a work each by Hunter and Peploe. Fergusson was quick to clarify with the Musée du Jeu de Paume, where the paintings were hung, that they were Scottish not English artists. He explained: 'as a race, nationality and temperament, it is completely different, we are all greatly influenced by French art and not at all by English art. And we are proud to be in your museum as old allies of France.'[49] Fergusson was praised by the French critic Maximilien Gauthier who wrote in his review of the exhibition that the artist knew 'how to add the supple charm of deep blacks, underpinned with light beiges, to elegant geometrical compositions'.[50] This was to be the last time Fergusson showed with Hunter, Peploe and Cadell before their deaths, later that year, in 1935 and in 1937 respectively.

The work Fergusson made in the early 1930s reveals an accomplished engagement with the Art Deco movement, as seen in *Grace McColl* [37] and *The Quay at Dinard* [70]. The term originates in the landmark *Exposition international des arts décoratifs et industriels modernes* held in Paris in 1925. Its style was spread through magazines such as the *Gazette du Bon Ton* and was pioneered by artists including Georges Lepape (1887–1971) and Jean Dupas (1882–1964). Fergusson's sitter was the wife of his friend from pre-war Paris, the Scottish businessman Harry McColl, whom Fergusson described as 'the man I like best. Quite wonderful.'[51]

Fergusson was soon galvanising artists to join forces to exhibit their work. By 1936 he was President of Le Groupe d'Artistes Anglo-Américains, albeit with 'Ecossais' in brackets after his name in the list of members. His associates included Winifred (1893–1981) and Ben Nicholson (1894–1982), Victor Pasmore (1908–1998) and John Piper (1903–1992).[52] The group aimed to 'obtain and present, by means of two or more exhibitions each year in Paris, an accurate and balanced cross section of present day painting and sculpture by English and American artists living in France' and its first exhibition was held in 1935.[53] Fergusson's profile remained high in London where he had four solo exhibitions between 1932 and 1939; three of paintings and sculptures and one dedicated to his watercolours, a medium which became increasingly important to him.

The ambitious *Bathers: Noon* [40], in which Fergusson and Morris take centre stage, is a summation of their relationship and belief in a healthy, outdoor lifestyle, conducted in the heat of the south of France coast. *Lilies* [38] marked a rare return to the genre of the still life. With its sexual, particularly phallic references, combined with a sense of the fecundity of nature, it shares the sensuality which informed much of Fergusson's work. However, the originality of

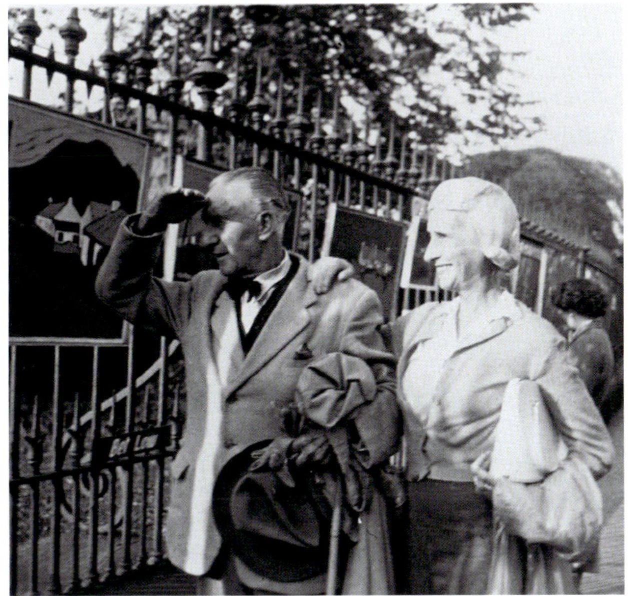

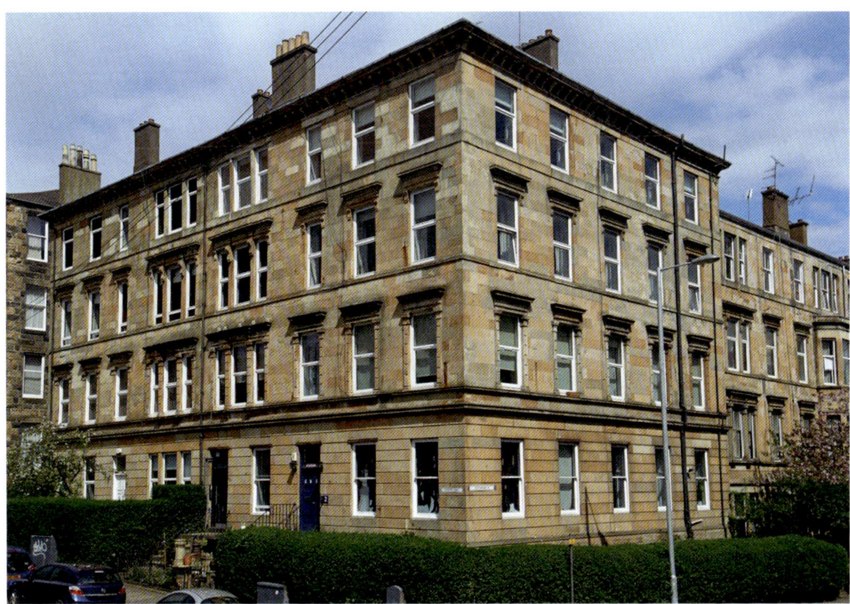

[15] J.D. Fergusson and Margaret Morris looking at works by the New Scottish Group, hung on the railings of the Botanic Gardens, Glasgow, 1951
Photograph by J. Morris McChlery
Private collection, courtesy Lyon & Turnbull

[16] 4 Clouston Street, Glasgow, Fergusson's home from 1939 until his death. He lived in the top-floor corner flat.

his earlier career was not sustained, with one critic bemoaning in 1932 that he 'does not seem to have anything new to say or anything that is not repeated to the point of irritation'.[54] Another world war once again forced Fergusson to leave France. This time, he and Morris settled in Glasgow, which he believed was the most Celtic city in Scotland and was where her one remaining school survived, at 299 West George Street.

GLASGOW

Fergusson was of retirement age when he returned to live in Scotland for the first time in over thirty years. 'Fergus and Meg', as the couple became affectionately known, moved to a top-floor flat at 4 Clouston Street, overlooking the Botanic Gardens [16]. Fergusson had a light and spacious corner studio [75], with views over the River Kelvin to the university. Morris had a dance studio in which she fitted a wall-length mirror that reached from floor to ceiling, as well as a 'sun room'. Visitors remarked on the flat's unusual decoration, with white walls, bare floorboards and sparse furnishing. Indeed, the couple never had much money, but 'they had what they needed for life' and continued to pursue their vocations with vigour.[55] Fergusson developed a distinct late style, which reached its apotheosis in the majestic *Danu, Mother of the Gods* in 1952 [104]. By this point, he had eliminated black from his palette, declaring 'there is no such colour as black, black is an absence of light'.[56]

In 1946 Fergusson wrote: 'The Scotland I'd like to see from the Art point of view, would be a Scotland liberated from the stranglehold of Academic Art, and where there was, if not a square deal, at least a fair fighting chance for the Independent Artist.'[57] He and Morris played a vital part in the renaissance of the arts in Glasgow during this period. In 1940, Morris founded the Celtic Ballet Club and together they were co-founders of the New Art Club, created to offer affordable exhibiting opportunities and evenings of 'free discussion'.[58] In 1942 the New Scottish Group was formed, with Fergusson as President. Its mission was to focus on exhibitions of work by members, without selection by a jury and with a modest hanging fee. Eight exhibitions were held between 1943 and 1956 and on one occasion work was hung along the railings of the Botanic Gardens [15]. Members included Donald Bain, Louise Annand (1915–2012) and James Morrison McChlery (1924–1969). Fergusson was particularly supportive of Bain's career, going so far as to write to Picasso in 1950, urging him to visit Bain in Cagnes on the French Mediterranean coast.[59] Indeed, many people remember the couple's kindness, encouragement and hospitality. In 1947, Fergusson wrote a foreword for a book about the New Scottish Group, which was published, like his 1943 monograph *Modern Scottish Painting*, by William MacLellan.[60] In a repeat of his involvement with the journal *Rhythm*, Fergusson was Art Editor of MacLellan's radical journal *Scottish Art and Letters*, which ran from 1944 until 1950.[61]

The artist Josef Herman (1911–2000) recalled Fergusson during his early Glasgow years:

> *J.D. Fergusson was good looking and immaculately dressed. His light grey suit, the white shirt and the deep blue tie were all in the right degree of tonality and beautifully matched together ... The white hair had a pearl-like gleam and lay smoothly on the head. Elegance suited him and was the introduction to his gentle manner.*[62]

Fergusson was revered for his professional achievements and for his personal link with early Modernism. A major retrospective exhibition of his work opened in Glasgow in 1948 and toured to Aberdeen, Ayr, Carlisle, Paisley and Belfast. It was greeted warmly in the press, with *The Scotsman*'s critic writing 'to pass into this exhibition out of the grime and rain of Glasgow is to come into Rivieran sunshine, eternal youth and happiness. Fergusson is old in years, but he is young in spirit and he is still very much the modern Painter.'[63]

In 1949 and 1957, Fergusson had selling exhibitions at T. & R. Annan & Sons, the leading gallery in Glasgow following the demise of Reid & Lefèvre in the city in 1932. Beginning in 1949 and continuing for eight years, Fergusson regularly consigned paintings to Annans, mainly of the pre-First World War period. Prices achieved ranged from £7 7s Od to £175, a far cry from the £500 Fergusson asked in vain for *The Red Shawl* when it was exhibited in London in 1912.[64] In 1952 the Hazlitt Gallery held a solo exhibition of his work, initiated by the Scottish writer Crieff Williamson, which resulted in the sale of four works for a total of £230.[65] After a gap of sixteen years, the Lefèvre Gallery held their last exhibition of Fergusson's work in 1955, which consisted of thirty-two paintings.

The 1950s saw a flurry of recognition from the establishment against which Fergusson had fought for so much of his life. In 1950, he was bestowed with an honorary LLD by the University of Glasgow; two years later he was awarded a Civil List pension of £300 per annum for his services to art, whilst a major touring retrospective exhibition, organised by the Scottish Committee of the Arts Council of Great Britain, began in Aberdeen in 1954 and ended in Glasgow in 1956.[66] Fergusson and Morris spent many summers in Antibes during the 1950s [17]; their last visit was in 1960, not long before Fergusson's death from chronic bronchitis in Glasgow, on 30 January 1961.

CONCLUSION

Fergusson's death was marked by obituaries in newspapers including *The Times*, *The Scotsman* and the *New York Times*.[67] A touring memorial exhibition was organised by the Arts Council, which started in Edinburgh in November 1961 and finished in Eastbourne in June 1962. According to Fergusson's wishes, his ashes were scattered over Schiehallion in Perthshire, whose Gaelic name translates as 'the fairy hill of the Caledonians'. He left an estate valued at £2,687:18.3, of which Morris was the sole beneficiary.[68] However, in his will Fergusson stated that none of her inheritance was to be spent on 'theatrical befittings', and that the residue after expenses 'for her personal benefit' was to be used to:

> *further Independent Scottish painting and sculpture according to my views clearly set forth in my book Modern Scottish Painting. Grants made from funds must be on purely artistic merits and not influenced by political, religious or academic distinction, no one being a member of or benefiting from any Academy to receive any benefit.*[69]

Morris was 'utterly devastated' by Fergusson's death, but between 1961 and her own death in Glasgow on 29 February 1980, made huge efforts to secure his reputation.[70] Some ninety works entered public collections throughout the United Kingdom during that period, including the Scottish national collection, in no small part due to Morris's endeavours.[71] In 1968 she presented fourteen paintings to the newly established University of Stirling and in 1974 she published a 'biased biography' of Fergusson.[72]

In 1963, Morris established the J.D. Fergusson Art Foundation to look after the works and archival material she had inherited. Its two aims were 'to establish ... a permanent memorial of two galleries, one to contain a representative collection of the work of J.D. Fergusson; the other to exhibit the work of progressive artists of Scottish descent'.[73] The Fergusson Gallery opened in Perth in 1992 (which sadly Morris did not live to see) and the J.D. Fergusson Arts Award Trust supports artists, including the opportunity to exhibit in the gallery.[74] As Fergusson's friend from pre-First World War Paris André Dunoyer de Segonzac prophesied in 1961: 'his work will triumphantly overcome the test of time for it is authentic, full of life and truth'.[75]

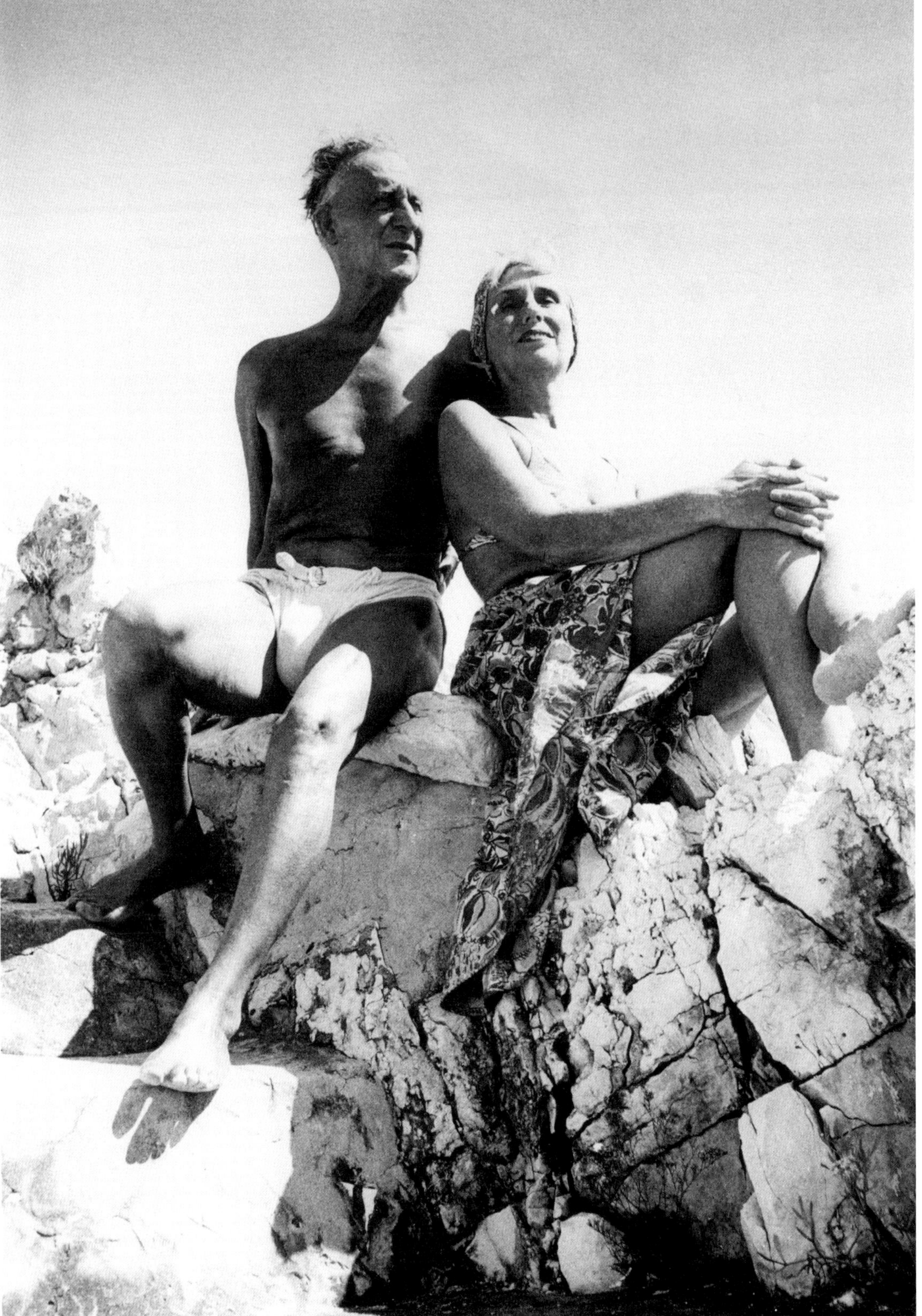

[17] J.D. Fergusson and Margaret Morris, Antibes, 1958
The Fergusson Gallery, Perth & Kinross Council

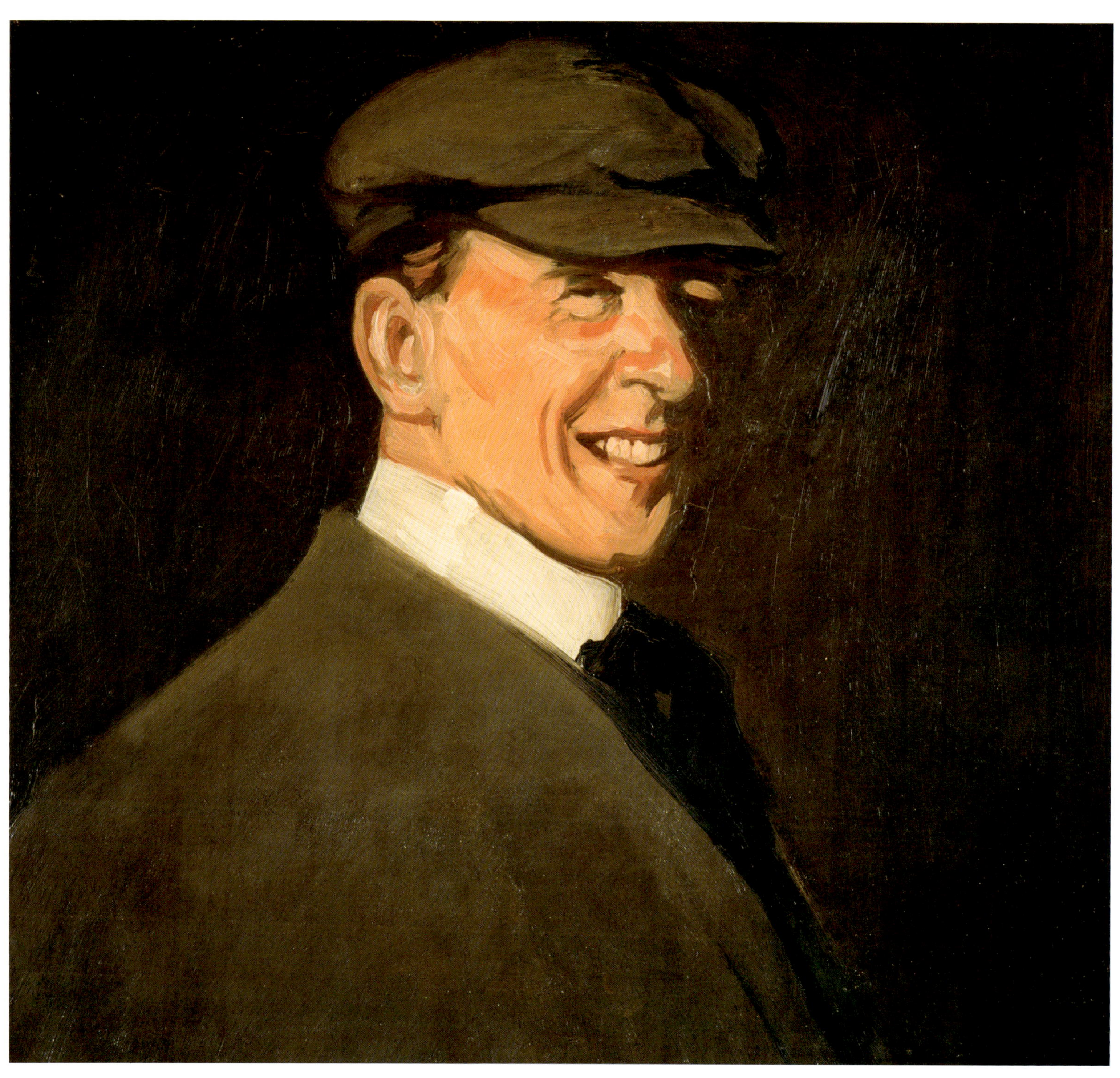

[18]

Self-portrait, *c.*1902

Oil on canvas, 50.8 × 56.4
Scottish National Portrait Gallery, Edinburgh, purchased 1982

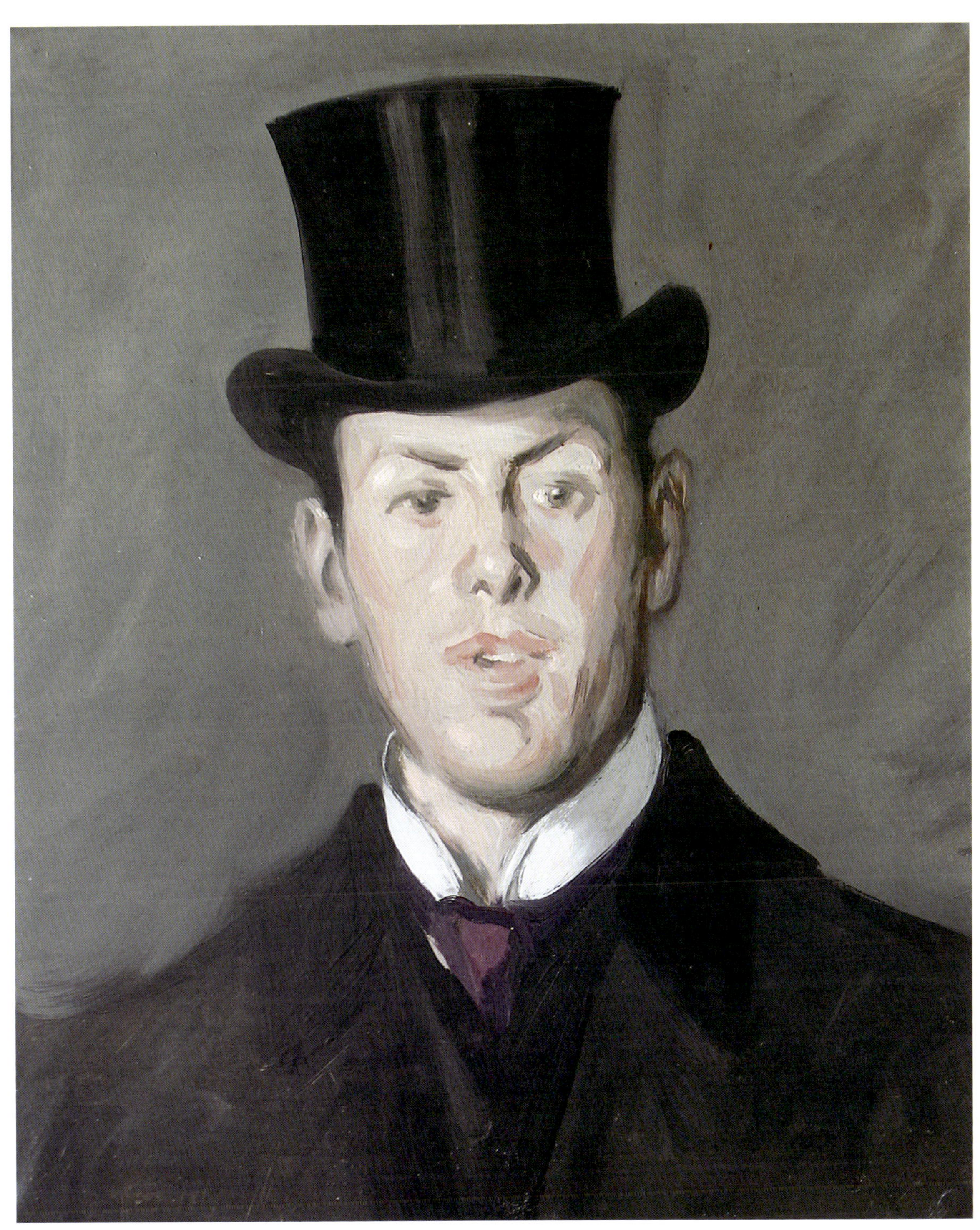

[19]
The Silk Hat, 1903
Oil on canvas, 61 × 50.5
Llangoed Hall Hotel, Brecon, Powys

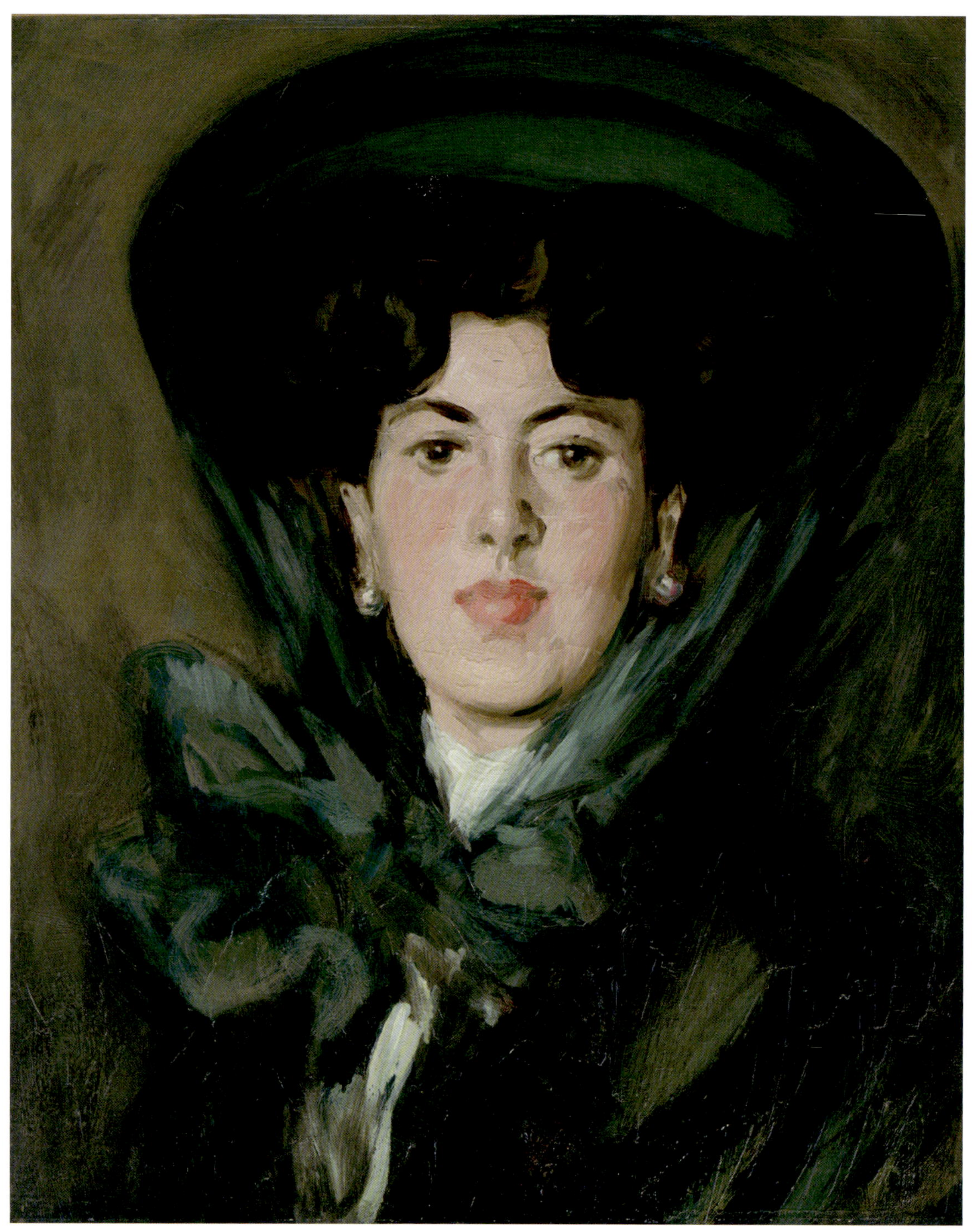

[20]

Jean Maconochie, *c.*1902

Oil on canvas, 60.9 × 50.8
The Fleming-Wyfold Art Foundation, purchased 1981

[21]

The White Dress: Portrait of Jean, 1904

Oil on canvas, 178 × 120.5
The Fergusson Gallery, Perth & Kinross Council
presented by the J.D. Fergusson Art Foundation 1991

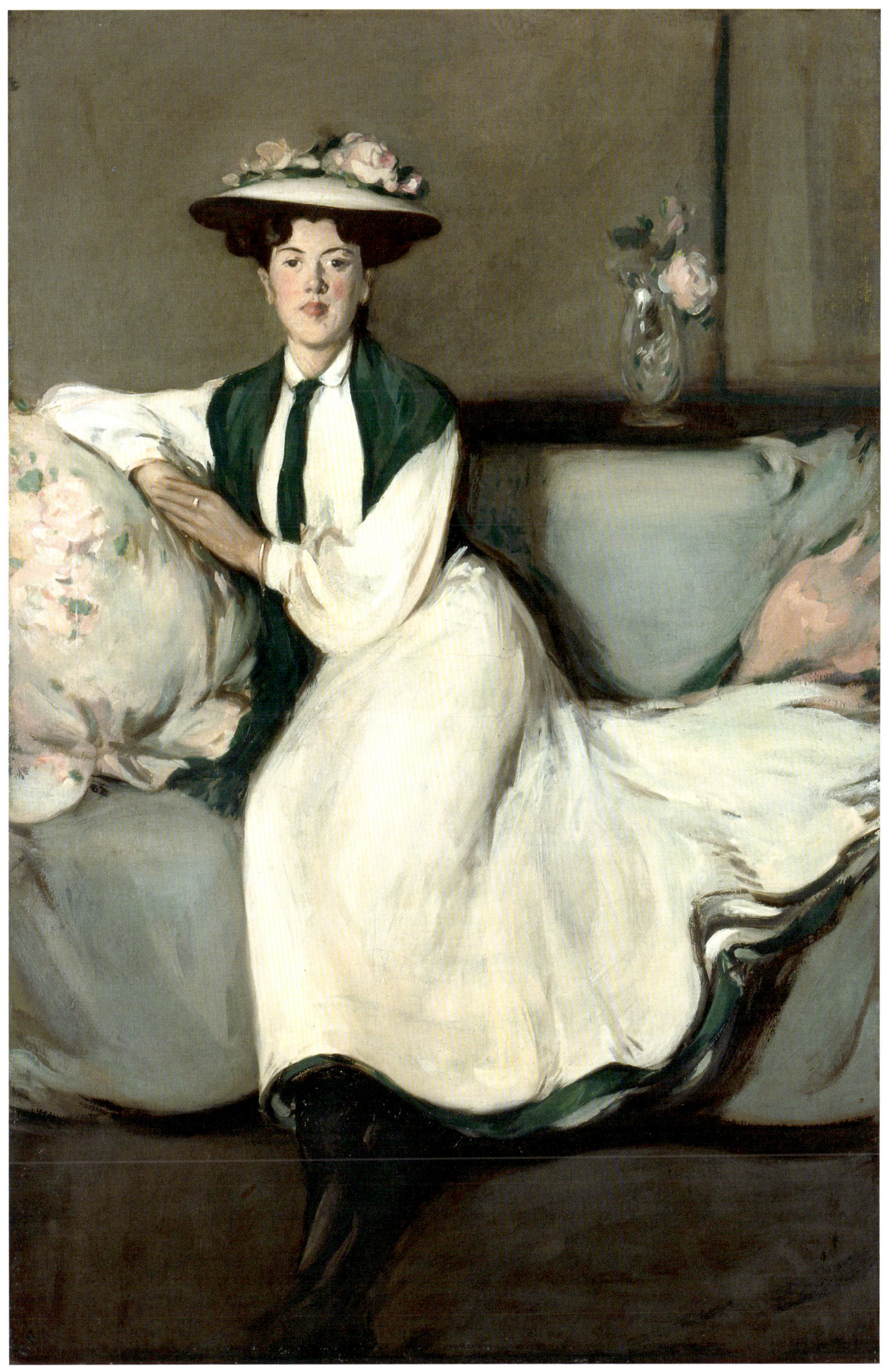

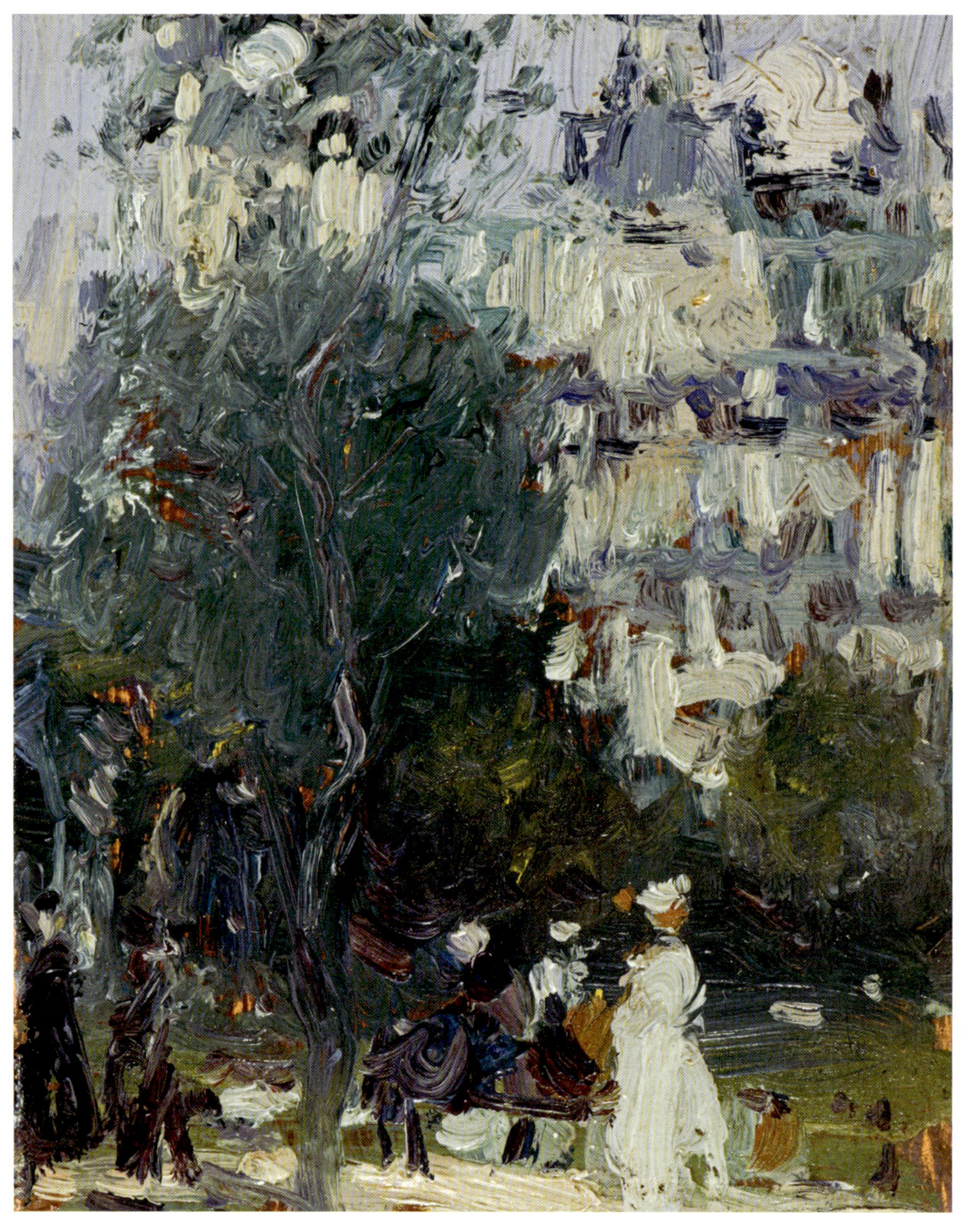

[22]

Bank of Scotland from Princes Street Gardens, early 1900s

Oil on board, 13.7 × 11
Scottish National Gallery of Modern Art, Edinburgh
presented anonymously 2006

[23]

Dieppe, 14 July 1905: Night, 1905

Oil on canvas, 76.5 × 76.5
Scottish National Gallery of Modern Art, Edinburgh
purchased 1978

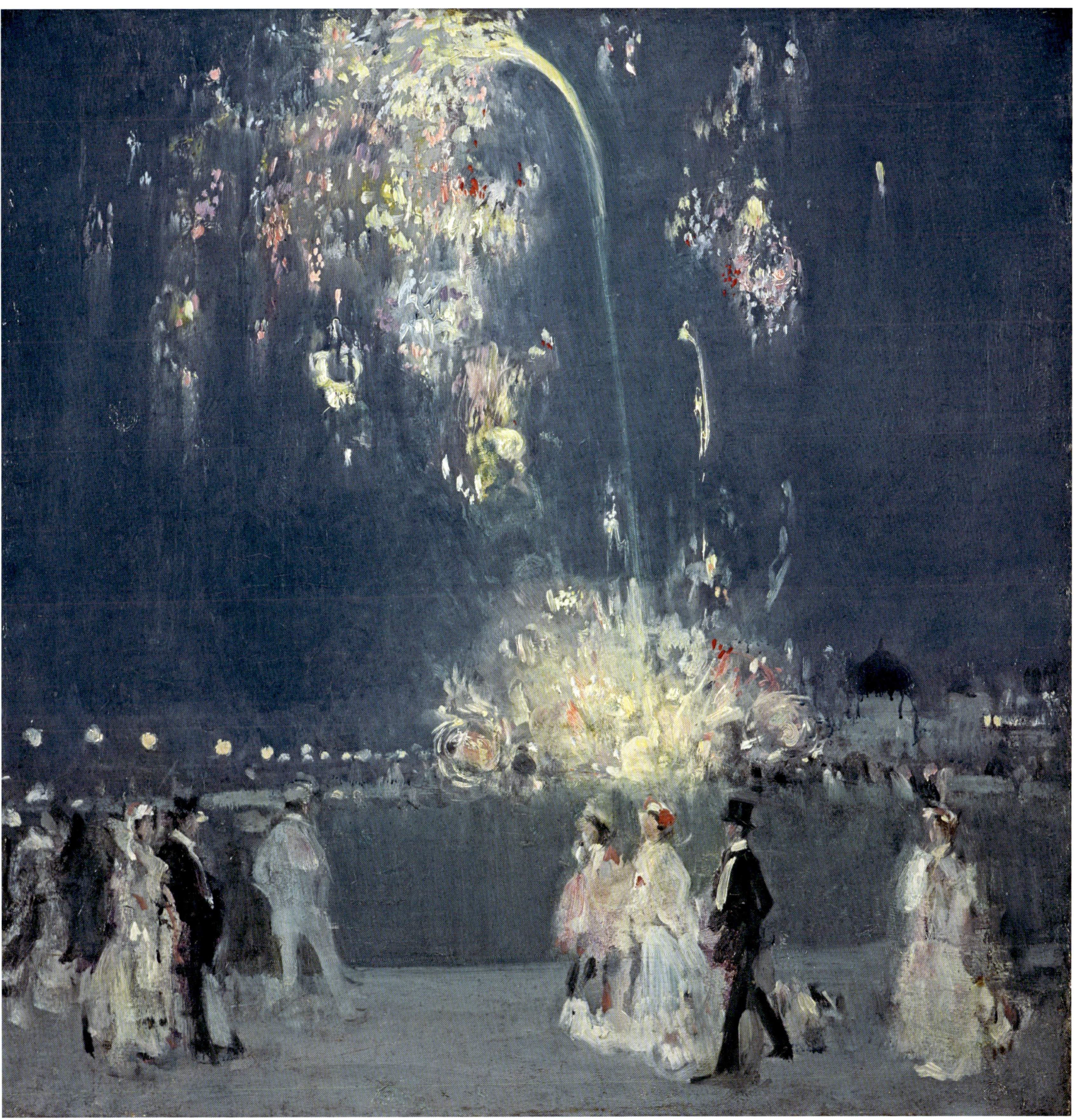

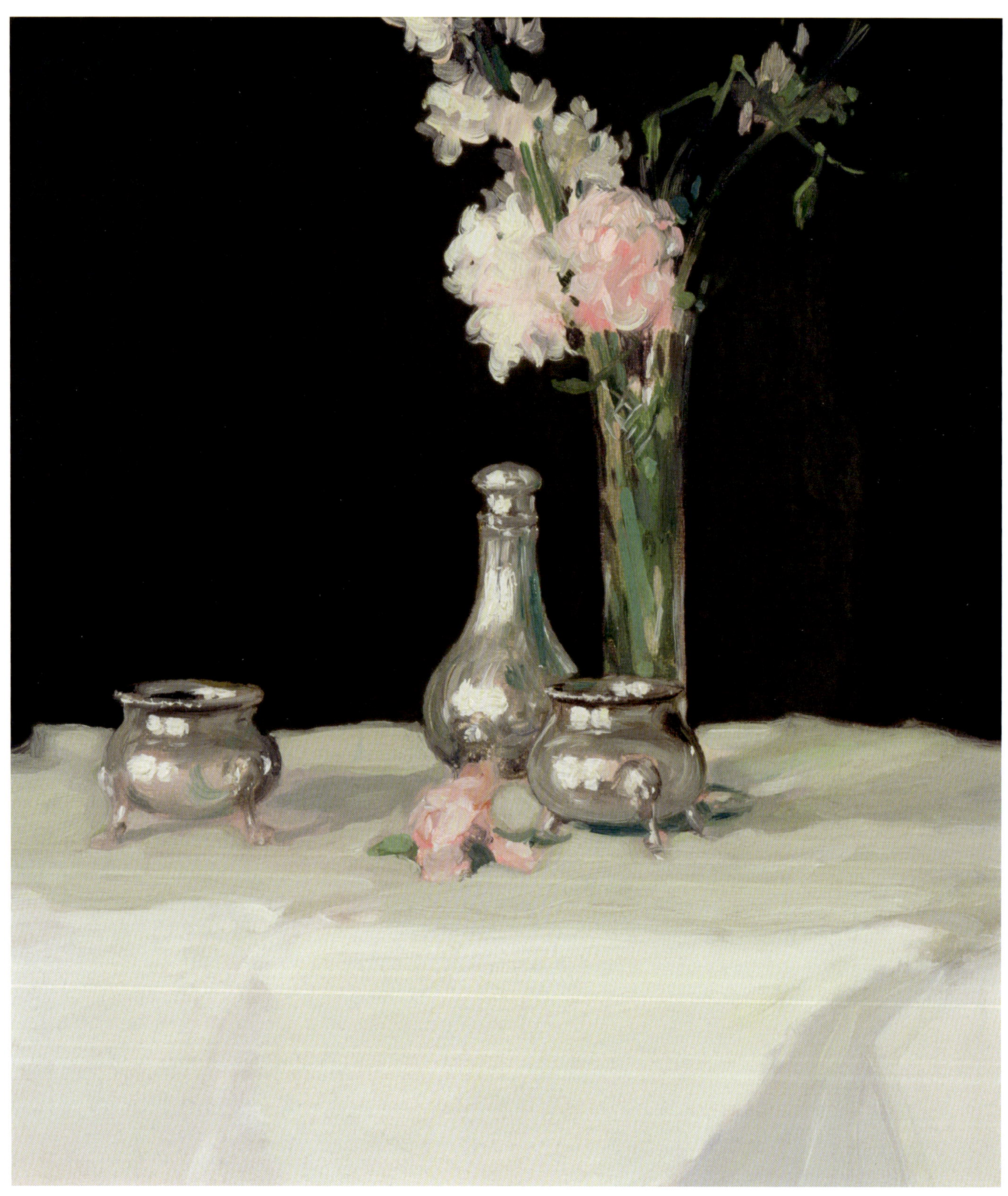

[24]

Jonquils and Silver, 1905

Oil on canvas, 50.8 × 45.7

The Fleming-Wyfold Art Foundation, purchased 1971

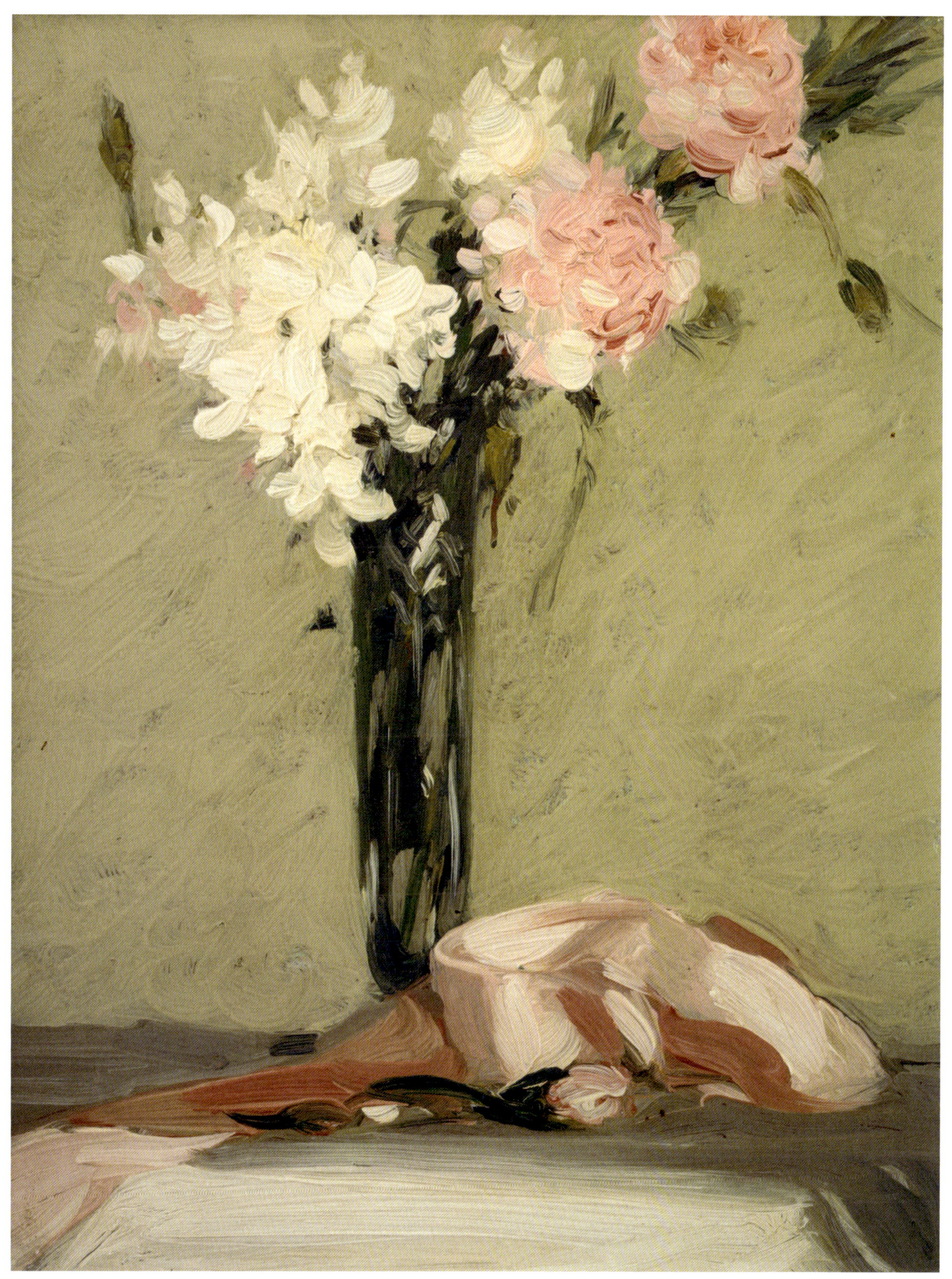

[25]
Carnations and Narcissus, *c.*1905
Oil on board, 35 × 27
Private collection

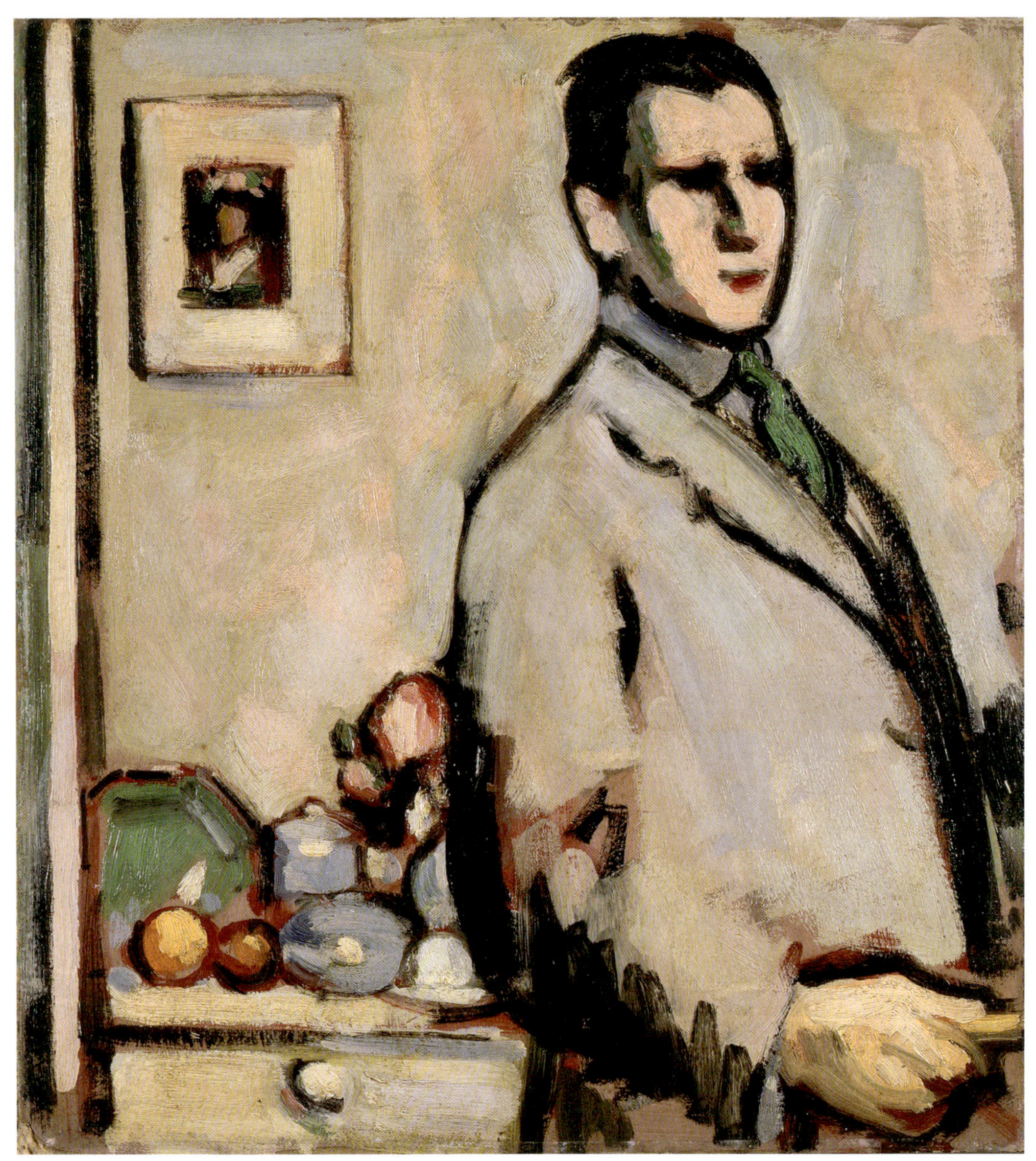

[26]

Self-portrait, 1907

Oil on canvas, 54 × 51
The Fergusson Gallery, Perth & Kinross Council
presented by the J.D. Fergusson Art Foundation 1991

[27]

The Red Shawl, 1908

Oil on canvas, 200 × 84.8
University of Stirling
presented by Margaret Morris and the J.D. Fergusson Art Foundation 1968

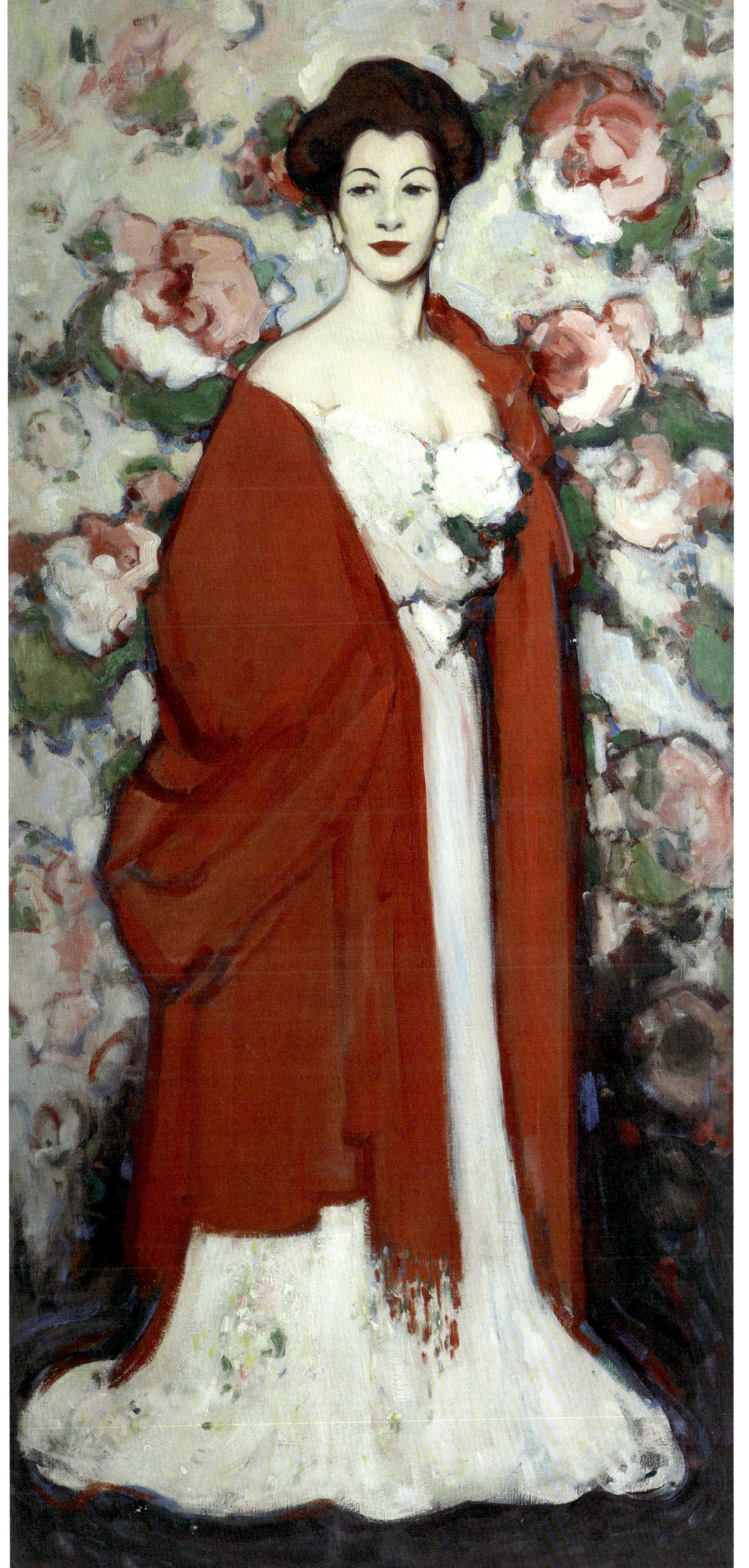

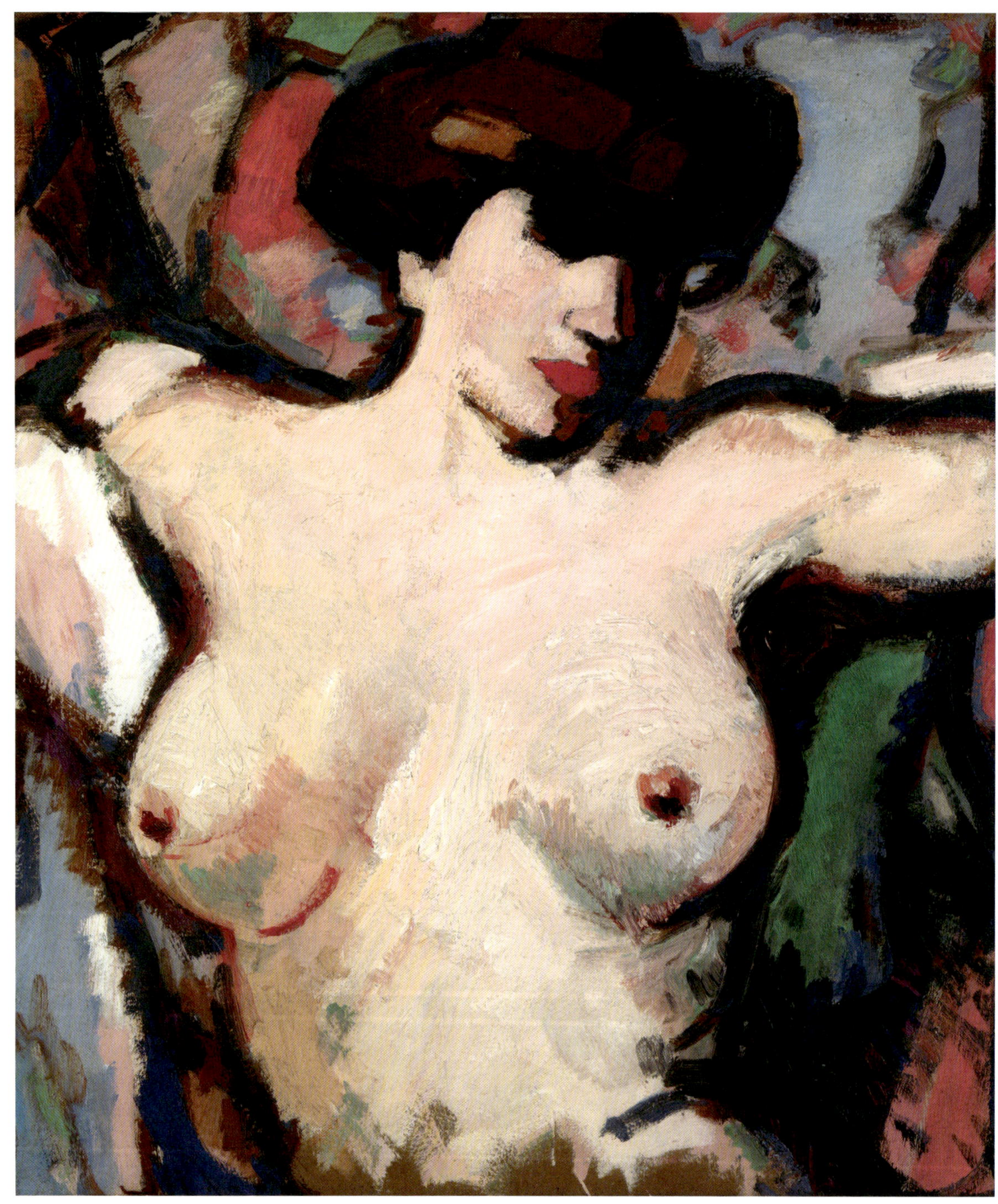

[28]

Torse de Femme, *c.*1911

Oil on panel, 66 × 55.9
Glasgow Life (Glasgow Museums) on behalf of Glasgow City Council
purchased from Mrs Margaret Morris Fergusson 1963

[29]

Voiles indiennes, *c.*1910

Oil on cardboard, 64.8 × 55.6
University of Stirling
presented by Margaret Morris and the J.D. Fergusson Art Foundation 1968

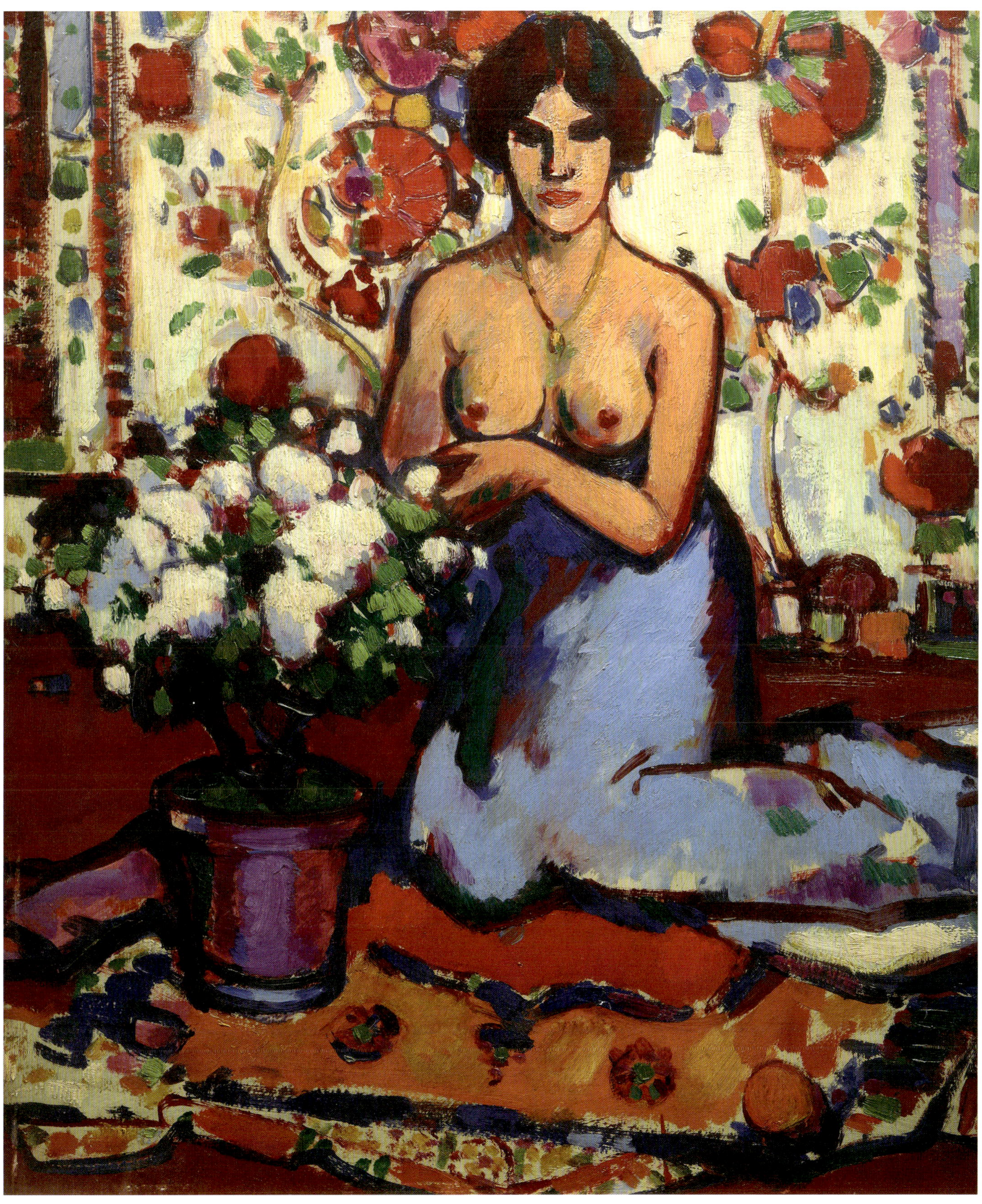

[30]

Simplicity, 1916

Oil on canvas, 48.7 × 43.2
Private collection
courtesy The Fine Art Society
London and Edinburgh

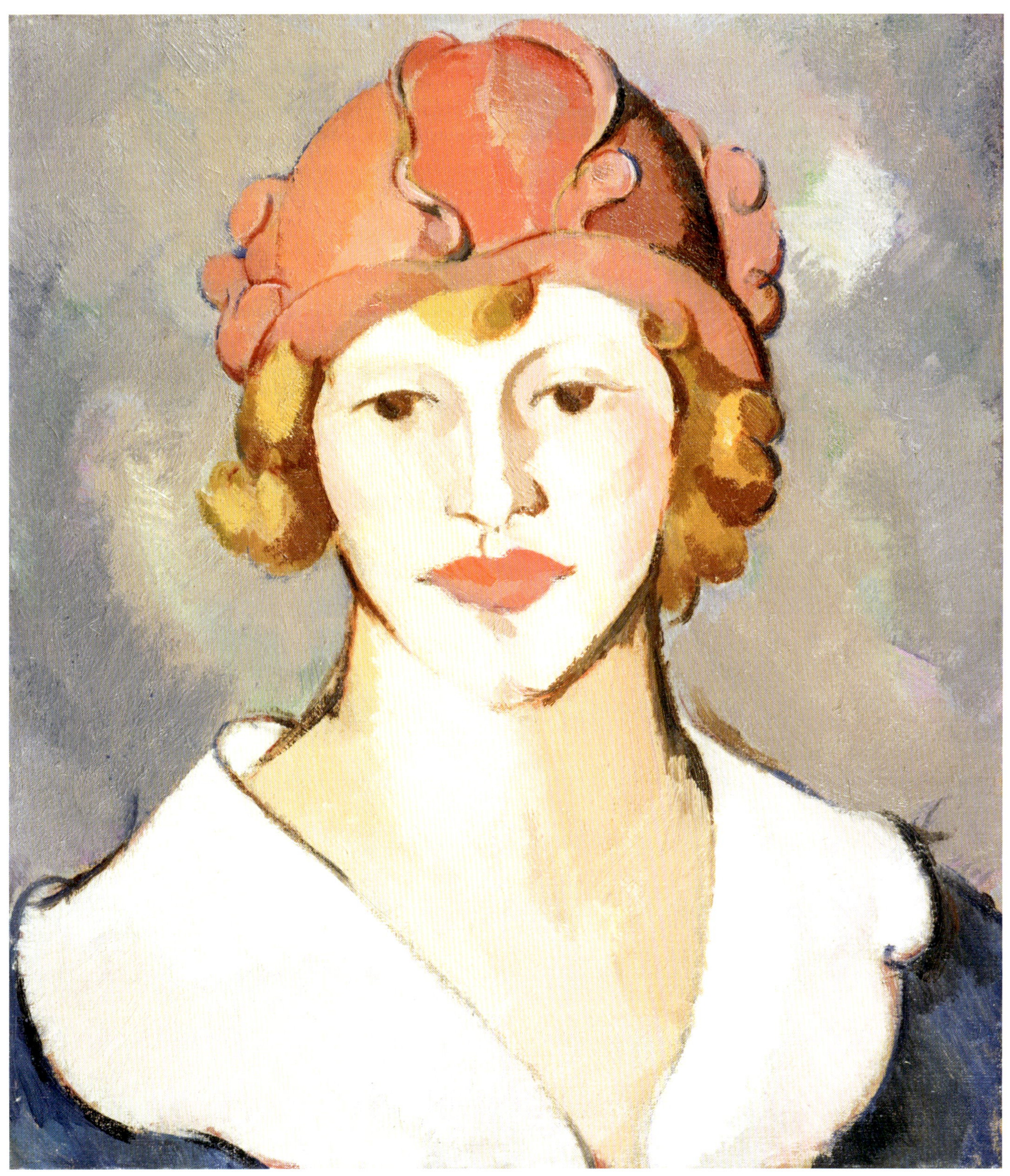

[31]

A Lowland Church, 1916

Oil on canvas, 50.8 × 55.9
Dundee Art Galleries and Museums (Dundee City Council)
purchased from the J.D. Fergusson Art Foundation
with the assistance of the National Fund for Acquisitions 1968

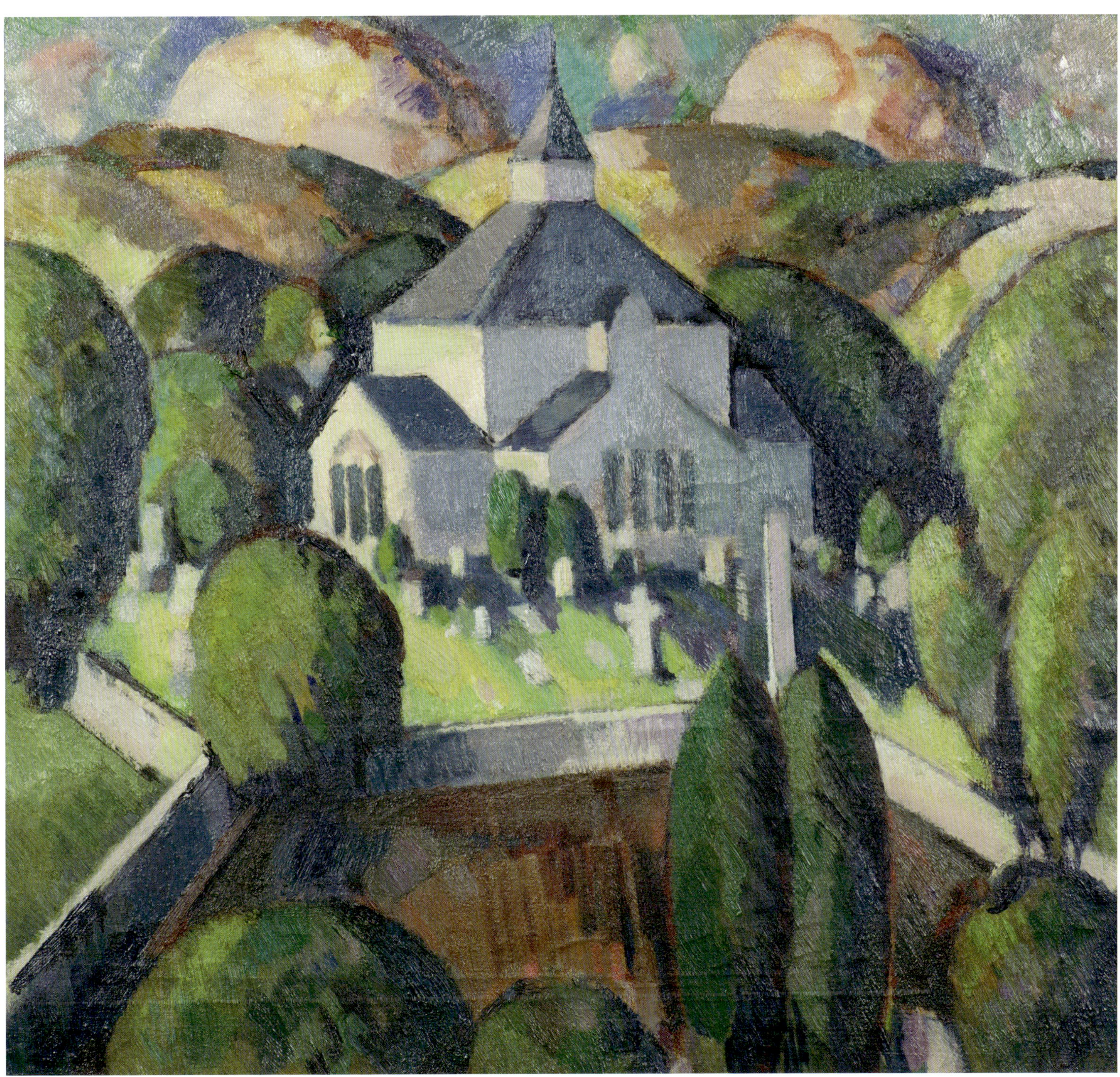

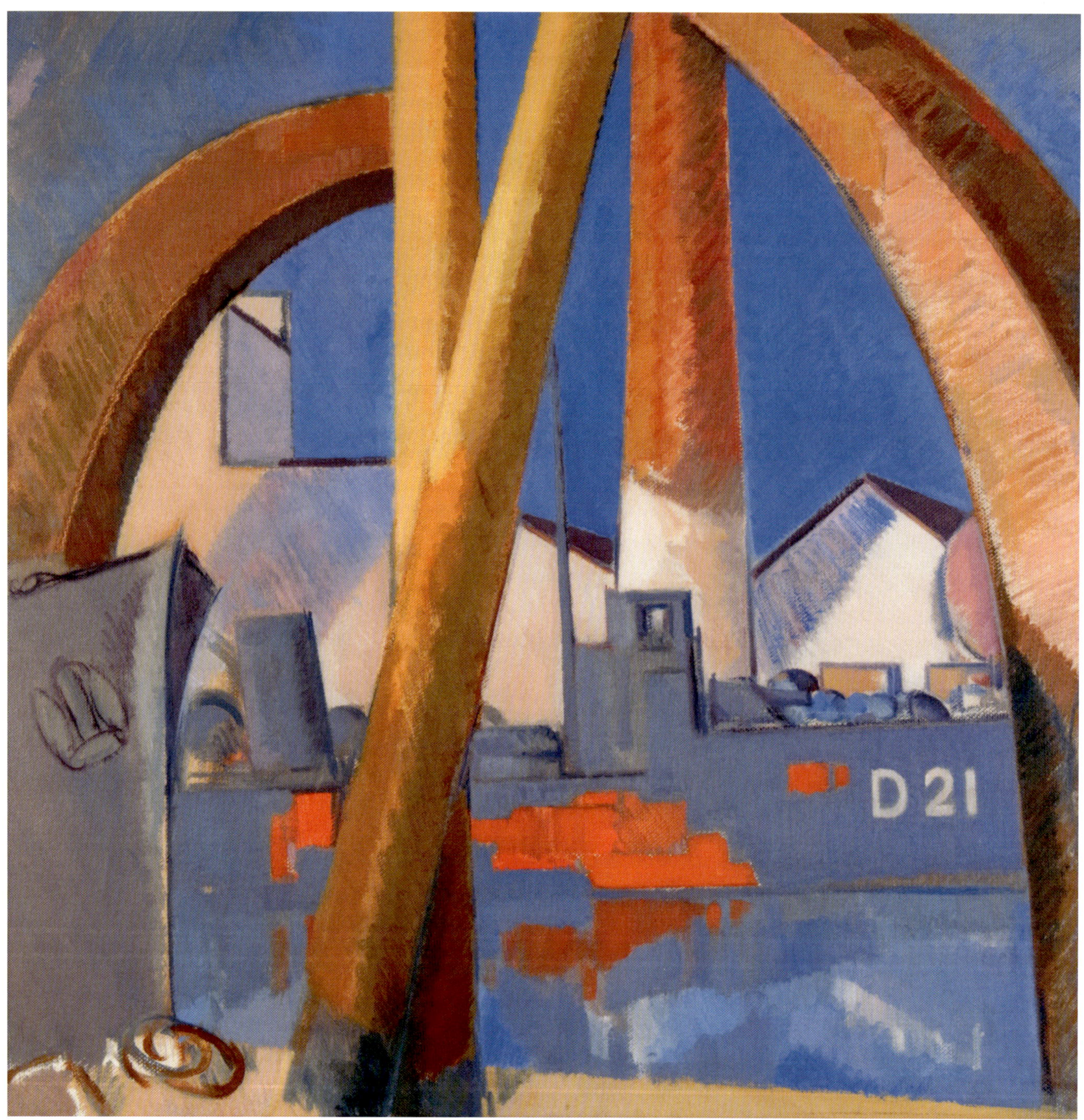

[32]

Damaged Destroyer, 1918

Oil on canvas, 73.6 × 76.2
Glasgow Life (Glasgow Museums) on behalf of Glasgow City Council
presented by Glasgow Art Gallery and Museums Association 1976

[33]

Portsmouth Docks, 1918

Oil on canvas, 76.2 × 68.6
University of Stirling, presented by Margaret Morris and the J.D. Fergusson Art Foundation 1968

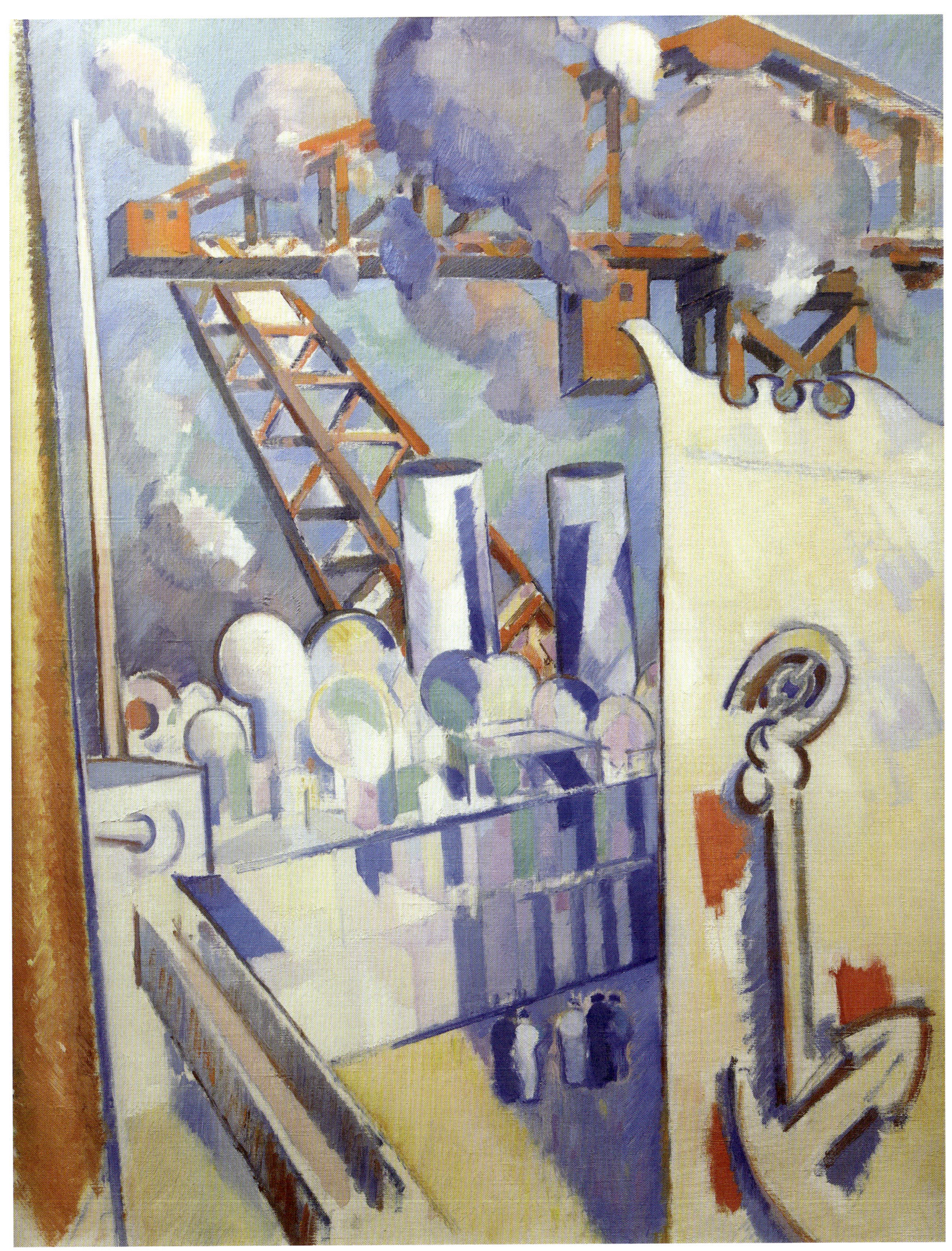

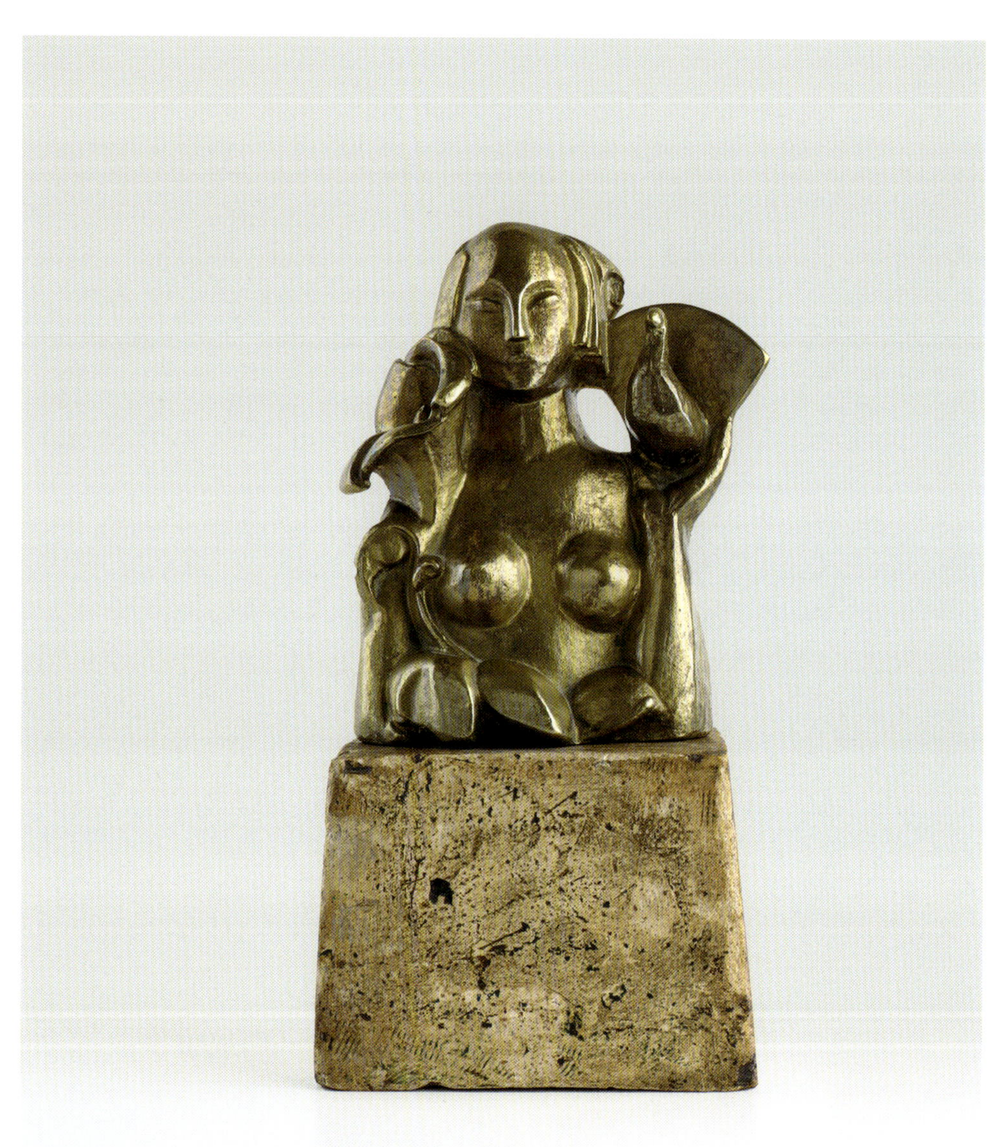

[34]

Philosophy, 1919 (cast at a later date)

Bronze on plaster base made by the artist, 13 × 11 × 7 exc. base, 22.5 × 13 × 9.5 inc. base
Private collection

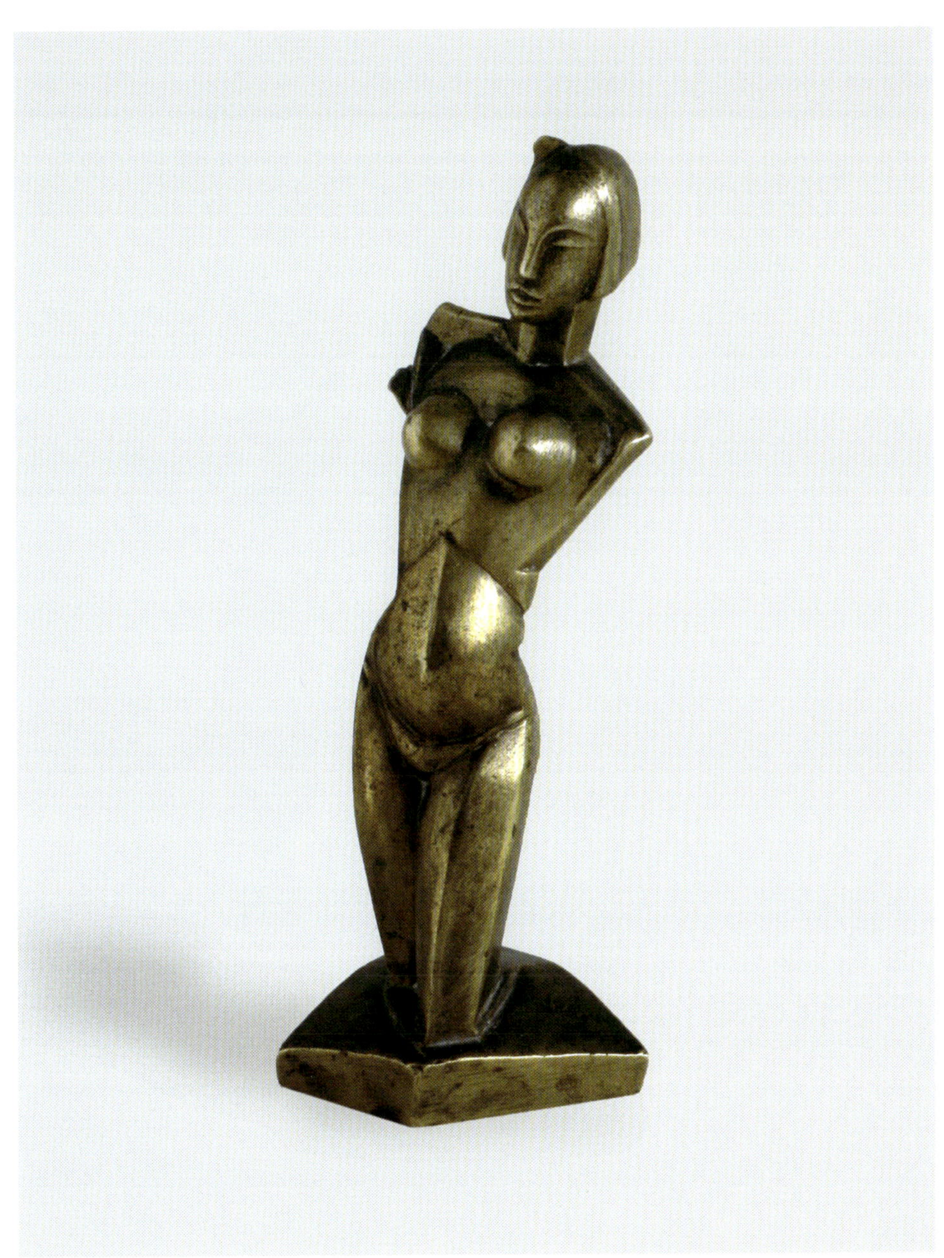

[35]

*Standing Female Nude, c.*1920 (cast at a later date)

Bronze, 23 × 8.5 × 8.5
Private collection

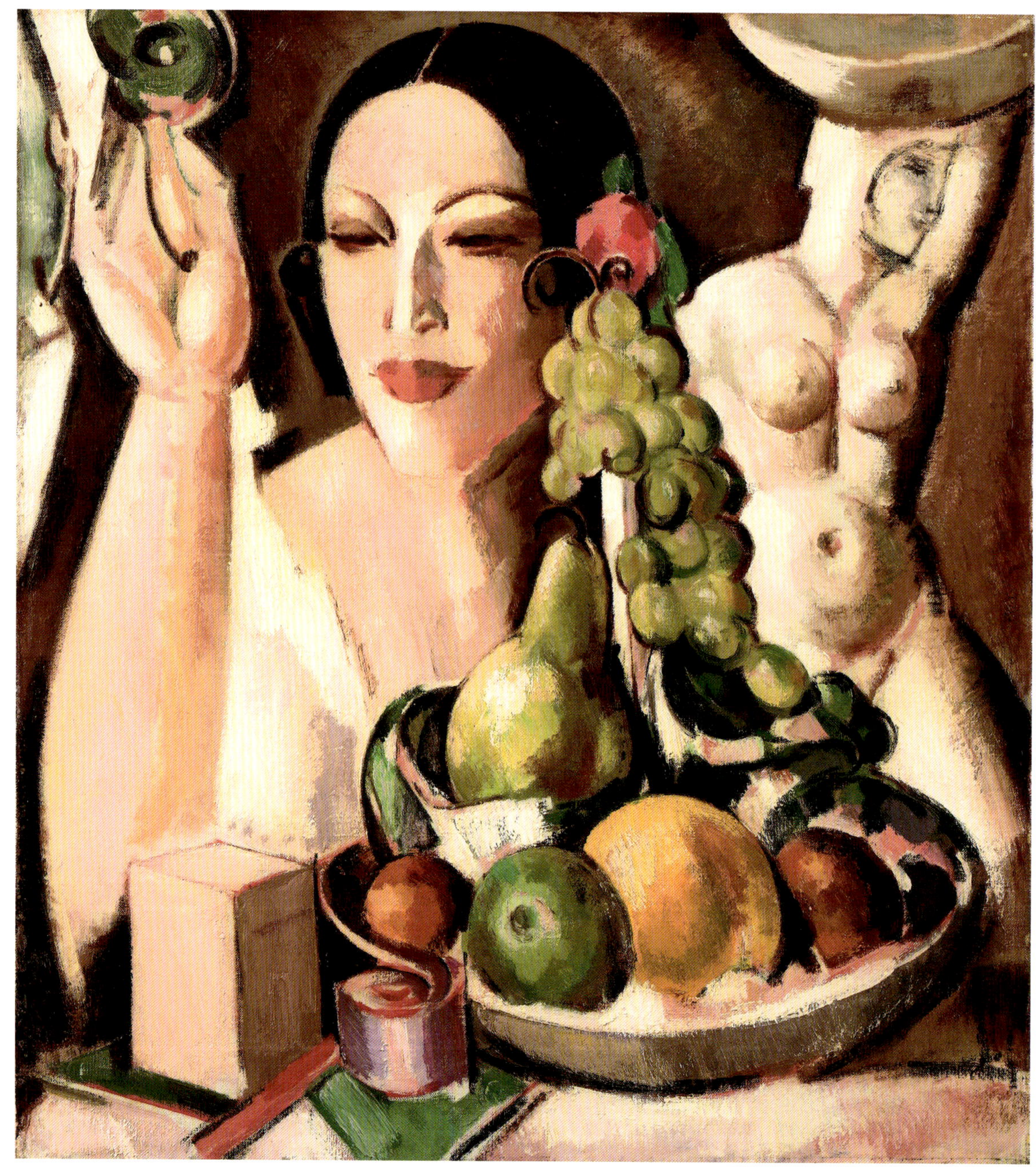

[36]
S.S. Transylvania Souvenir (*The Pink Box*), 1929
Oil on canvas, 61 × 56
Private collection, courtesy Christie's

[37]
Grace McColl, 1930
Oil on canvas, 91.5 × 73.7
Private collection, courtesy the Richard Green Gallery, London

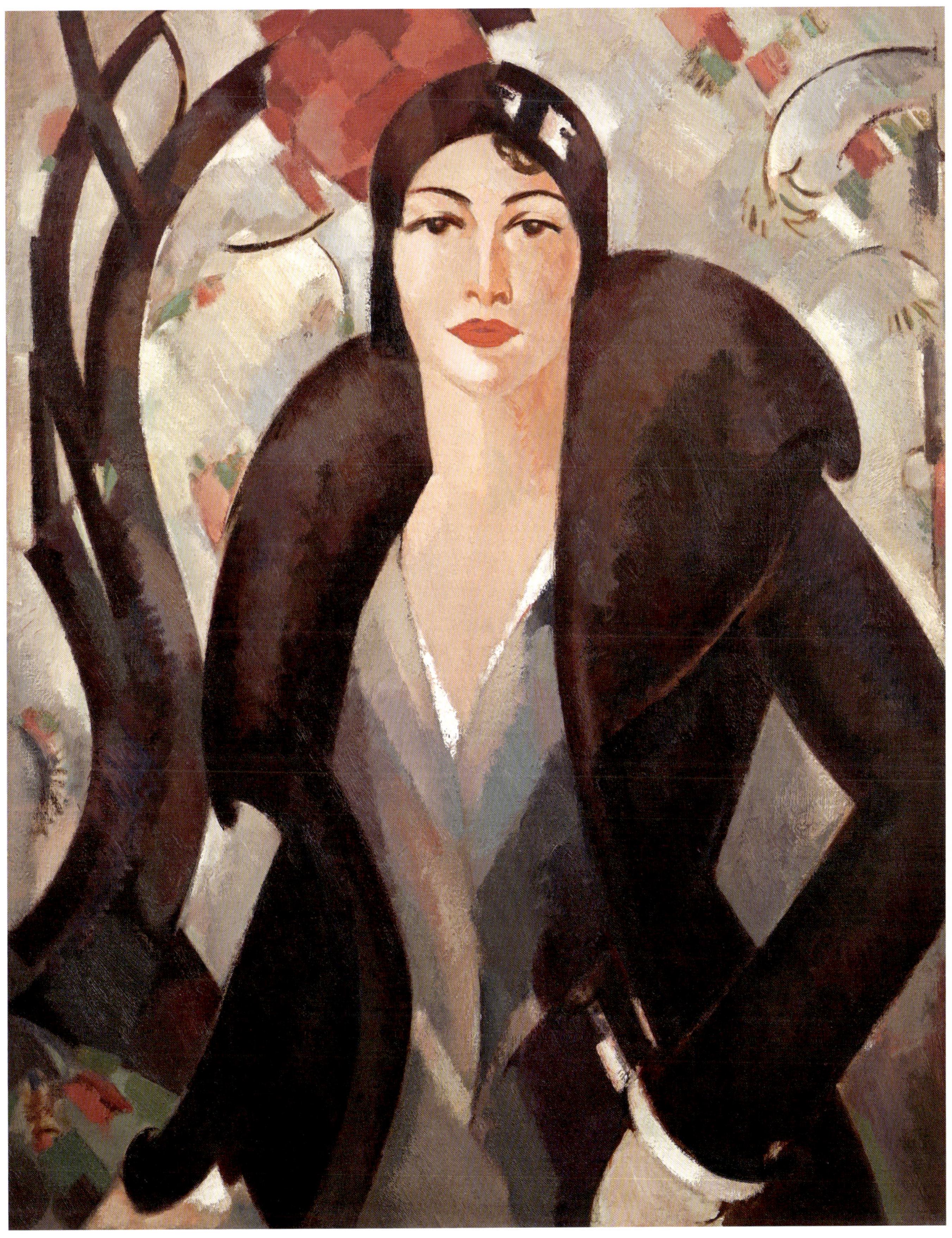

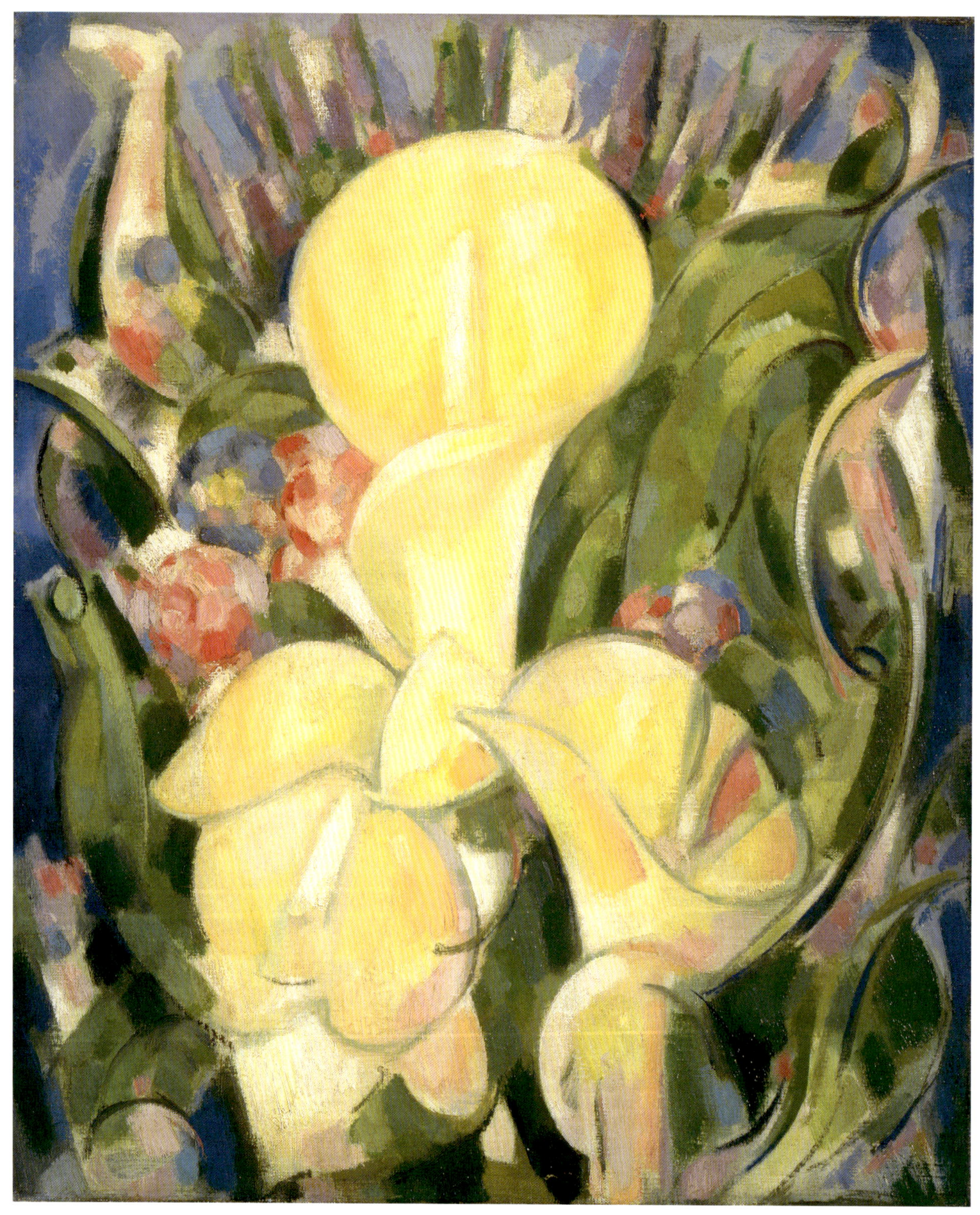

[38]

Lilies, 1938

Oil on canvas, 92 × 73.5
The Fergusson Gallery, Perth & Kinross Council
presented by the J.D. Fergusson Art Foundation 1991

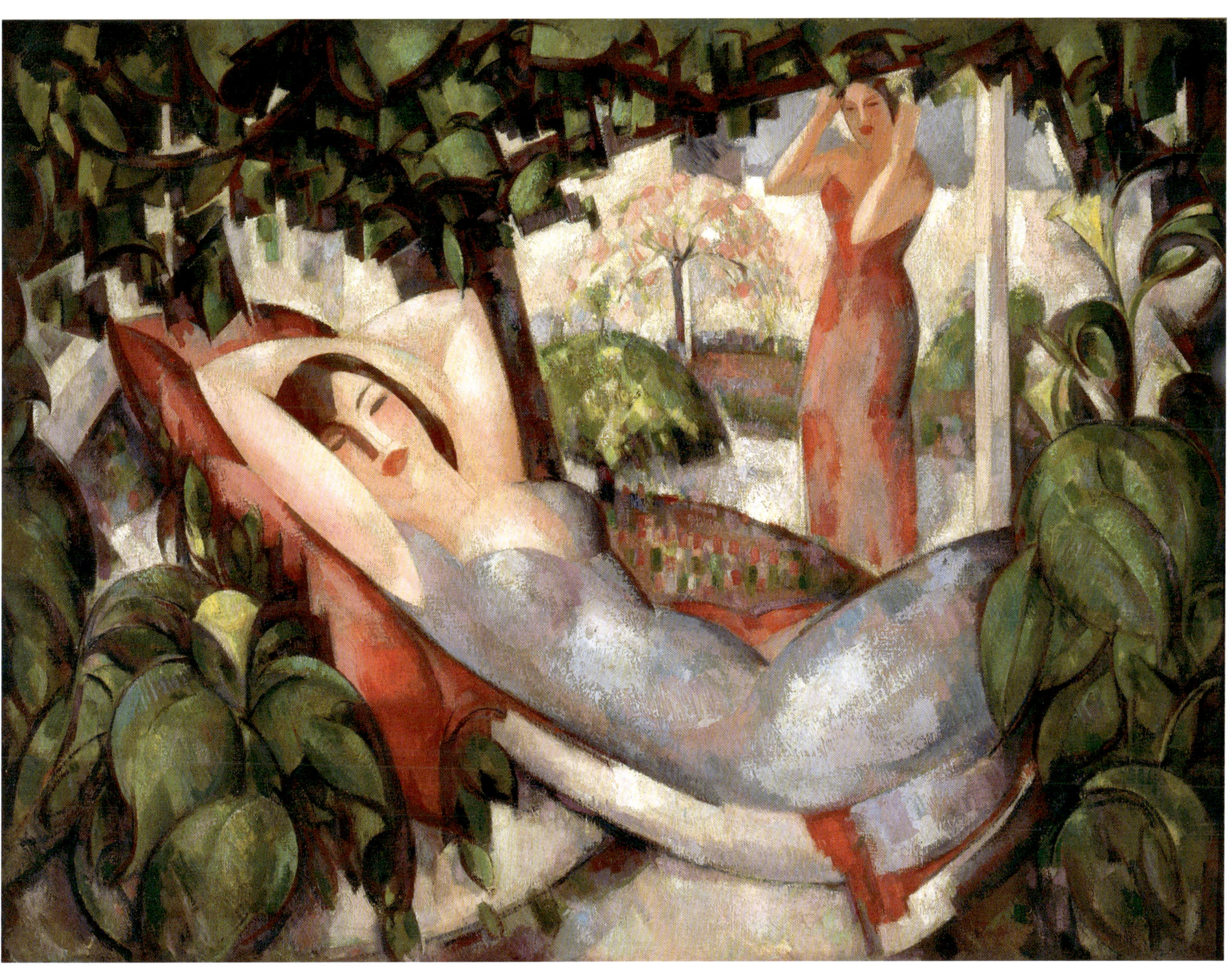

[39]

Summer, 1914, 1934

Oil on canvas, 88 × 113.5
The Fergusson Gallery, Perth & Kinross Council
presented by the J.D. Fergusson Art Foundation 1991

[40]

Bathers: Noon, 1937

Oil on canvas, 115.3 × 146.4
University of Stirling
presented by Margaret Morris
and the J.D. Fergusson Art Foundation 1968

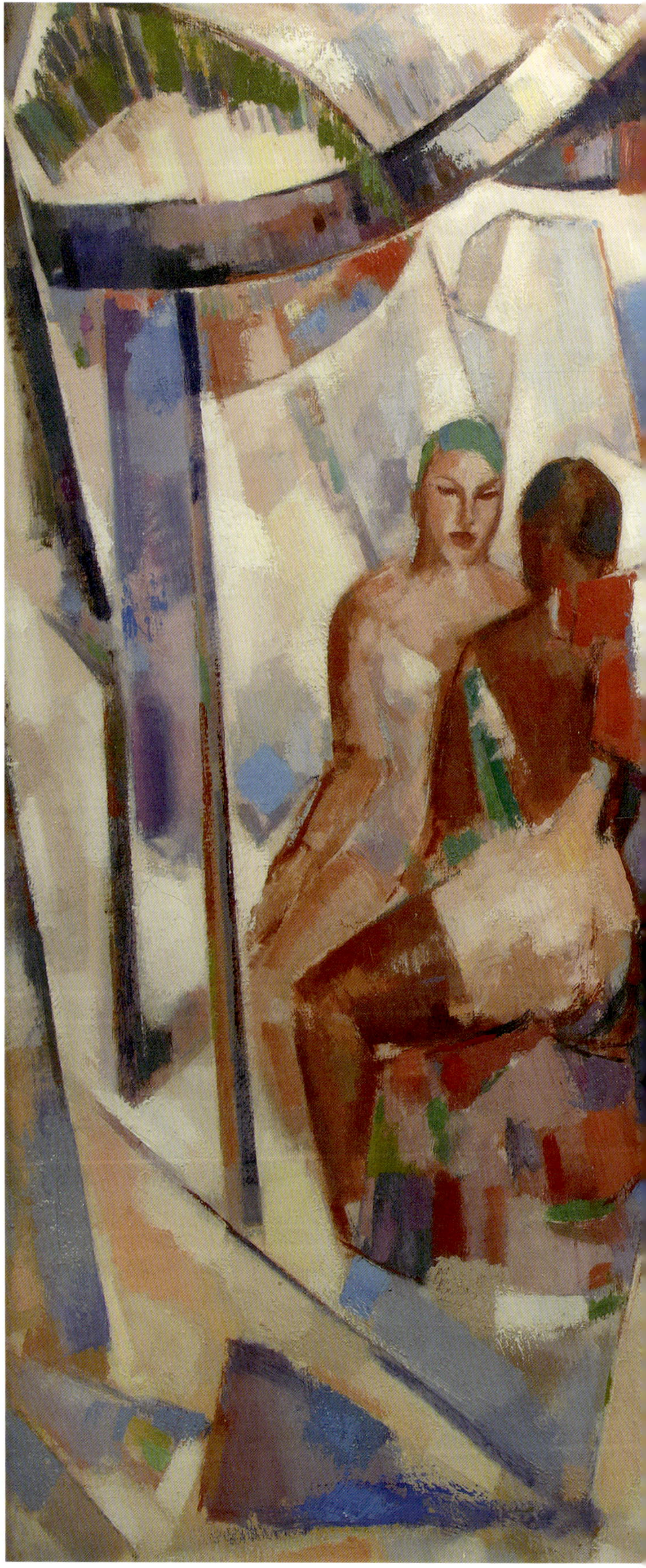

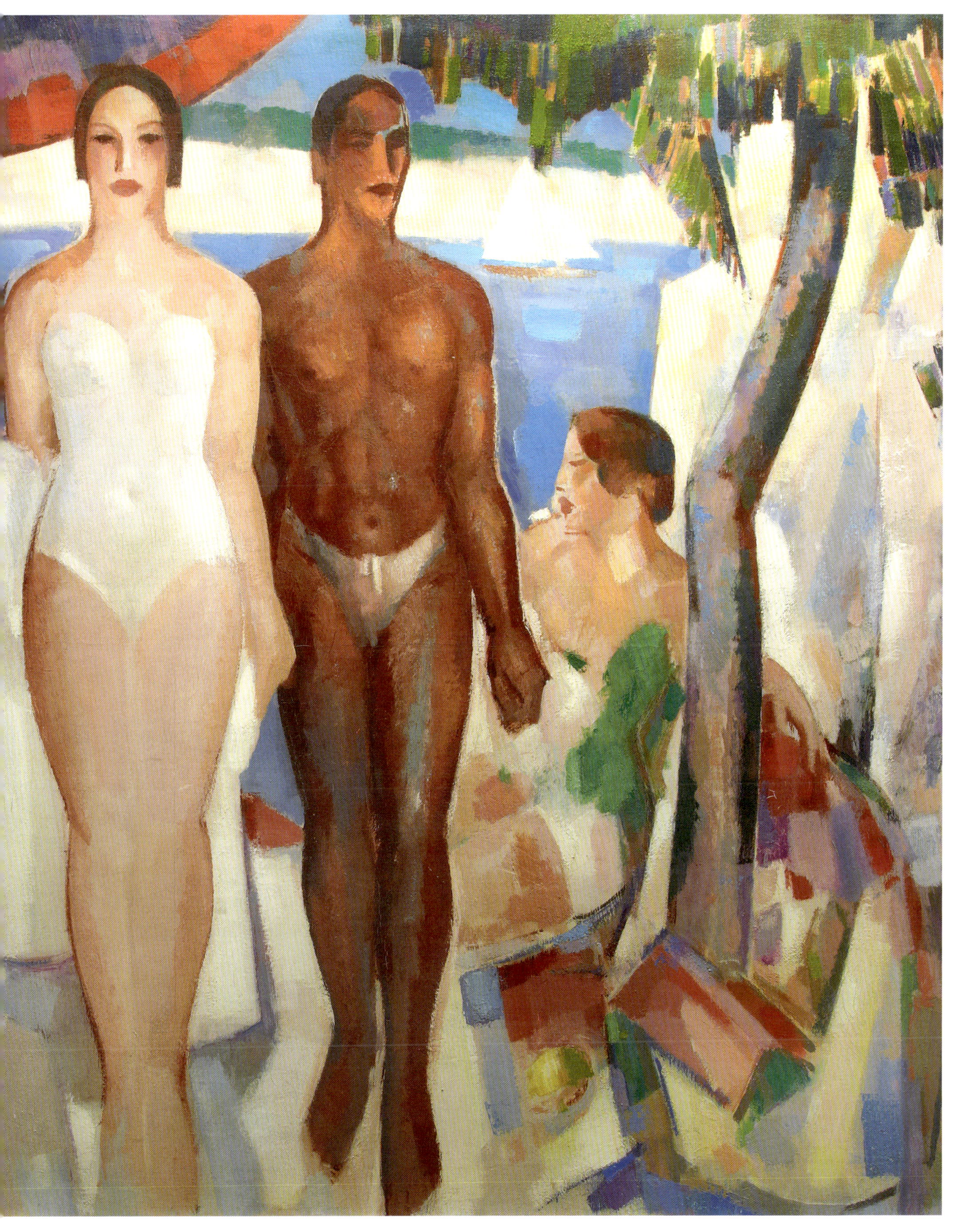

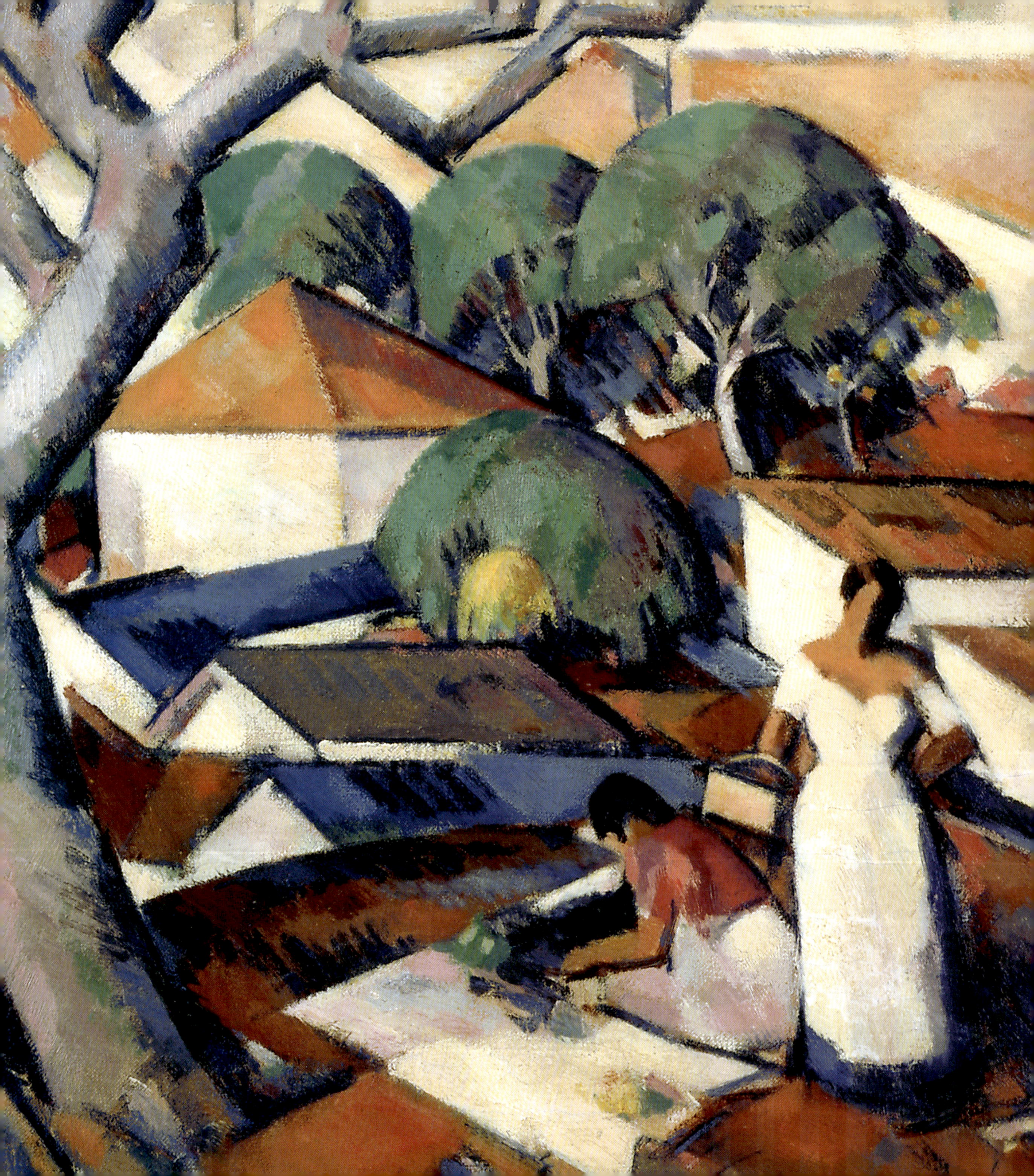

3 · La vie de bohème: Fergusson in France

ELIZABETH CUMMING

In 1961 the artist André Dunoyer de Segonzac contributed a foreword to the catalogue for the Memorial Exhibition. A friend for half a century, he warmly referred to Fergusson as a born painter, and to his work as having a directness that required no explanation.[1] France had become Fergusson's second, perhaps his true, home. He was attracted by its culture, its artists and the sheer openness of its thinking, its debating of new ideas. Even on early visits to Paris from the late 1890s and in the 1900s to the northern resorts such as Paris-Plage he found a simultaneously relaxing and stimulating attitude to life and art that would soon deepen [42]. His first visit in 1897 resulted in paintings of Paris and Rouen sent to the RSA and the SSA, the following year; thereafter he went to Paris every May with money which his father had given him.[2] His first visit had introduced him to the Latin Quarter on the Left Bank, at the heart of which was the Palais du Luxembourg: its paintings and surrounding park would provide inspiration right up to the First World War.[3] As he later recalled, Paris also provided that sympathetic 'ambience' which Robert Burns had called 'a "clime", – "a happy fireside clime for weans and wife"' and that made it 'so easy to work in'.[4]

While Fergusson was committed to being a professional artist, his early painting was not particularly innovative but rather reflected his attraction to the art of others. His first preferred medium, watercolour, soon felt old-fashioned and was replaced by oils, with thickly applied pigments jotting down his impressions on cigar box lids: these Scottish and French scenes capture the effect of light and local colour, a sense of time and place. Keen for experience in art, Fergusson absorbed and adapted what he found particularly stimulating. As a measure of his commitment to painting, the catalogue of his exhibition in May and June 1905 at the commercial London gallery of John Baillie (1866?–1926) lists fifty-six paintings – portrait studies, still lifes, scenes of Edinburgh, Aberdour and Burntisland, Valencia, Étaples, Paris-Plage and Paris. These were small-scale works, made for British taste, honest recordings of light and local colour, painted *en plein air* (grains of sand settled on the paint in some sketches) and largely traditional in their ambition [52].

The show's catalogue tells a different story. Here Fergusson published his credo that would set the scene for his ambitious future work. In part, his attitude to painting is that of the Impressionists, as he writes that 'the artist is not attempting to compete with the completeness of the camera, not with the accuracy of the anatomical diagram' but rather 'for truth, for reality through light'. However, he also states that 'what is on the surface may explain everything to one with real insight' and that 'art is purely a matter of emotion, sincerity in art consists in being faithful to one's emotions' and 'to restrain an emotion is to kill it'.[5] Fergusson was aware of the radical new art which within months was being labelled as the work of '*les Fauves*' (wild beasts).[6] Although some visitors referred to the paintings of Matisse and Derain as 'madness', and another critic the 'barbaric and naive games of a child ... playing with a box of colours',[7] artists such as Maurice Denis (1870–1943) recognised in such works 'an emotion from nature'.[8] Fergusson felt an affinity with the insight into true reality offered by such vibrant colour and free painting.

Fergusson's decision to settle in France was of course also the result of meeting Anne Estelle Rice at Paris-Plage. Rice had first been sent with her journalist colleague Elizabeth Dryden to Paris in 1905 by Philadelphia's *The North American* to illustrate the latest fashion trends.[9] Rice's established style of

[41] Detail from *Christmas Time in the South of France,* 1922 [71]

drawing for publication was heavily contoured with 'simplification of interior detail and shading'.[10] A light yet clear touch was required for sketches for a ladies' journal. This plain way of working, when applied to painting and allied to a fresh new 'Fauve' approach to art or the more restrained manner of such painters as Auguste Chabaud, began to give Fergusson's art a more expressionist edge. His low-toned and relatively modest *Self-portrait* of 1907 [26] paved the way. Made as a first formal statement of his new settlement in Paris, its composition is seemingly casual yet it is also a fine balance of figure and still life caught in a studio mirror, with a framed study of a woman's head, probably of Rice, on the wall behind and the black left edging acting as compositional counterweights to the figure. The painting has a formal structure compared with many of his oil sketches of Paris and his celebrated study of Rice herself outside the café at the south-east corner of the gardens of the Palais du Luxembourg that was frequented by poets and artists, *Anne Estelle Rice, Closerie des Lilas* [43], which declared his adoption of core Fauvism in its bold green facial shadow.

Fergusson obviously much enjoyed the company of women and often created a sense of theatre from their personal elegance and dress. His art at this time combines freely painted studies and traditional portraiture. *The Green Bird* [53], a further intimate study of Rice, is so very different from the glamorous, formal portraits of Elizabeth Dryden such as *La Cocarde* [54] and the anonymous *Portrait de Mademoiselle H.*. As well as a number of paintings of the glamorous women he encountered, Fergusson also turned his eye to his adopted country, capturing its liveliness in a number of small pieces such as *Paris* [55] and *The Open Air Fête, Armenonville* [56], *Carrefour de l'Observatoire* and, not least, *Closerie des Lilas*. These blend traditional recording of place and local colour with a new palette of greens, pinks and blues. Fergusson now blocked in colour with Fauvist simplicity, his paintings becoming increasingly vibrant and decorative as he recorded his response to his surroundings rather than its surface appearance. Symbolic of this new attitude to form and colour is *Hortensia* [57], where the facial features are ambitiously reduced to a mask set against the billowing blossoms of a late spring or summer garden.

Immersing himself in the life of the city, Fergusson had started to send to the Salon d'Automne in 1907, with *Hortensia* displayed there in 1910. In 1909, the year he was elected one of the Salon's *sociétaires*, he reviewed the annual exhibition for London's *Art News*.[11] *La Terrasse, Café d'Harcourt* [58] was one of six paintings[12] he showed that year; *Le Cocher: Crépuscule* (*The Coachman: Dusk*) [59] is a quick, evocative study of a hansom cab and driver. Of them all, *Café d'Harcourt*, possibly painted in late 1907,[13] probably played a significant part in his election for it is a powerful, iconic work, boldly uniting Parisian nightlife with the world of couture. Situated on the boulevard Saint-Michel east of the Luxembourg and north of the Closerie des Lilas, this was one of the liveliest night spaces in Paris; the English writer John Middleton Murry, who met Fergusson and Rice there in 1910, described it as 'the last resort of the *petites femmes* of the Left Bank ... Big hats and muffs were the mode that year, and some of the faces they framed were charming indeed'.[14] Fergusson painted the view from inside the café, looking out to the tables and awning spilling over the pavement. Many of the women represented are milliners, each crowned by one of their own creations. The glare of the artificial lighting equalises all those present.

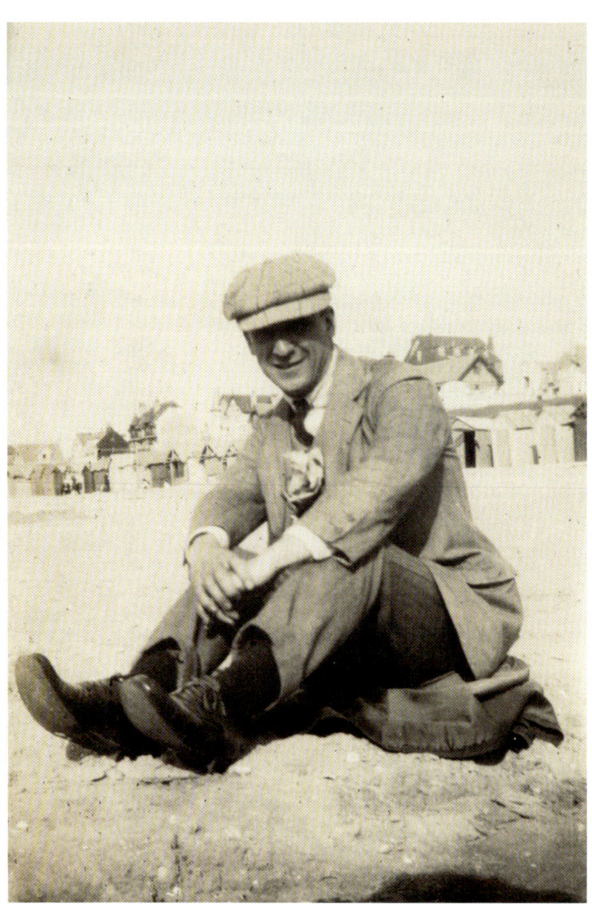

[42] J.D. Fergusson at Paris-Plage, *c.*1907
The Fergusson Gallery, Perth & Kinross Council

[43] *Anne Estelle Rice in Paris* (*Closerie des Lilas*), *c.*1907

Hunterian Art Gallery, University of Glasgow, bequeathed by Gilbert Innes 1971

Some girls share tables with male companions, others casually mill around.

This recording of a café at night conflates various aspects of cultural modernity. Placed centrally and forward, eye to eye with the viewer, is a woman dressed in pink, the flatness and incompleteness of her dress a reminder of Rice and Dryden's fashion sketches and also of Paris's indigenous street art – the art of the poster. Two large and major single studies of women, the elegant Dryden in *The Red Shawl* [27] and Rice in the delicious *Le Manteau Chinois* [64] unite the worlds of haute couture with floral, feminised backgrounds, and in the latter faux Chinese abstracted motifs, to reflect their characters. The sheer voluptuousness of these is in contrast to the plainness of the Sargentian swagger of the earlier full-lengths of Jean Maconochie such as *The Feather Boa* of 1904, exhibited at the 1907 Salon d'Automne. *Le Manteau Chinois* is one of Fergusson's essays in uniting traditionalism with Fauvism, the shadow facial skin tones green but less obvious than in *Anne Estelle Rice, Closerie des Lilas*. These were formal exhibition pieces for Paris and

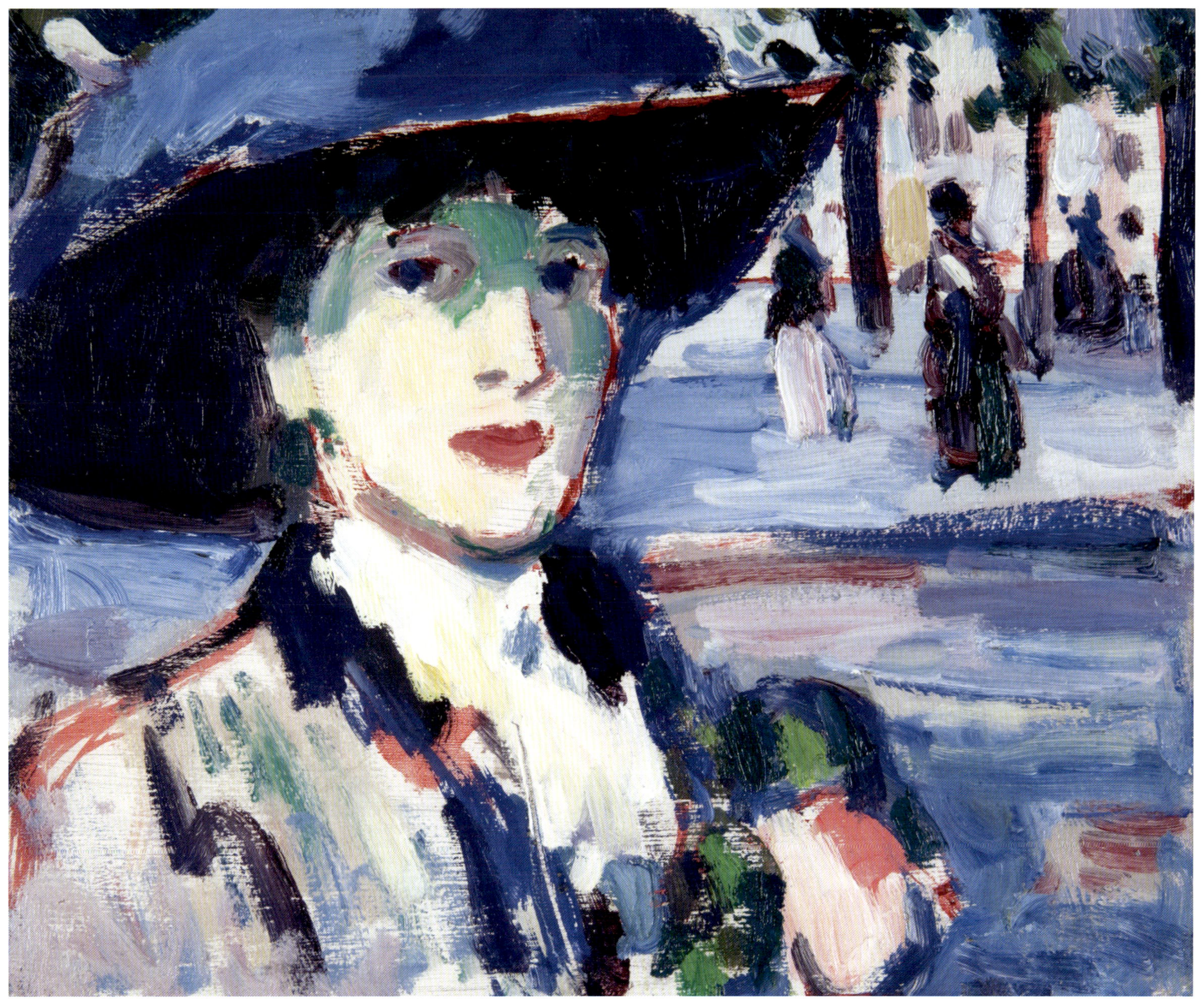

London[15] that displayed one aspect of Fergusson's professional ambition, but their formalism also conveys the totality of vision required for poster art.

More than any other, the art of Henri de Toulouse-Lautrec (1864–1901), and in particular his posters featuring the cabaret dancer La Goulue, convey the immediacy and liveliness of the essential Parisian culture. Fergusson made several sketches of the famous poster of 1891 which show his interest in the dancer as the essential design element of its studied simplicity.[16] As Carol Nathanson has noted, Rice is known to have joined Fergusson and associates on a visit to a brothel to see some of the Frenchman's work in its natural habitat.[17] The art of the poster remained an interest, with both Fergusson and Rice contributing not only paintings but also lithographs printed by the firm of J. Minot to Frank Rutter's 1913 display of Post-Impressionist posters at his major *Post-Impressionist and Futurist Exhibition* at London's Doré Galleries. Most likely to have been those designed for Wanamaker's department store in Philadelphia, the titles of these posters indicate a shared world of pleasure and wellbeing: Fergusson's were *Happy Days*, *Paris Modes* and *Furniture Poster* and Rice's *Joy World* and *Summer Comfort*.

In 1908–9 Fergusson also sent illustrations to Wanamaker's, Rice's employer, for their trade journal. At the same date he made six strong ink and wash drawings of beach scenes, one of which he captioned '*Assiette au Beurre au Bains de Mer*' [44]. *L'Assiette au Beurre* was a fiercely satirical journal published in Paris between 1901 and 1912. Each themed issue was given to a leading artist to work on – for example, Kees van Dongen, an artist admired by Fergusson,[18] created the images for a 1901 issue on prostitution, while František Kupka (1871–1957) produced those on money in 1902 and on religion in 1904. The journal followed the French satirical tradition well established by the mid-nineteenth century. Fergusson's theme of seaside life and characters, if ever submitted (and this is highly unlikely), lacked the expected political bite. Nonetheless, many of his numerous quick sketches of urban café and night life such as *Chez Maxim* [60] do verge on the grotesque and were his personal response to both the French journal and the *Yellow Book*, first enjoyed years earlier in the Edinburgh public library on George IV Bridge: the sale of his own complete run of the *Yellow Book* may have partly financed his move to Paris.[19]

These seemingly ephemeral artworks, with their acute observations of French everyday life, are in fact a key to Fergusson's painting at this time. Two *intimiste* works from 1909, *St Jacques Studio* [61] and *The Blue Hat, Closerie des Lilas* [63], although different in scale, capture what now seems the intoxicating atmosphere of Paris's studios and café society. The latter is an ambitious study of Yvonne de Kerstrat, a fashion designer and future wife of his friend, the American sculptor Jo Davidson who quoted Fergusson as saying that she had 'no drawing in her face'.[20] It is a scrupulously arranged pose set out across a shallow plane: combined with an overquick, thick application of oil paints[21] it turns a café sketch into a piece of serious painting. It announces a series of medium-size, academic pieces

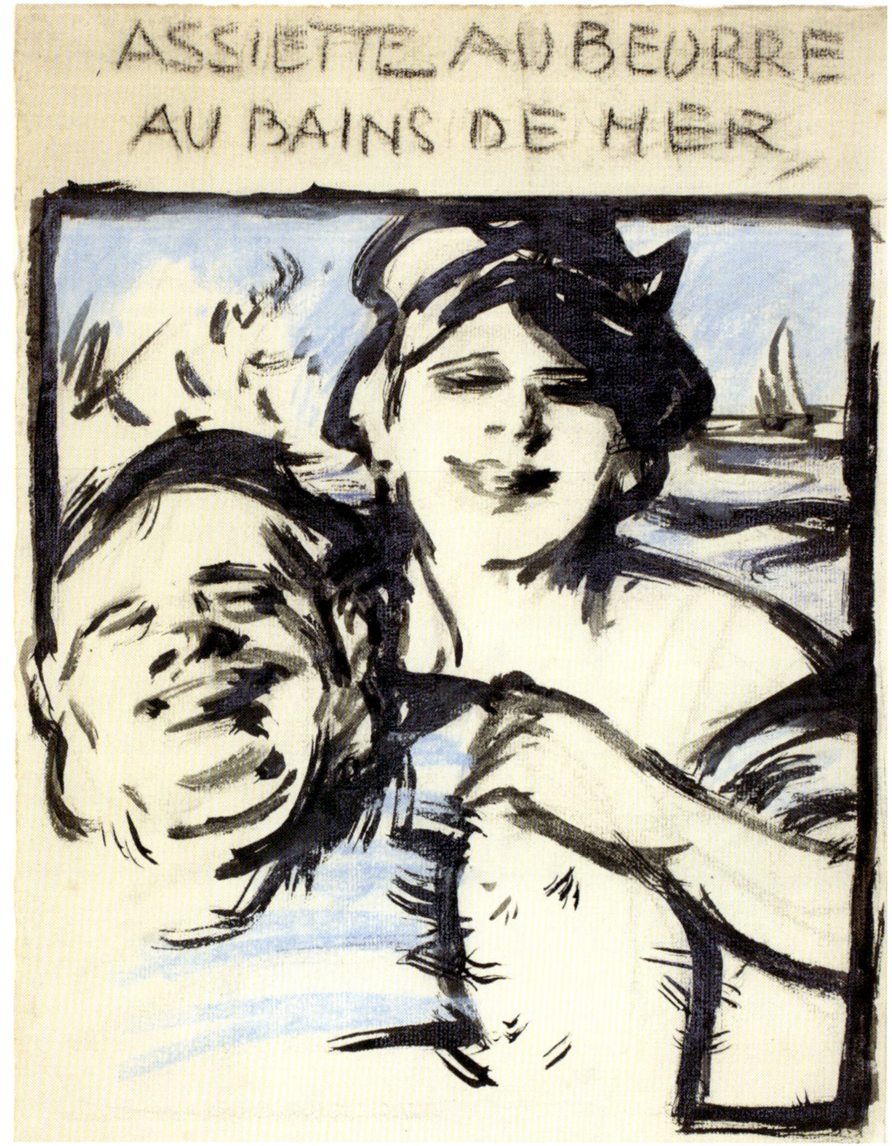

[44] Design for *Assiette Beurre au Bains de Mer*, *c.*1908
The Fergusson Gallery, Perth & Kinross Council

in which Fergusson set out to explore the richness of form and our experience of it. *Voiles indiennes* [29] was inspired directly by Matisse's joy in colour, women and textiles, with an anonymous semi-nude placed in an exotic setting and tending white flowers in a blue pot. The flat backcloth patterning of nature links it and *The Red Shawl* to Rice's 1909–13 panels for Wanamaker's Philadelphian store where figures in eighteenth-century dress are set within decorative floral backgrounds. *La Bête violette* (*The Violet Beast*) [62] is one of a series of studies in which still-life elements dominate, their carefully chosen bright colours and forms together creating a vibrant sense of immediacy. It was among those works sent with his large, academic piece *Rhythm* [66] to the 1911 Salon d'Automne but – in an intentional shift to engage in current Parisian intellectual debate for the earlier Salon des Indépendants that year – Fergusson selected *Torse de Femme* [28] and an abstract study for *Rhythm*.

Teaching English-speaking pupils in his own studio and at the private Académie de la Palette[22] provided Fergusson with both a regular income and a source of further cultural exchange and stimulation. Among the other tutors was the cubist Jean Metzinger (1883–1956). Until 1912, when Henri Le Fauconnier (1881–1946) took it over, the school was run by Jacques-Émile Blanche (1861–1942), a lifelong Anglophile and a painter perhaps now mainly remembered for his celebrated 1892 portrait of Marcel Proust. As a boy, Blanche had been taught English by the poet Stéphane Mallarmé and his schoolmates had included both Proust and Henri Bergson. In Fergusson's day Bergson was the leading philosopher of the age, a man whose ideas of the importance of intuition countered the strict analysis of experience currently being promoted by Freud and others. For Bergson, the creative arts defied such careful compartmentalisation but rather presented the inexpressible. A key idea was the sense of a life force, the *élan vital*, which was expressed through the participant's projection of him – or herself into a painting or poem, an object or a piece of music. To read Bergson's key work, *L'Evolution Créatrice* (1906), in the Frenchman's own city had been the declared reason for Murry's visit to Paris in late 1910 when he met Fergusson.

Not surprisingly, the idea of somehow connecting and conveying sensation, time and the power of creativity was attractive to progressive artists. Fergusson's first such experimental paintings include *At my Studio Window* [65] where the figure became an element of the outside natural world whose shimmering colours enter the studio: interior and exterior making one space, time paused as imagination takes over. It found full expression the following year when Murry appointed Fergusson Art Editor of his new London journal of art, music and literature, *Rhythm*, the title of which again echoes time, evolution and the embedded constant change of music and life.[23] Running from 1911 to 1913, its contributors, such as the collector and Leeds academic Michael Sadler, saw Fauvism as the visual embodiment of Bergson and 'a reaction on the one hand against the lifeless mechanism of Pointillism, on the other against the moribund flickerings of the aesthetic movement', a view shared by Fergusson.[24] As Murry himself wrote in the first issue of *Rhythm*, Bergson's philosophy, in France at least, was:

> *a living artistic force. It is the open avowal of the supremacy of the intuition, of the spiritual vision of the artist in form, in words and meaning. He has shown that the concepts of the reason, while the reason remains untrue to itself, fail before the fact of Life.*[25]

According to the Canadian painter Emily Carr (1871–1945), Fergusson encouraged his students 'to see rhythm in nature'.[26] Nature, however, was only the starting point for expression through art: such works as *Rhythm* [66] and also works by Rice are modernist syntheses of form, line and colour.

The art of these 'Rhythmists' loosened tradition in academic subjects and encouraged experiment. According to the son of his lawyer from later London days (whose fees were paid in art), Fergusson would coat his fruit with paint before starting on a still life.[27] The intensity of his work at this period was reflected in the contents of his studio at this time, as recorded by the writer Katherine Mansfield:

> *Very beautiful, oh God is a blue teapot with two white cups attending, a red apple among the oranges, with pink and lilac notes recurring until nothing remains but them, sounding over and over. There are a number of frames ... and the picture of a naked woman with her arms raised, languid as though her heavy flowering beauty were almost too great to bear.*[28]

In this painting, *Torse de Femme* [28], and its companion piece *La Force* [67], the figure, primordial yet sophisticated, is thickly outlined in black to energise its form. The pose would be adapted in stone as *Paysanne, Roquegautier* (*Bust of a Woman*) in 1930, an instance of Fergusson reworking a powerful image into three dimensions.

The sexual potency of some of Fergusson's exhibited drawings and paintings of 1911–13 was a sign of his confident position within Montparnasse's liberal circles. His friends by now included De Segonzac, Othon Friesz, a Fauve painter and friend of Georges Braque (1882–1963), and Davidson, but perhaps more impressively he also knew Jacob Epstein, Pablo Picasso, to whose studio he introduced Peploe, and Gertrude Stein, the American writer and collector.[29] Another key person in Paris was the poet and director of the Théâtre d'Art, Paul Fort, who presented works by the writer Emile Verhaeren. Fergusson would recall how Fort, 'King of the Poets', hosted an 'open to all poets' evening each Thursday at the Closerie des Lilas. Much later, he asked Fort why they never chanced to meet, to which the poet replied that they had come there by different routes, himself by that of the poets, Fergusson by '*la route des Rois*' [the way of the Kings].[30] His sketchbooks from this date also note addresses for the writer Jean Cocteau (12 rue d'Anjou) and the businessman Auguste Pellerin (57 boulevard Haussmann), a famous Cézanne collector and patron of Matisse. When it came to selecting artwork for *Rhythm*, Fergusson requested pieces from modernist artists including Picasso, Derain, his pupil Jessica Dismorr and his friends De Segonzac, Rice and Peploe, although, as many scholars have remarked, these were by no means all new artworks.

The energy of many of the paintings and some drawings of these years is obvious. In his designs for *Rhythm*'s cover [45], the figure is placed within nature as a nude in her sexual prime, a token of the fecundity of the natural world. Expanded to life size as a painting, the figure becomes monumental, the curves of her body echoed in the organic forms of nature. A related painting called *Eve* was also made around 1912 and was shown in London only in 1913 – one of four pieces including *Rhythm* selected for Rutter's *Post-Impressionist and Futurist Exhibition* where they kept company with Cézanne, Matisse, Paul Gauguin (1848–1903), Camille Pissarro (1830–1903) and Pierre Bonnard (1867–1947).

Yet such ambitious paintings were created alongside more modest work. The paintings made at Royan on the Gironde Estuary and at nearby Saint-Palais in

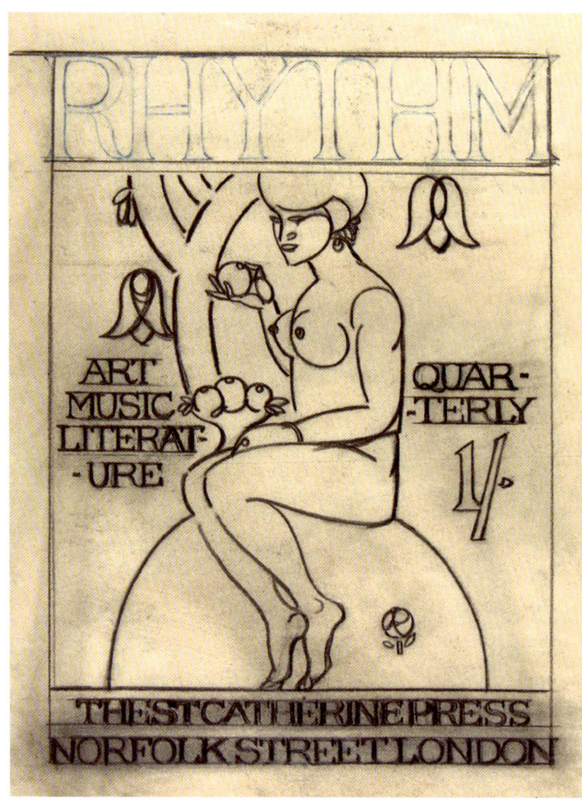

[45] *Study for* Rhythm *cover*, 1911
Private collection, courtesy Alexander Meddowes Fine Art Broker, Edinburgh

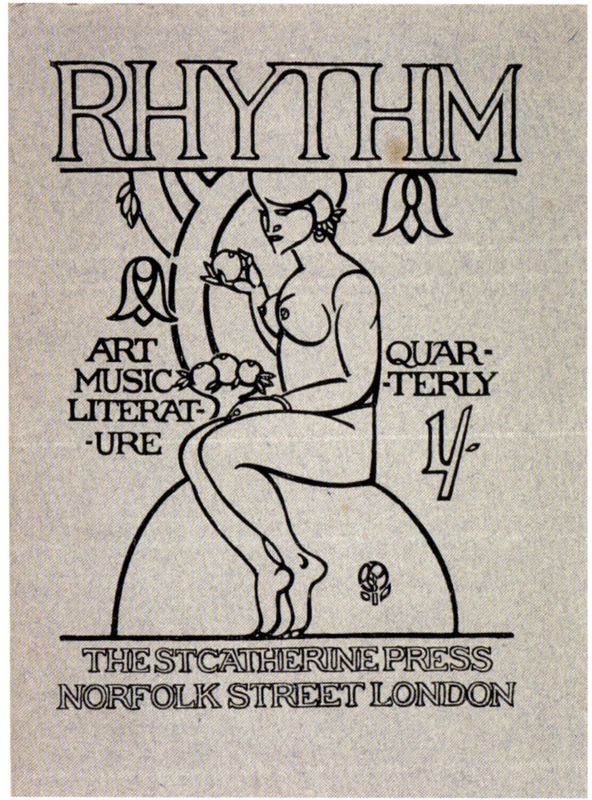

[46] Cover of *Rhythm*, vol.1, no.1, published Summer 1911
Private collection

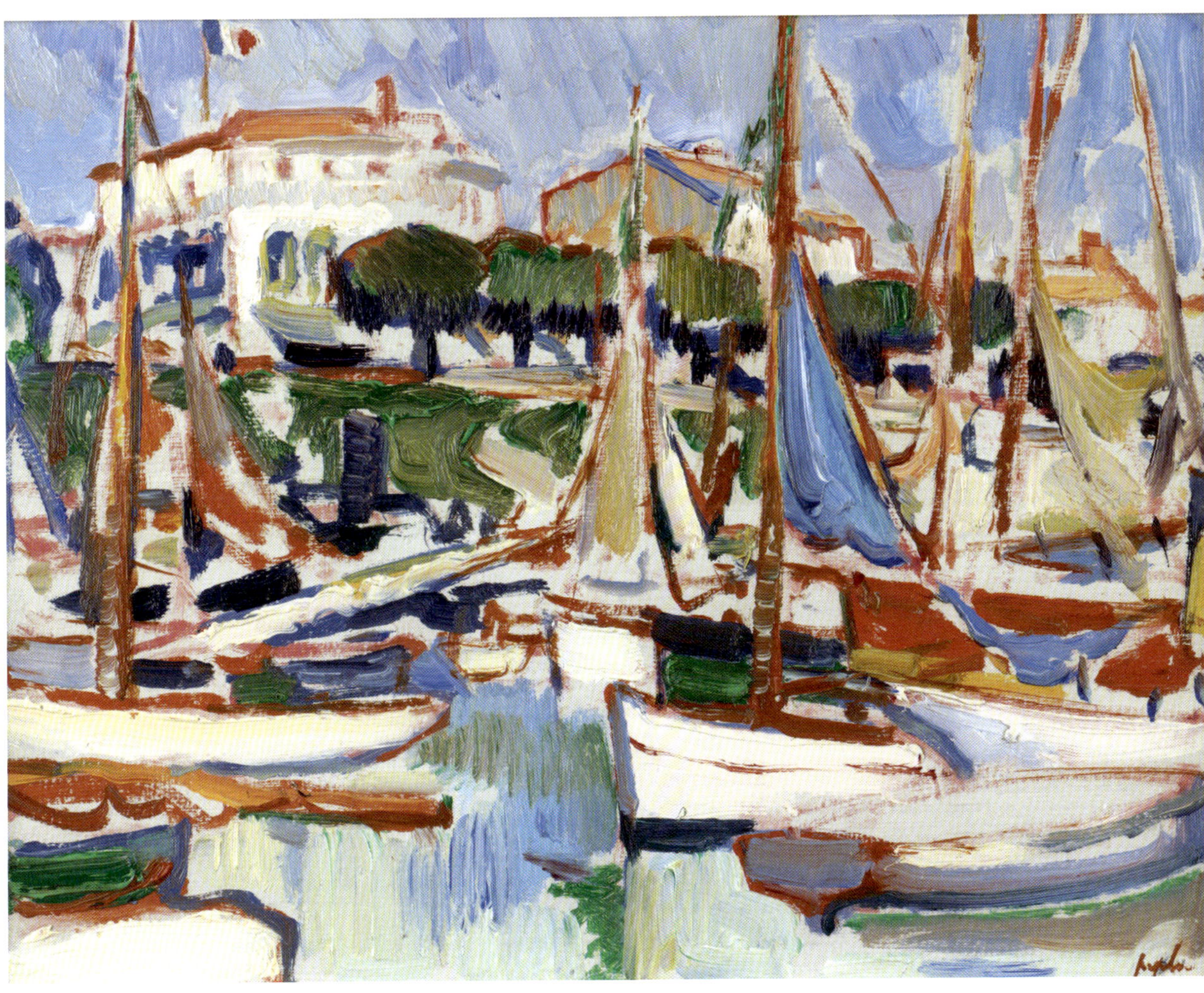

[47] S. J. Peploe
Boats at Royan, 1910
Private collection

the summer of 1910 alongside Peploe and Rice have enriched colours, strong blues and reds or blacks edging the forms of the harbour, sailing craft and sails and people to capture an essence of place [50, 51, 47]. In the summer of 1911 Fergusson and Peploe also painted together at the picturesque Ile de Bréhat on the Brittany coast, where again the distinctive colour, light and atmosphere were inspirational. Few exhibited titles relate to these visits: perhaps they were simply sold more informally or kept as mementos of good times. Other subjects appear in exhibition catalogues including the results of further visits to Paris-Plage. With his ambition to compete with native *artiste-peintres*,[31] Fergusson seems to have edited the number of pictures submitted to the main Paris shows. He had sent as many as thirty-nine portraits and town or landscapes to the Baillie Gallery in 1908, and his submission to the Salon des Indépendants in 1911 included a painting of azaleas, a view of Montmartre alongside *Etude de Ligne* and *Etude de Rhythme*. Some titles such as *Portrait* or *Girl with Camelia* (shown with the AAA, 1911) are, like many exhibition catalogues of the period, frustratingly vague. Few were illustrated in the Paris press, but the fashionability of the 'rhythmist' style in London circles was recorded by the novelist Ada Leverson for her appreciative readership. In *Tenterhooks* (1912) her heroine Edith Ottley (who lives in a chic white, if regrettably small, Knightsbridge flat) asks her less worldly friend Grace Bennett to find her two or three tea-gowns 'in straight lines ... in red, blue and black' which, although made of a Liberty satin 'with a dull surface', must also have 'a hard outline like a Fergusson'.[32] Edith also reads *Rhythm*, given to her 'to convert her to Post-Impressionism' – in preparation for a visit to Roger Fry's *Second Post-Impressionist Exhibition*.[33] And in *Rhythm* she might have come across London critic Raymond Drey's review of that year's Salon d'Automne, in which he commented on the range of ideas put forward in Fergusson's work and the balance of his strong contour and modelling achieved by subtle lighting.

Drey's review mentions that the larger of the two paintings shown at this Salon was 'a study of a nude dancing figure, painted in strong outlines'. This painting, entitled *Le Printemps*, had been on the easel as Igor Stravinsky was writing his orchestral work *Le Sacre du Printemps* [The Rite of Spring]. Fergusson, like Rice and Peploe, had been elected a *sociétaire* of the Salon d'Automne[34] and as such was offered free tickets for performances of Sergei Diaghilev's Ballets Russes. Fergusson would recall wonderful evenings immersed in these total works of art, and may also have enjoyed a camaraderie beyond the pleasure of observing performances, for the company's key designer, Léon Bakst (1866–1924), was elected a fellow *sociétaire* of the Salon d'Automne. From the evidence of his sketchbooks and correspondence Fergusson seems to have seen a number of productions including *Schéhérazade*, *Pétrouchka* and *Le Sacre*, and some more than once. It is known that he was to attend the penultimate evening of the season when the programme may have been the same as the following one – *Salomé*, *L'Après-midi d'un Faune*, *Le Sacre*, *Le Spectre de la Rose* and *Prince Igor*.[35]

Among the sketches Fergusson made of Ballets Russes productions are several of *Cléopatre* from 1909. This production, which had introduced Bakst to Paris, also inspired Rice's *The Egyptian Dancers* [48] of 1910, a stylised painting which had a mixed critical reception at the time but, in its figural angularity, successfully encapsulates the theatrical sense of another world, as does the later *Les Eus* [68]. Developed from his own work, *Le Printemps*, this would be the largest and most important painting Fergusson ever produced. Showing a bacchanalian dance in a forest glade, *Les Eus* reflects many of his current interests – the energised totality of nature, primitivism, and the expressive dance then taking Paris by storm. In addition to performances by Isadora Duncan and the Ballets Russes there was the eurhythmics movement led by Émile Jaques-Dalcroze which promoted the understanding of music through physical movement. Quite apart from his direct influence on dance, Jaques-Dalcroze had advised Diaghilev and his dancer-choreographer Vaslav Nijinsky on the steps and movements to be used in *Le Sacre*. Fergusson's curious title for the picture certainly best relates to eurhythmics and again suggests the notion of time, the nude dancers those who both 'have' and 'have had', the repetition of the figures symbolic of moment succeeding moment, a robust and classical alternative to cubism's semi-mechanical, cold façades. It might also mean 'those who have everything' which comes closest to the artist's own note of 'The Healthy Ones', as quoted in his partner, the dancer Margaret Morris's biography.[36]

To an extent *Les Eus* may also reflect Fergusson's awareness of the local Arcadian tradition which had produced such classical paintings as Nicolas Poussin's (1594–1665) *A Dance to the Music of Time* in the 1630s and more recently infused the fauvist vision of *bonheur de vivre* from the mid-1900s, inspired in part by Charles Baudelaire's poem 'L'Invitation au Voyage' in his *Les Fleurs du mal*. However, as Nijinsky had written to Stravinsky that their *Le Sacre* would be 'new, beautiful and utterly different – but for the ordinary viewer a jolting and emotional experience',[37] so *Les Eus* also diverts from recent French tradition. It may in fact date from the summer of 1913 and after the première of *Le Sacre* on 29 May, for Stravinsky's proud 'new language of rhythm',[38] so raw and repetitive as it heads towards the ballet's sacrificial climax, its choreography and Fergusson's nudes are equally charged with heavily muscular energy – what Stravinsky called 'the mystery surge of the creative power of Spring'.[39] *Les Eus* also presents a radically different concept from another large but feminised panel of dancing figures, this time made by Rice as part of her decorative programme for Wanamaker's Philadelphian store. A 1913 dating for *Les Eus* makes further sense in terms of detail as the facial features of the far left figure resemble those of the young dancer Margaret Morris, a recent pupil of Isadora Duncan's brother Raymond, whom Fergusson met in January of that year – and in homage to *Le Sacre* Morris would soon create a ballet called *Spring*.

The meeting of Fergusson and Morris brought a new dimension to both of their lives. Rice would remain a friend but married Raymond Drey in late December of that year, a matter of months after a last summer spent painting in Cassis with Fergusson and Peploe. This was where, as Rice wrote to Theodore Dreiser, 'the sun shines eternally, where the artist's vision has a chance to expand'.[40] By the winter, his Paris studio having been demolished, Fergusson was in Cap d'Antibes where he invited Morris to spend Christmas with him. Here he too enjoyed 'the wonderful heat, sunlight and sense of certainty of the settled sunshine of the south'.[41] Finding a villa in Cap d'Antibes

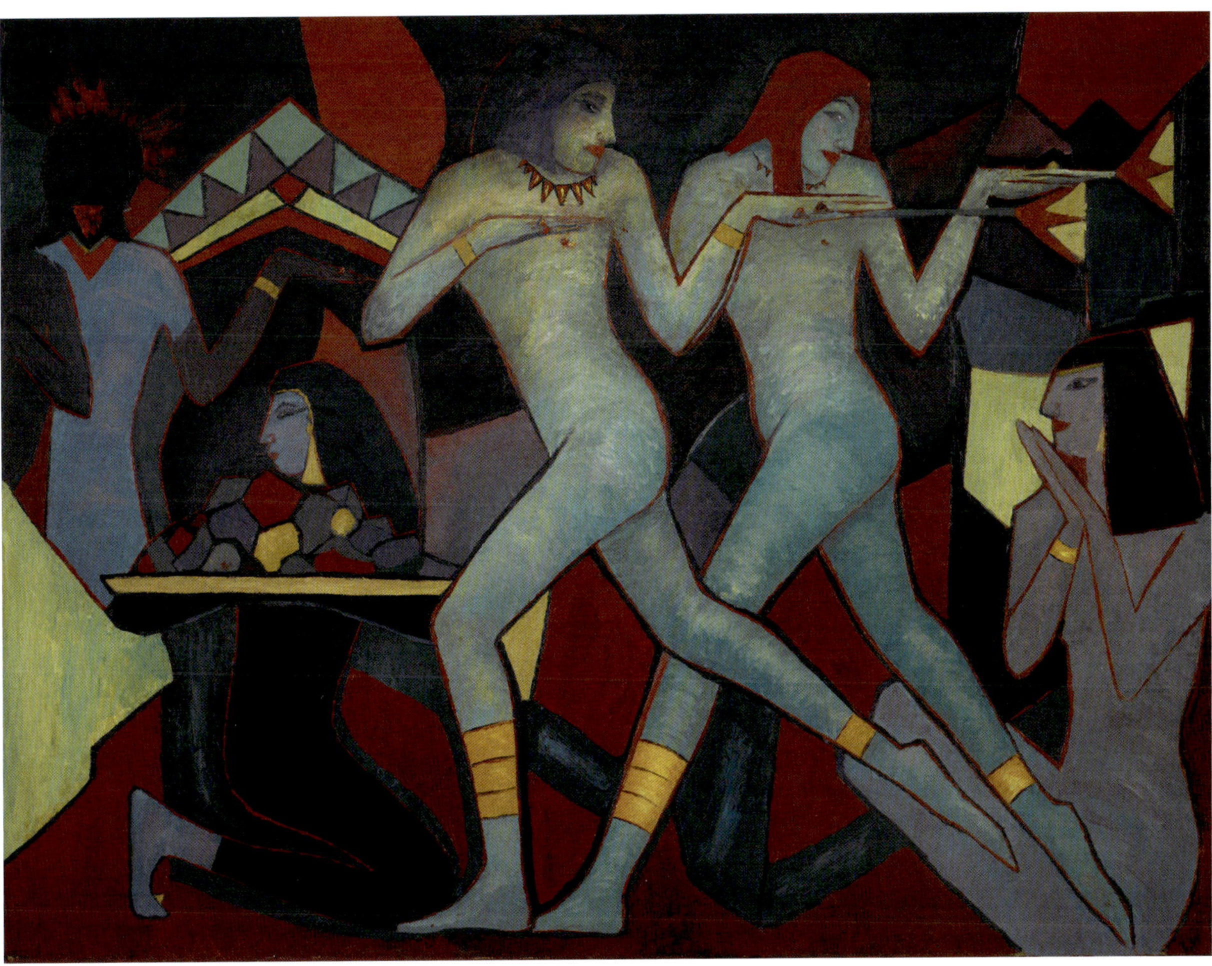

[48] Anne Estelle Rice
The Egyptian Dancers (*Two Egyptian Dancers*), 1910
Brooklyn Museum, New York, Dick S. Ramsay Fund, 2007.51

brought a base for fresh thinking and a new attitude to art. As he wrote to Morris in early December:

> *The place here has given me quite a new start, a different feeling altogether about painting, or rather it has given me what I have been trying to make out of nothing – the colours, the shapes, everything that I was developing by sheer sweat and labour is here. The light that one snatched with excitement when it happened once in a blue moon, is here even in winter.*[42]

His house was modest, only two rooms but opening directly on to that southern landscape, its vibrant colour, sounds and heat. His oil sketches from this time are much to do with the essence of the world about him, excluding the pretentious or academic, and point to future satisfaction. It can be said that he never fully regained the ambition of his earlier work, with much of his later work becoming more decorative than dynamic.

Back in wartime London Fergusson applied a French attitude to form, shape and colour to his geometricised paintings of shipping. He and Margaret tried to recapture the cultural dynamism of Paris through the Margaret Morris Club. In addition, he attempted to revitalise the AAA exhibition as a version of the Salon des Indépendants, calling it 'The London Salon of the Independants'.[43] Intended to show paintings, sculpture and 'craftwork of every kind', he formed a committee which included various friends and associates such as Rutter, Charles Rennie Mackintosh, Frank Dobson, the painter Charles Ginner (1878–1952) and the graphic artist E. McKnight Kauffer (1890–1954). It never got off the ground due to not finding the right venue.

An interest in sculpture had been first kindled through museum collections and friendship with Jo Davidson and Epstein. There are many potential influences on Fergusson's choice of materials and style. As Sheila McGregor has noted, Fergusson picked out the

Yugoslav sculptor Ivan Meštrović (1883–1962) for attention in his 1909 review of the Salon d'Automne and his work was on view at the Victoria & Albert Museum in 1915.[44] The figurative anonymity of *Plénitude d'Olivier* and *Eástre* (*Hymn to the Sun*) [93] reflects the legacy of *Rhythm* and connects with the post-war intercultural Classicism of Aristide Maillol (1861–1944) and the Art Deco style. *Eástre*, depicting the Saxon goddess of Easter, is superbly both ancient and modern: it can keep company with both Frank Dobson's modernist forms and shiny materials as well as the robot Maria in Fritz Lang's modernist film masterpiece *Metropolis*, also conceived in 1924 and made in 1927, the year *Eástre* was first cast.[45]

Although Fergusson would always remain a Francophile, his relationship with the country shifted as a result of the war and the manner of his partnership with Morris. He taught painting during her dance Summer Schools held at Harlech, north Wales, in 1919 and again in 1922, Dinard in 1920, Pourville in 1921, and Antibes from 1923. The generous support they received in Wales and then France from the retired businessman and philanthropist George Davison, first met in London during the war, was inestimable, allowing them to commit in advance to Morris's Summer Schools. Davison and his second wife would continue to support Morris and Fergusson generously into the 1950s.[46] In 1922 Davison bought the Villa Gotte in Juan-les-Pins, where *Christmas Time in the South of France* [71] was painted, an atmospheric semi-cubist study of home and landscape, and in its sense of wellbeing continuing the theme of health and good living. The 1923 summer school which followed was held across three sites in Cap d'Antibes: the Hôtel Beau Site, the Hôtel du Cap, where Picasso was staying, and the Château des Enfants, bought for restoration by Davison and which had substantial wooded grounds for dance.[47]

The year 1923 was a crucial and positive year for all four of the Scottish artists we now call the Colourists. Resuming creative links with France boosted Fergusson's recognition at home: he had his first commercial exhibitions in Scotland that year with La Société des Beaux-Arts (now largely directed by A.J. McNeill Reid) in Glasgow and The Scottish Gallery in Edinburgh. In 1924 he joined Peploe, Hunter and Cadell for their major group show in Paris with the Galerie Barbazanges as *Les Peintres de l'Écosse Moderne*, with a second group show following at the Hogarth Room of London's Leicester Galleries in January 1925: Fergusson here persuaded Walter Sickert to contribute a catalogue introduction. His work became more commercial in concept – gone was the fiercely intellectual ambition to be replaced by an overall lightness yet precision of pattern and design in keeping with the gay tone of Parisian art. This is seen particularly in his landscapes of the later 1920s and 1930s, such as his views of Dinard [70] which, like his war work, also contain a strictness of formal organisation shared with his friend Mackintosh. The palette of many of these, and a few late landscapes, including the exquisite *Wisteria, Villa Florentine, Golfe-Juan* [72], is as elegantly tuned as any of his career. There remained a side to Fergusson's work which showed the utmost sensitivity to the many women he painted: the subdued *Souvenir de Jumièges* from 1931 [69] is one such portrait.

During his 1920s summer visits and his second French residency from 1929 to 1939 Fergusson also persisted with figurative work. These were in a sense the heirs to his academic *Les Eus* but now such tableaux were simply evocations of the good life. The more successful of these, such as *Summer, 1914* [39], an elegant portrait of Morris painted just over twenty years after their first summer together, convey the heat and scent through colour and pose. *La Déesse de la Rivière*, again a portrait of Morris, was purchased by the French government from the Colourists' show with the Georges Petit Gallery in 1931. This exhibition was as important as their 1924 group show of *Les Peintres de l'Écosse Moderne*. The organiser, again McNeill Reid, had given Fergusson the name of the Luxembourg's curator, and a personal approach is likely to have engineered the acquisition. Although still making a financial loss for Reid,[48] the exhibition at the time was celebrated at home, with *The Scotsman* writing:

> *The Scottish painters' show created a buzz of excitement at the 'Vernissage', and is assured of success. A number of works have already been sold. Mr Fergusson attracting marked favour …* [49]

The London press also noted the unusual purchase of a painting by a foreign artist.

Naturally, perhaps, the Scottish press tended to romanticise Fergusson's reception in France with the English press more objective and analytical in their reports. In 1928 under the headline 'A Virile Scots Artist: Mr. Fergusson's Show in Glasgow', the

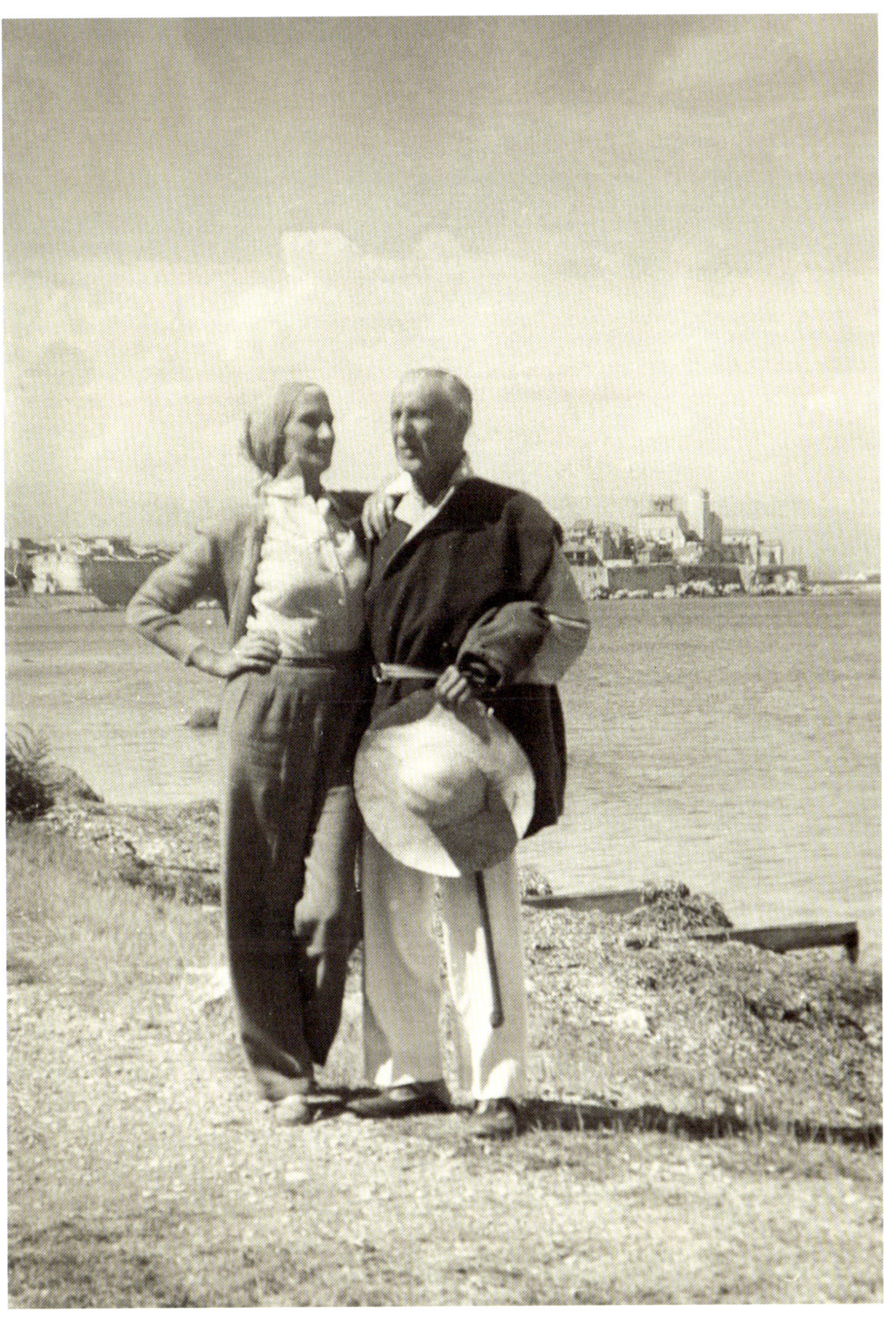

[49] J.D. Fergusson and Margaret Morris, Antibes 1956
Photograph by Professor James Fullarton Arnott
The Fergusson Gallery, Perth & Kinross Council

Glasgow Record commented that 'Fergusson has perhaps a greater artistic renown outside of Caledonia than within it'.[50] By contrast, Fergusson's canvases of groups of pale female and tanned male nudes, made in an age which was culturally promoting 'the body beautiful', were critically less well received in England, with his 1936 show at Reid & Lefèvre greeted in the *Manchester Guardian* with a demand for more landscapes and 'fewer of the rather obviously healthy Amazons'.[51] Fergusson never retired from his wish to promote sexuality in his art, with the exaggerated forms of his female nudes being commented on in London: Raymond Drey after Fergusson's death would write of his 'tendency to over-emphasise a voluptuous curve, and pigmentation of the lips, and to change slender necks into columns of sculptural form'.[52] This comment was applied especially to the portraits of women he made from the 1920s onwards and is a true one – yet in a way it misses the point. As in 1910 he had embedded a figure within its decorative setting, so these studies continued to encapsulate, enjoy and celebrate femininity and often reflect the gaiety and light good humour of his companions. Whether made in France or Scotland, the canvas never ceases to become a painting that is highly decorative in the best French sense. The wonderfully kaleidoscopic patterned *Blonde with Checked Sundress* of 1958 [73] is the final statement of this joie de vivre.

Writing his treatise on *Modern Scottish Painting* in the late 1930s, Fergusson plainly saw himself first and foremost as a Scottish artist, a painter in the country's common-sense tradition:

> *When I was leaving Scotland to settle in Paris I told our family lawyer and he said 'So you're going to be a Frenchman'. I said 'No! I hope I'm going to be able to persist in being a Scotsman'. Naturally the reply proved to him what he had suspected; that as I was an artist I was just daft.*[53]

For all his protestation that he had wanted to remain a Scot at heart, Fergusson never let go of French attitudes to art – and life, for his entire way of thinking had been more than enriched by the country. Although his art never recaptured that intellectual ambition of the pre-1914 years – by far the most important part of his entire career – his sunshine palette and patterning of form at its best continued to convey the essence of experience. Fergusson's clarity of expression and interest in the potential of paint on canvas had the power to sustain him, even on dour days in Scotland.

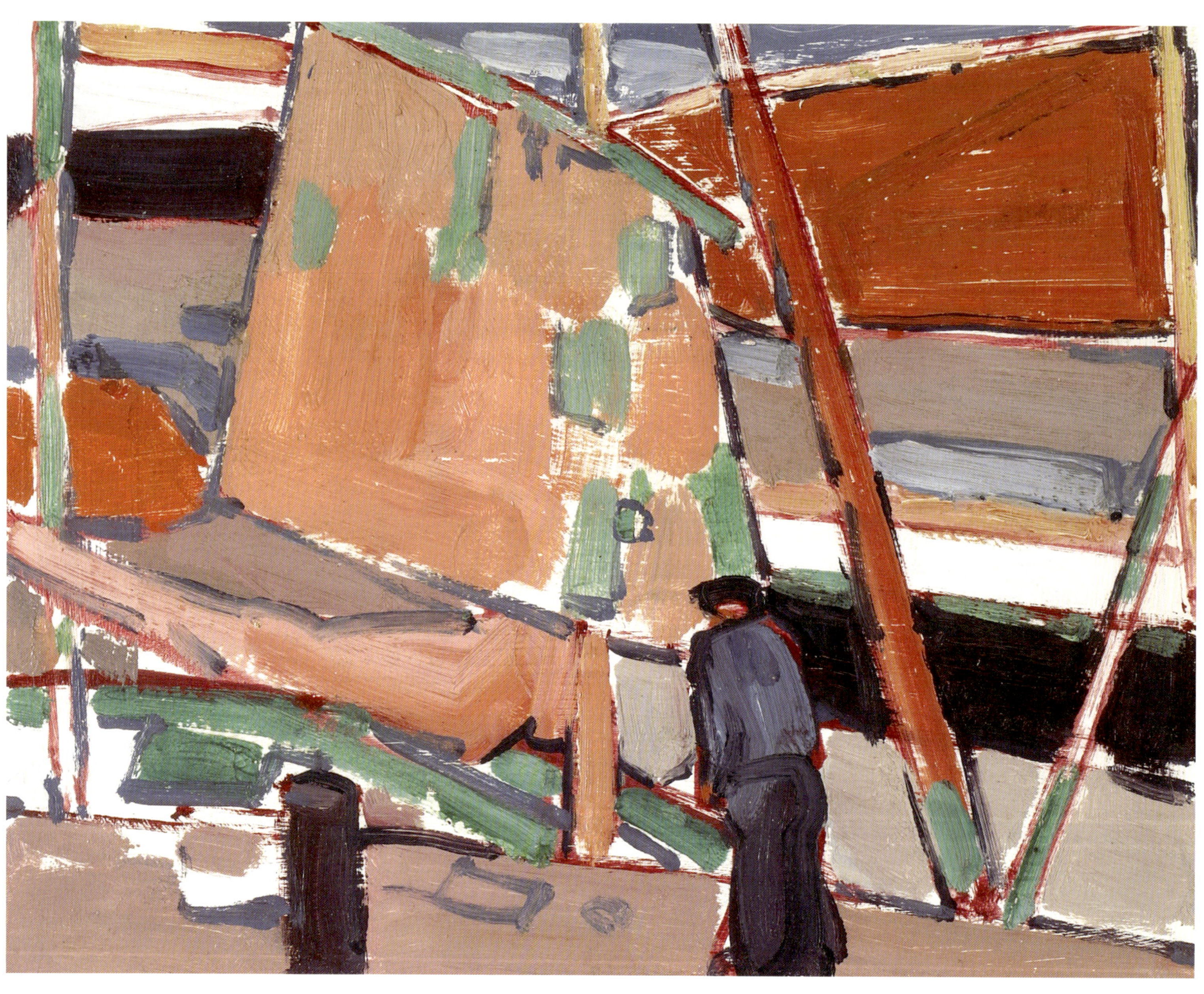

[50]

Royan, 1910

Oil on board, 27.3 × 35.5

Private collection

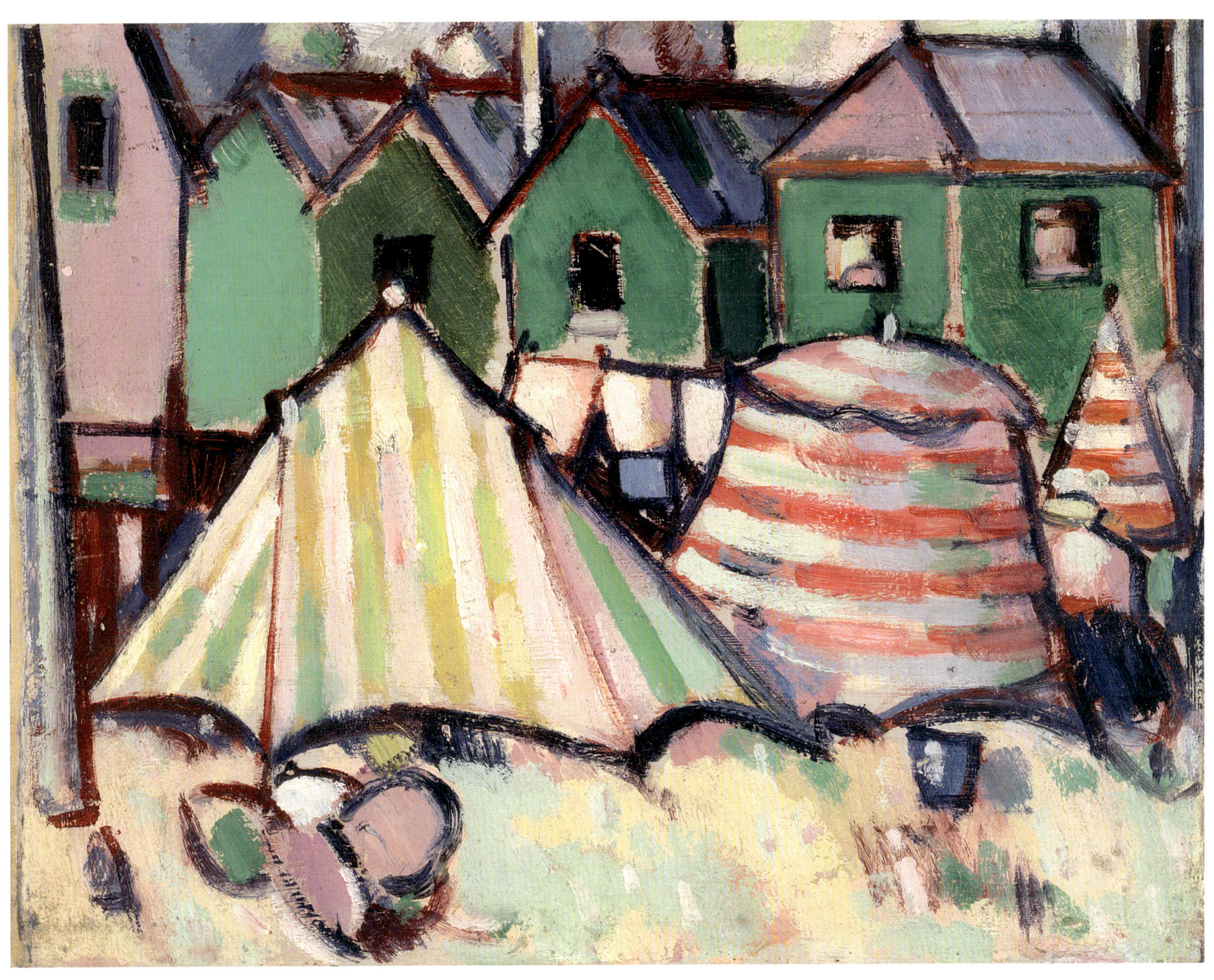

[51]
Bathing Boxes and Tents at St. Palais, 1910
Oil on board, 25.6 × 35.5
The Fergusson Gallery, Perth & Kinross Council
presented by the J.D. Fergusson Art Foundation 1991

[52]

Grey Day, Paris-Plage, 1906

Oil on canvas, 35.6 × 45.7
Glasgow Life (Glasgow Museums) on behalf of Glasgow City Council
presented by the Trustees of the Hamilton Bequest 1981

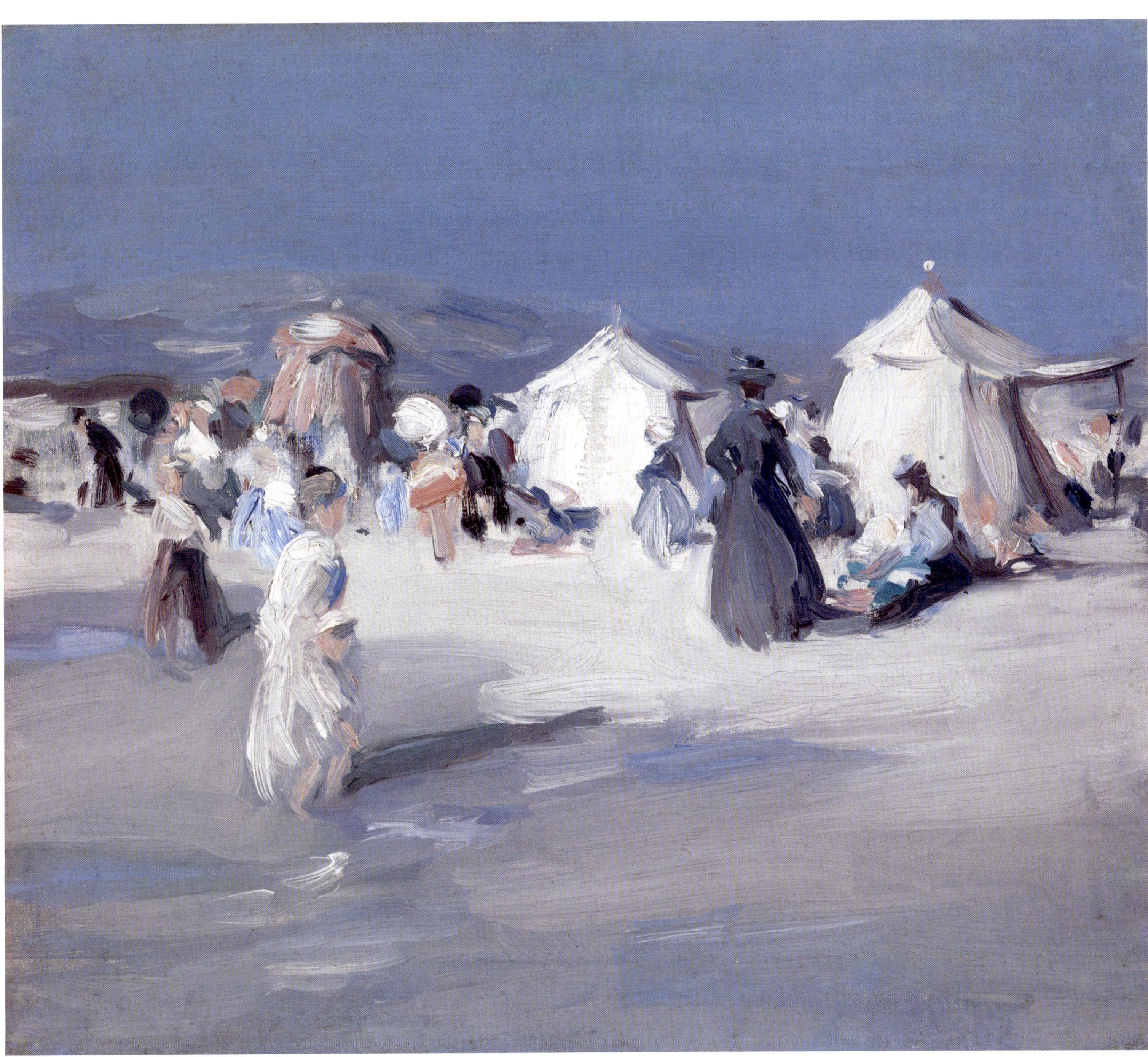

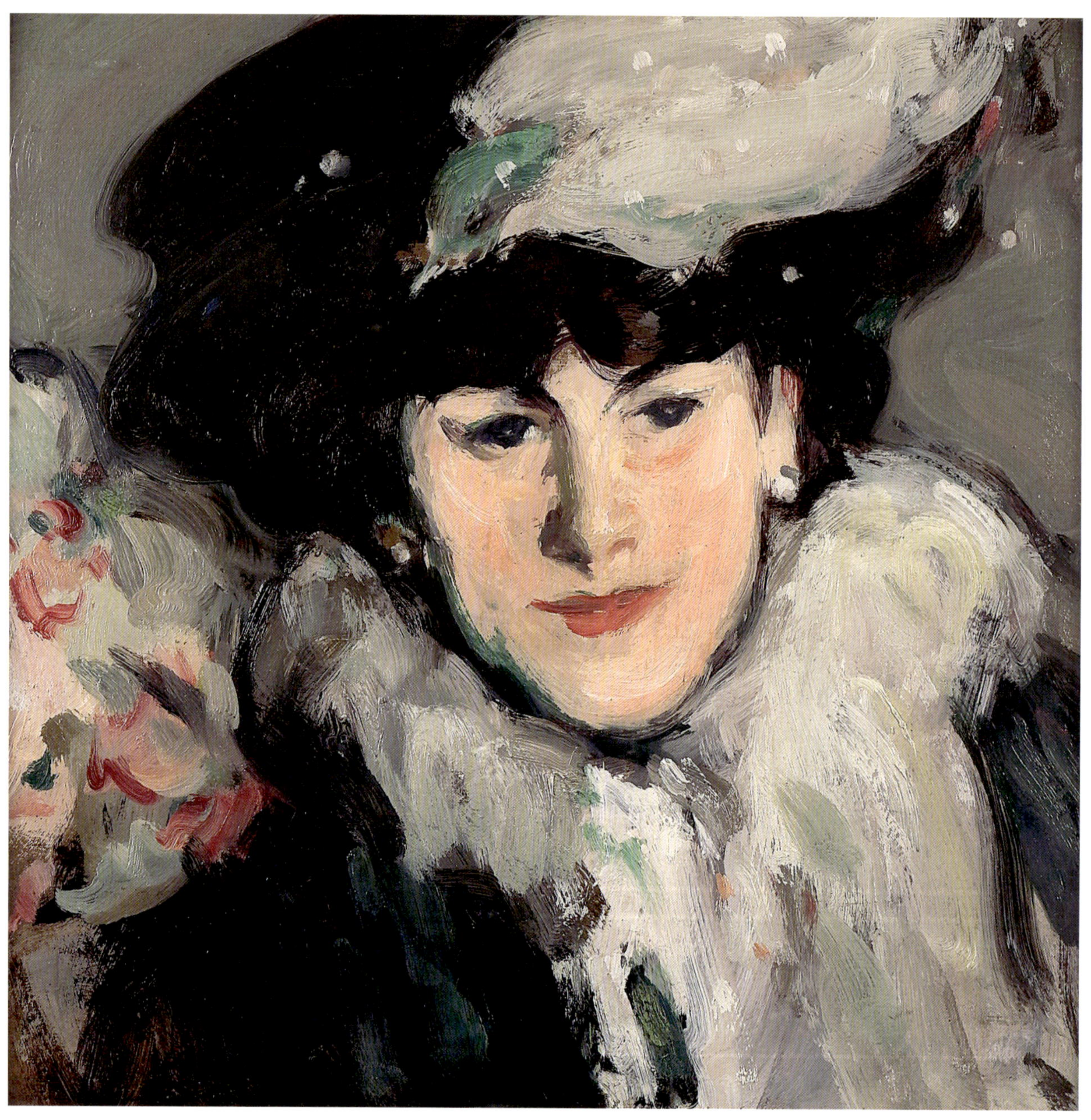

[53]

*The Green Bird, c.*1907

Oil on board, 37.5 × 37.5

Private collection, courtesy Duncan R. Miller Fine Arts, London

[54]

La Cocarde, 1910

Oil on board, 66 × 57.2

Private collection

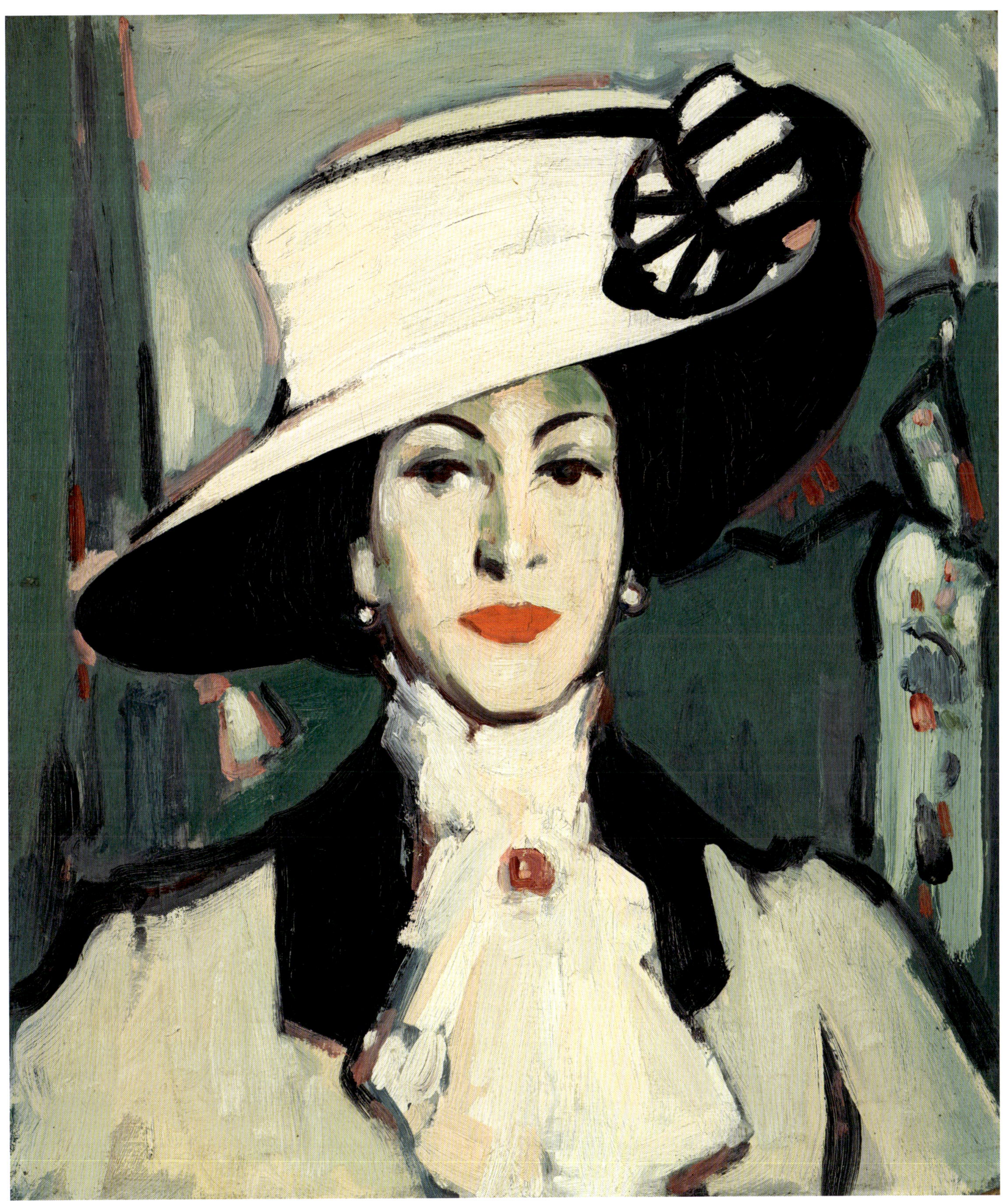

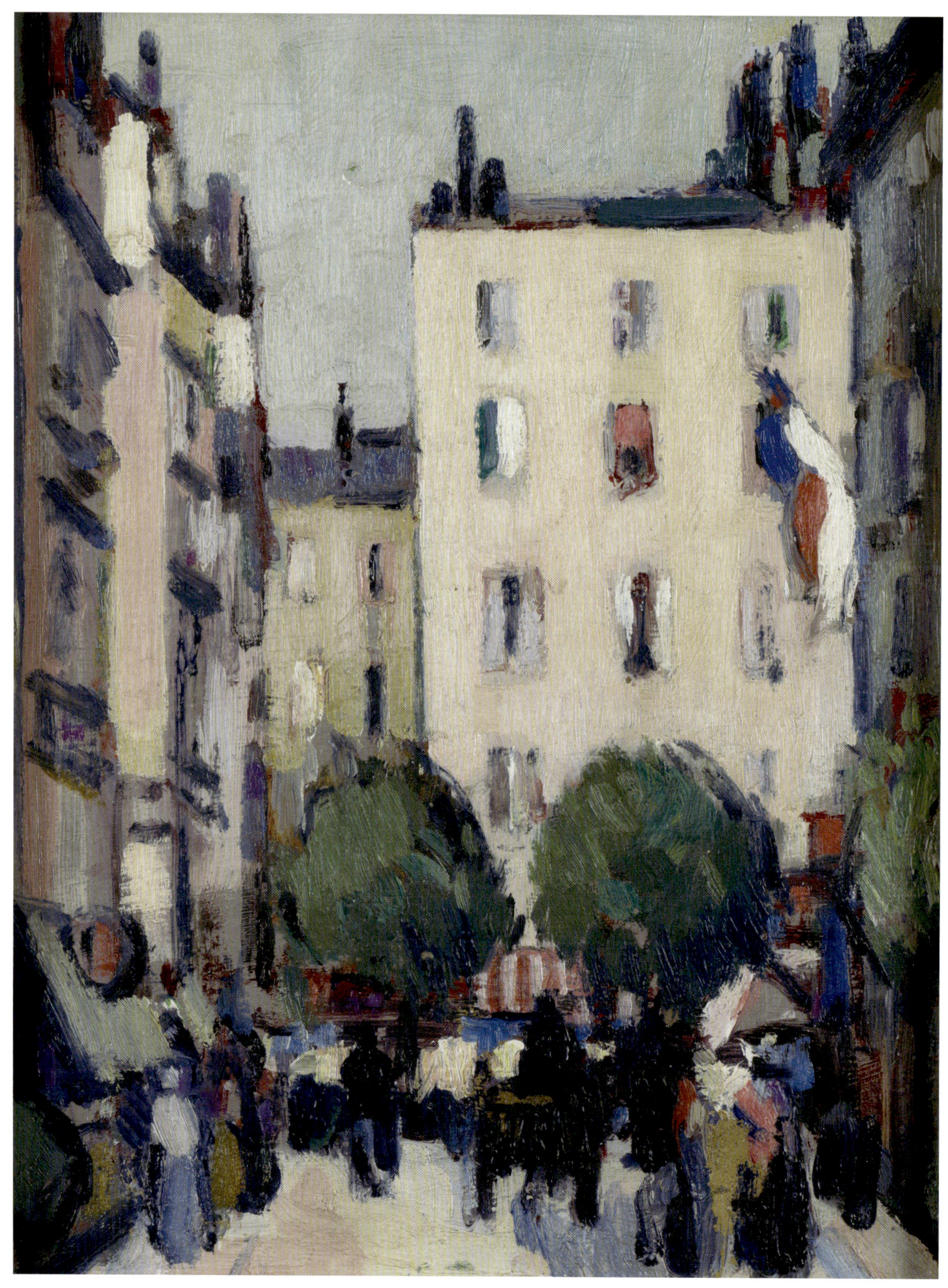

[55]

Paris, *c.*1907

Oil on board, 35 × 27.5
Private collection

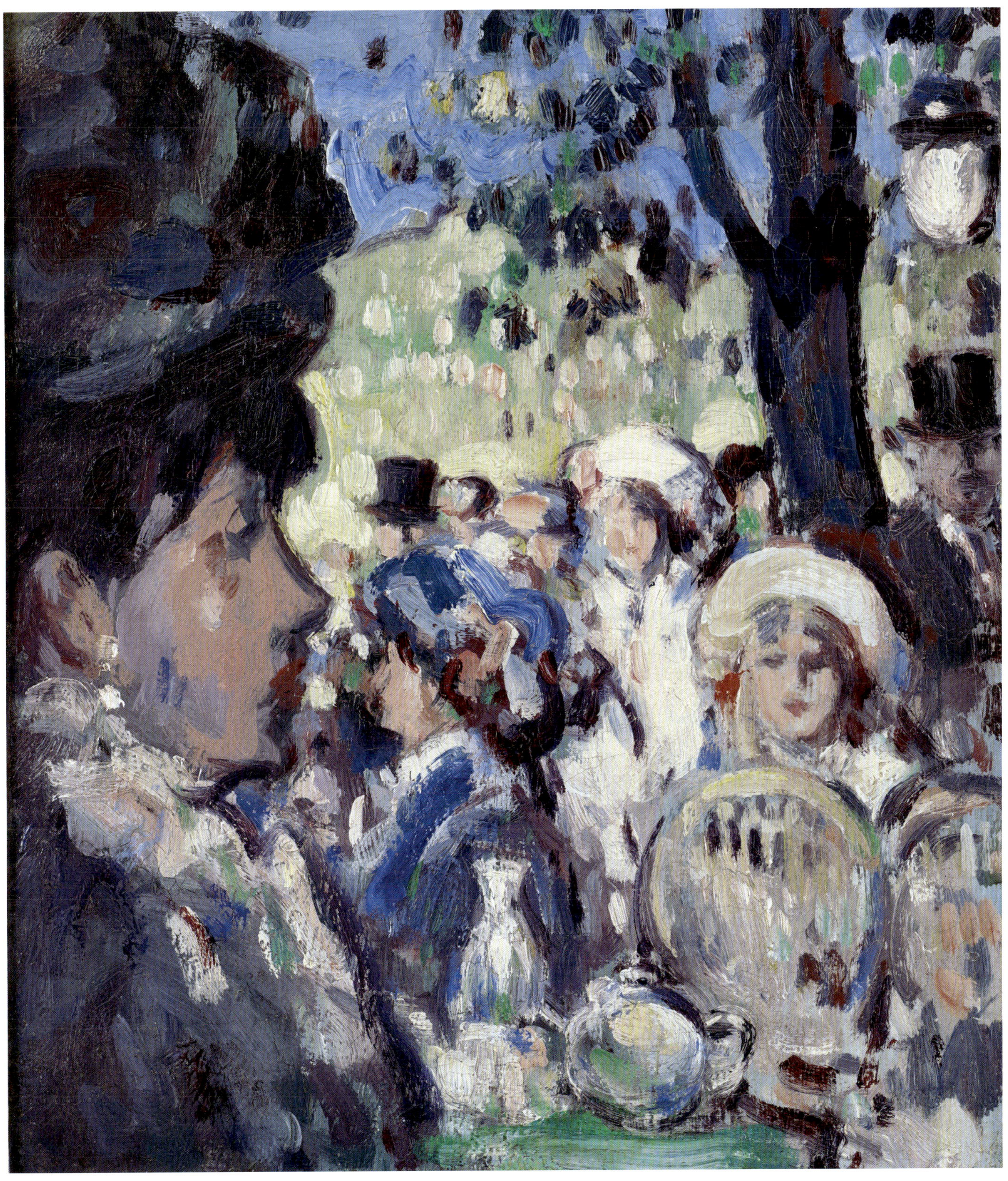

[56]

The Open Air Fête, Armenonville, c.1907

Oil on canvas, 40.8 × 35.7

Private collection

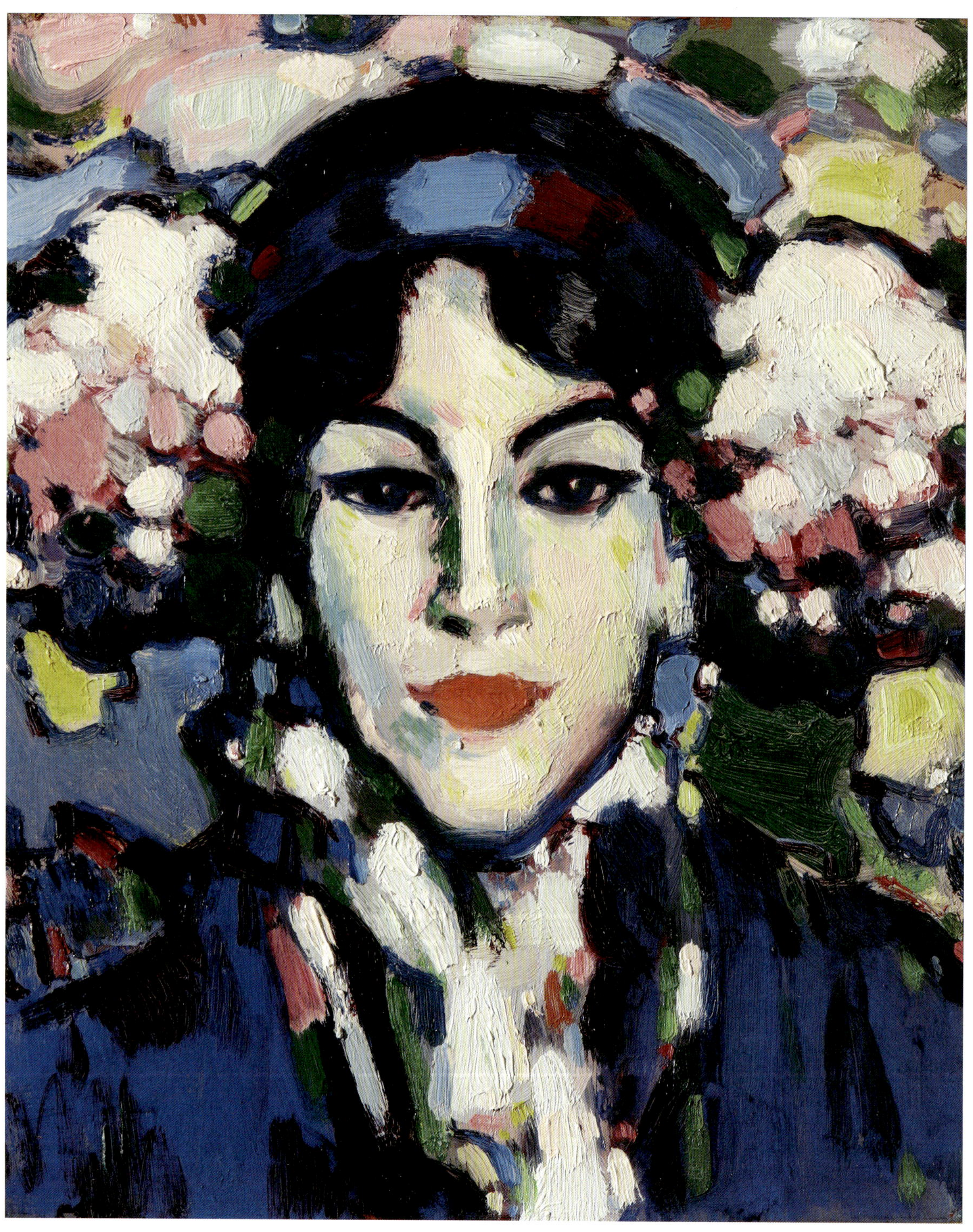

[57]

Hortensia, 1907

Oil on canvas, 43 × 38

The University of Aberdeen, bequeathed by Eric Linklater 1976

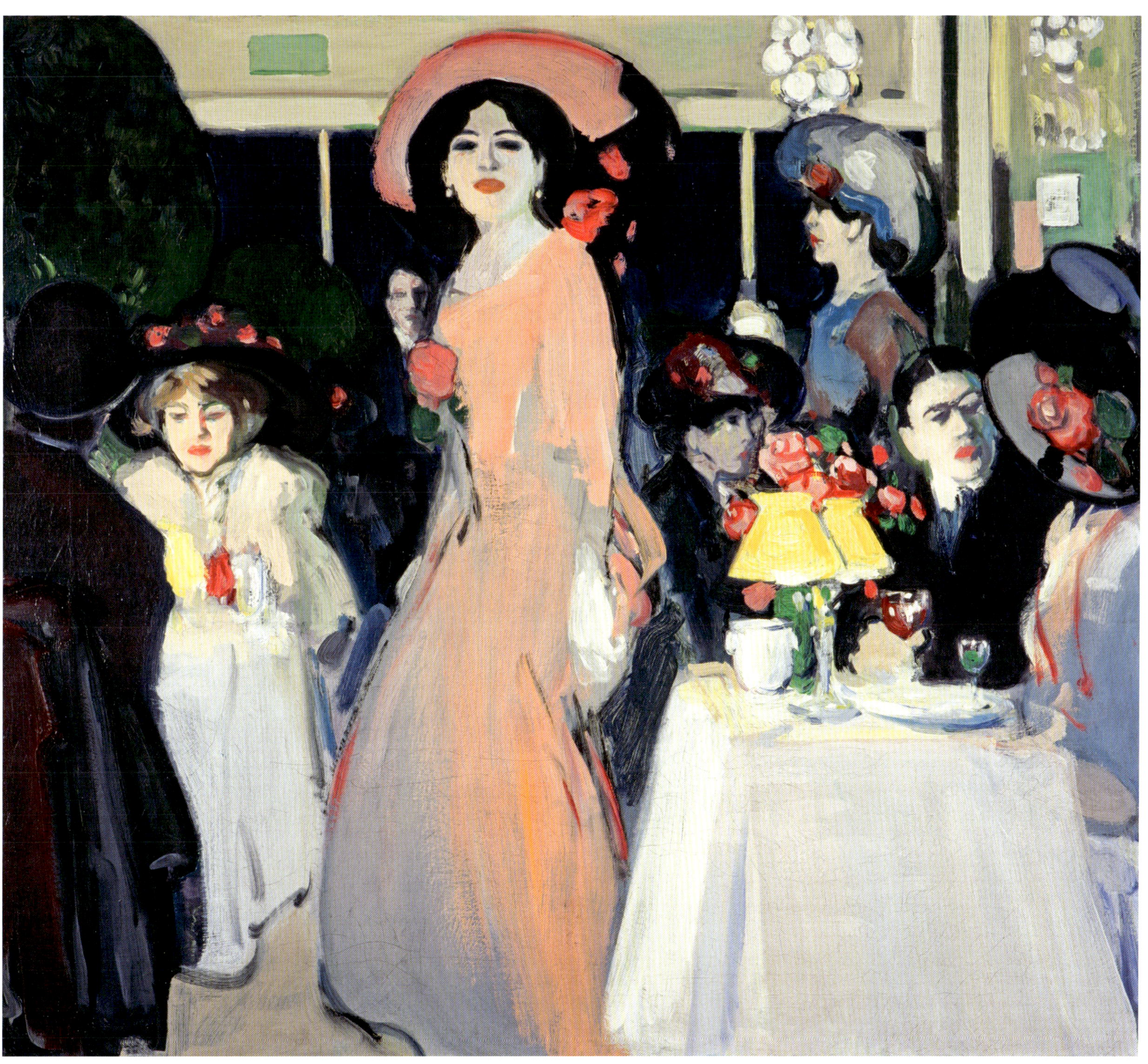

[58]

La Terrasse, Café d'Harcourt, *c.*1908

Oil on canvas, 108.6 × 122

Private collection on loan to the Scottish National Gallery of Modern Art, Edinburgh

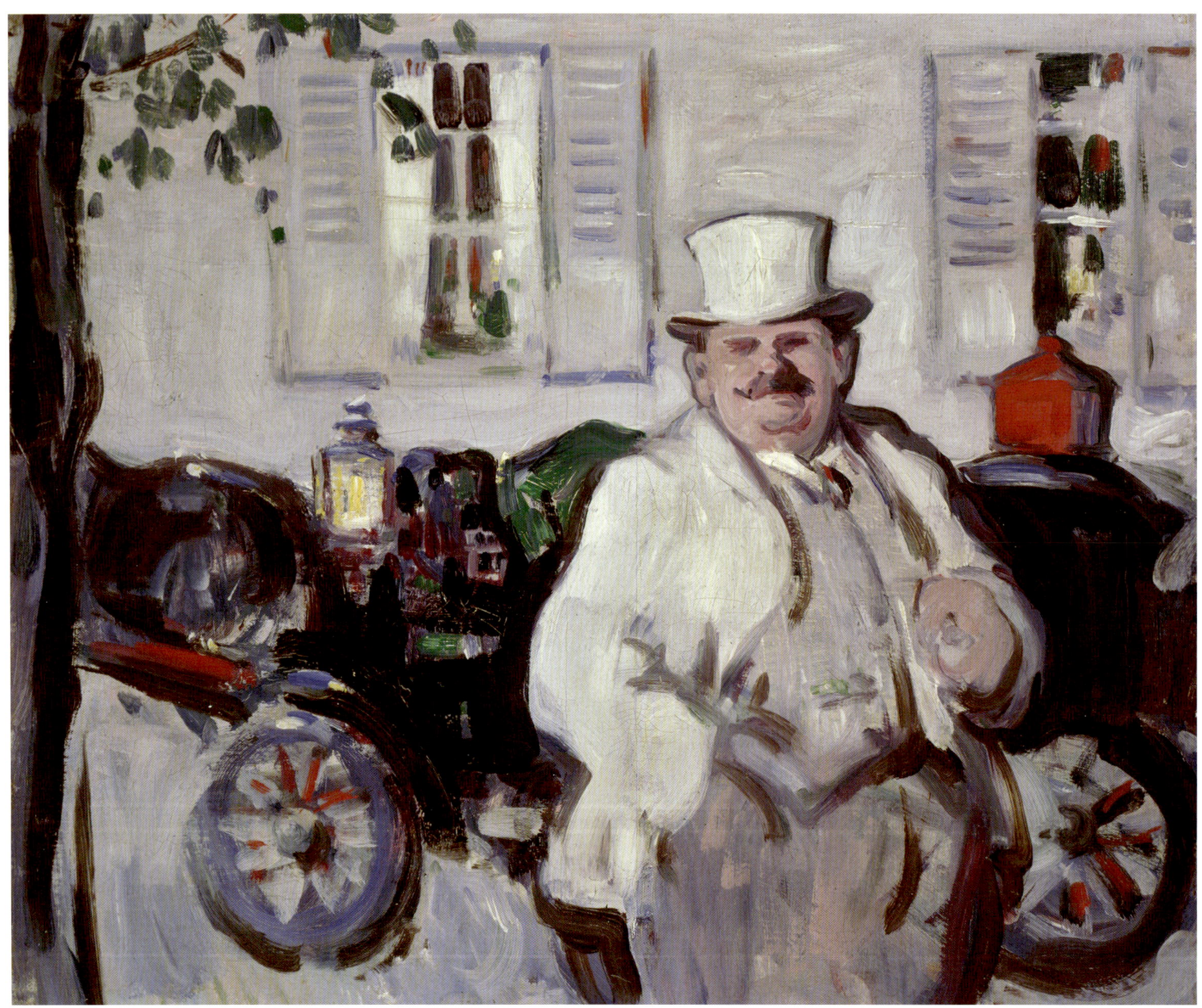

[59]

Le Cocher: Crépuscule, 1907

Oil on canvas, 63.5 × 76.3

Private collection, courtesy Duncan R. Miller Fine Arts, London

[60]

Chez Maxim, 1908

Conté and watercolour on paper, 37.5 × 30.2

Private collection, courtesy Duncan R. Miller Fine Arts, London

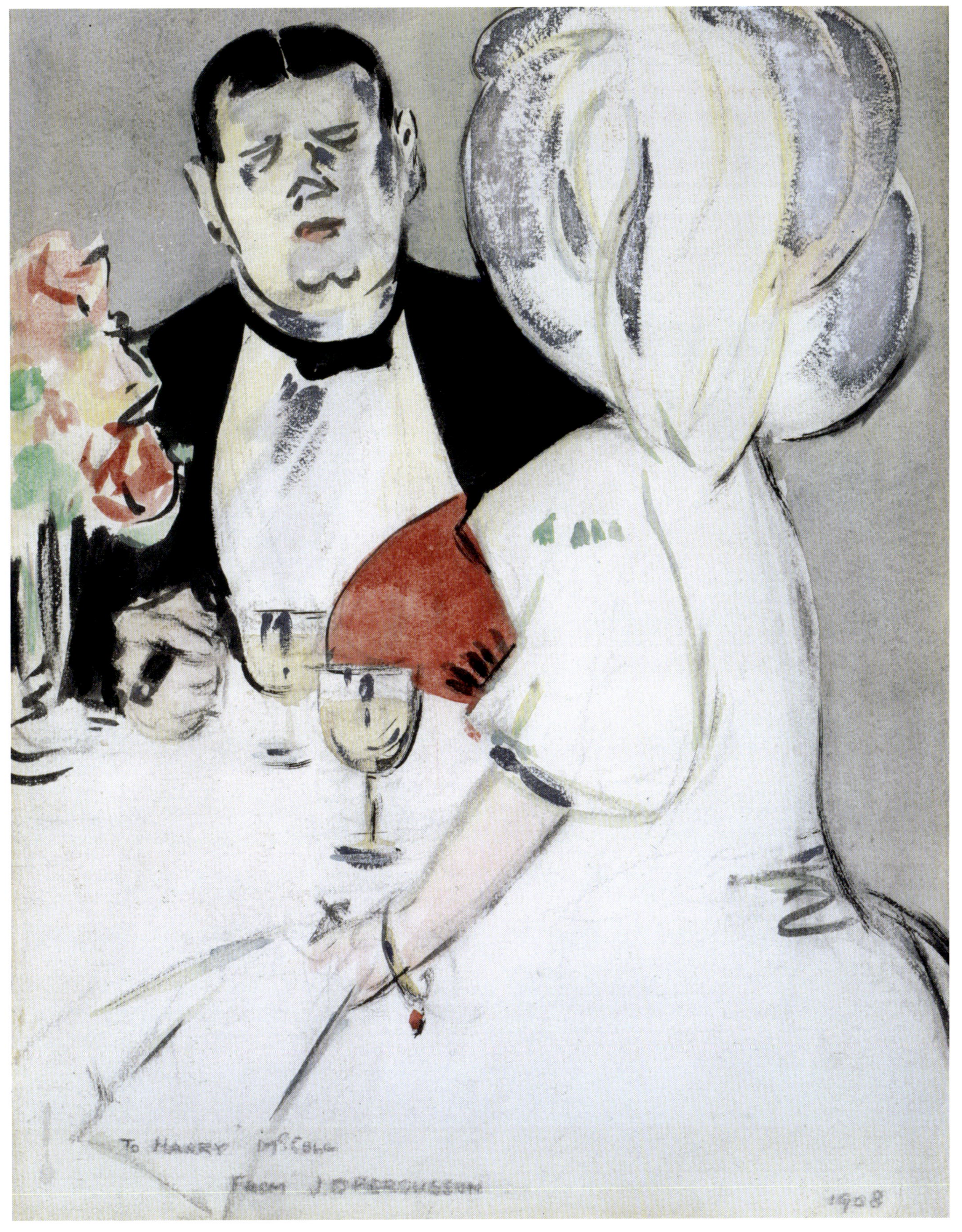
To Harry McColl
From J.D. Fergusson
1908

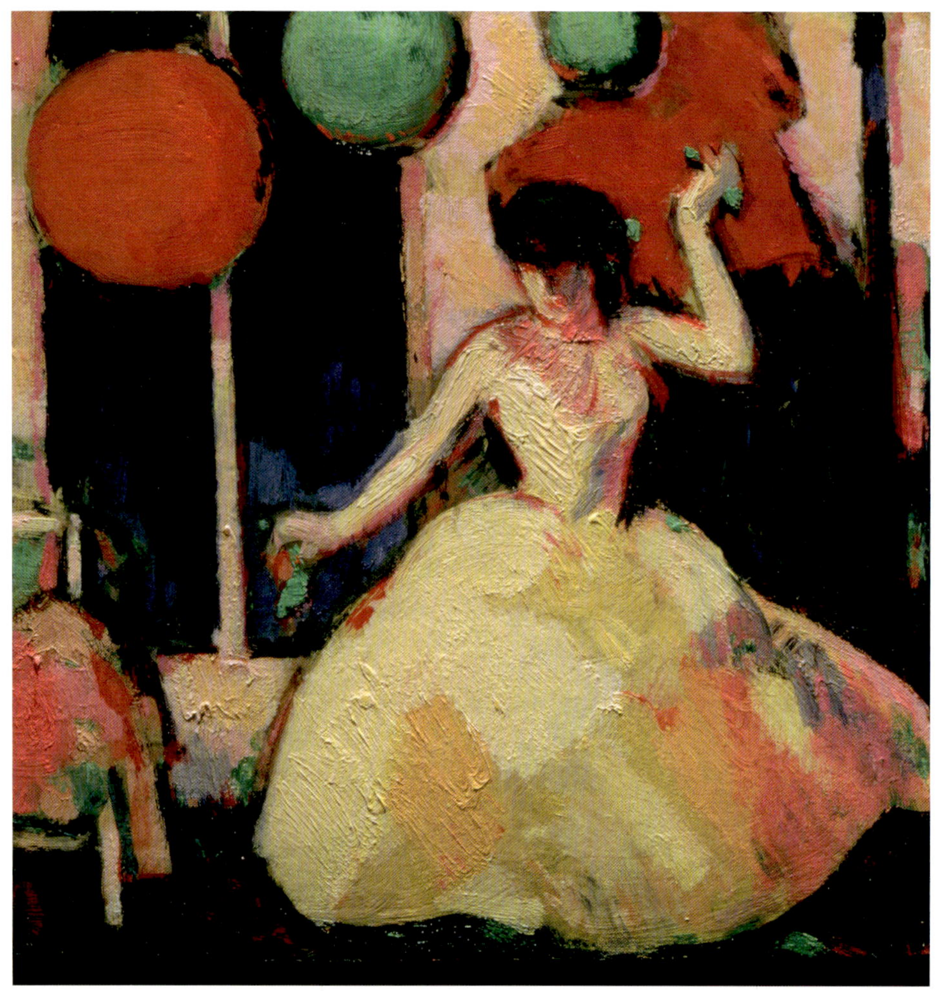

[61]
St Jacques Studio, 1909
Oil on panel, 37 × 37
Private collection

[62]
La Bête violette, *c.*1910
Oil on canvas, 77.5 × 77.5
Private collection

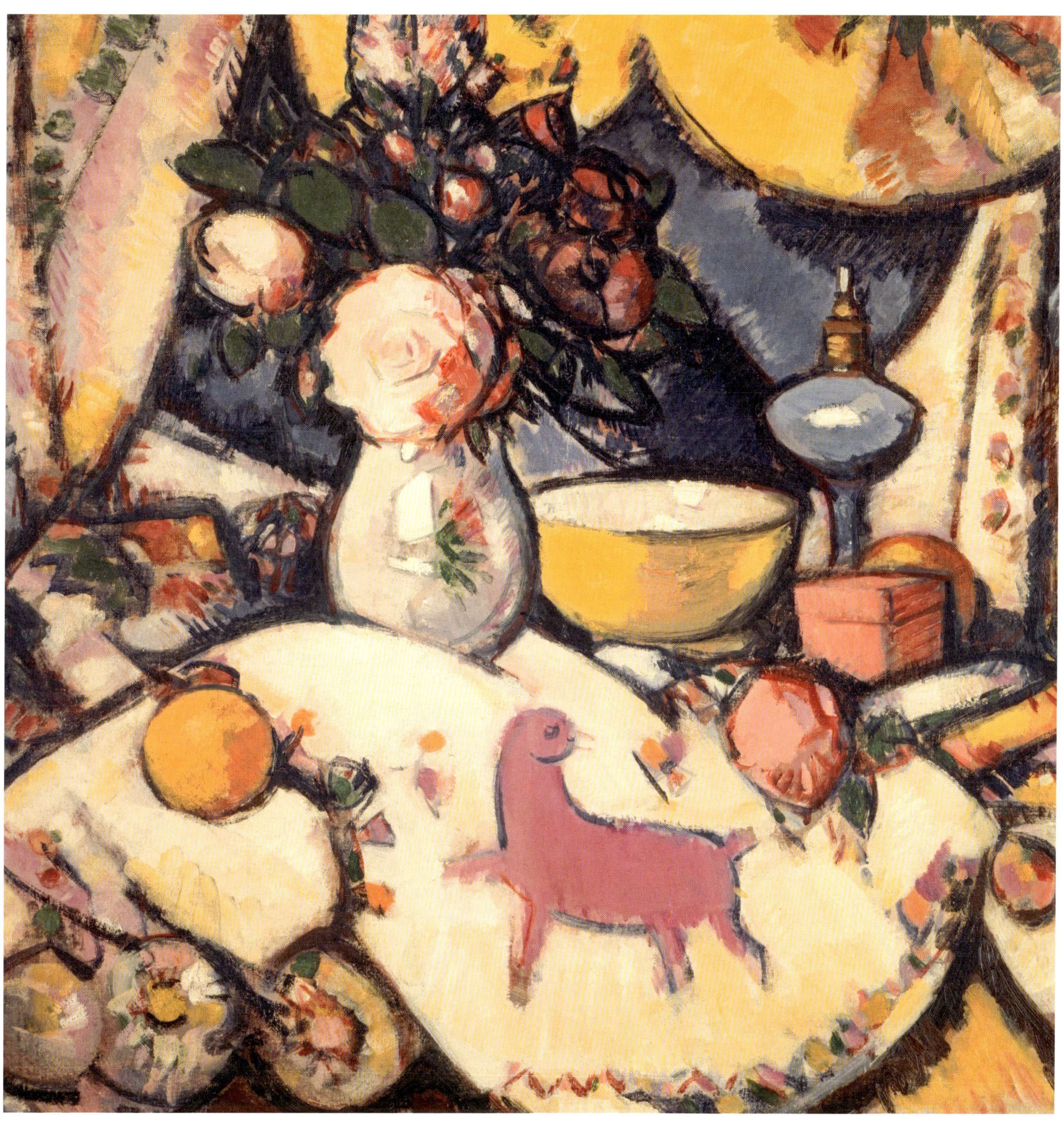

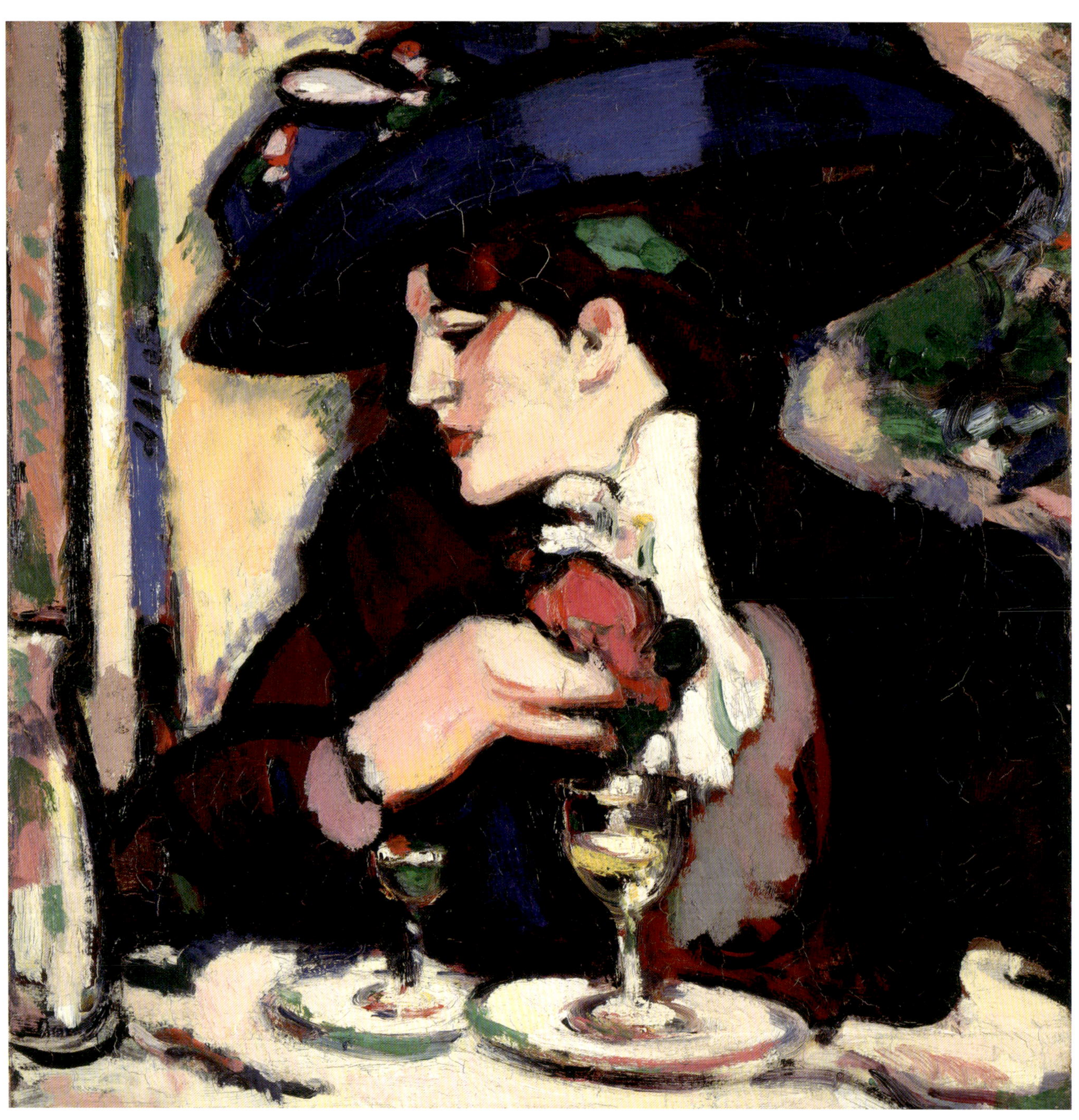

[63]

The Blue Hat, Closerie des Lilas, 1909

Oil on canvas, 76.2 × 76.2
City Art Centre, City of Edinburgh Museums and Galleries
purchased from Margaret Morris 1962

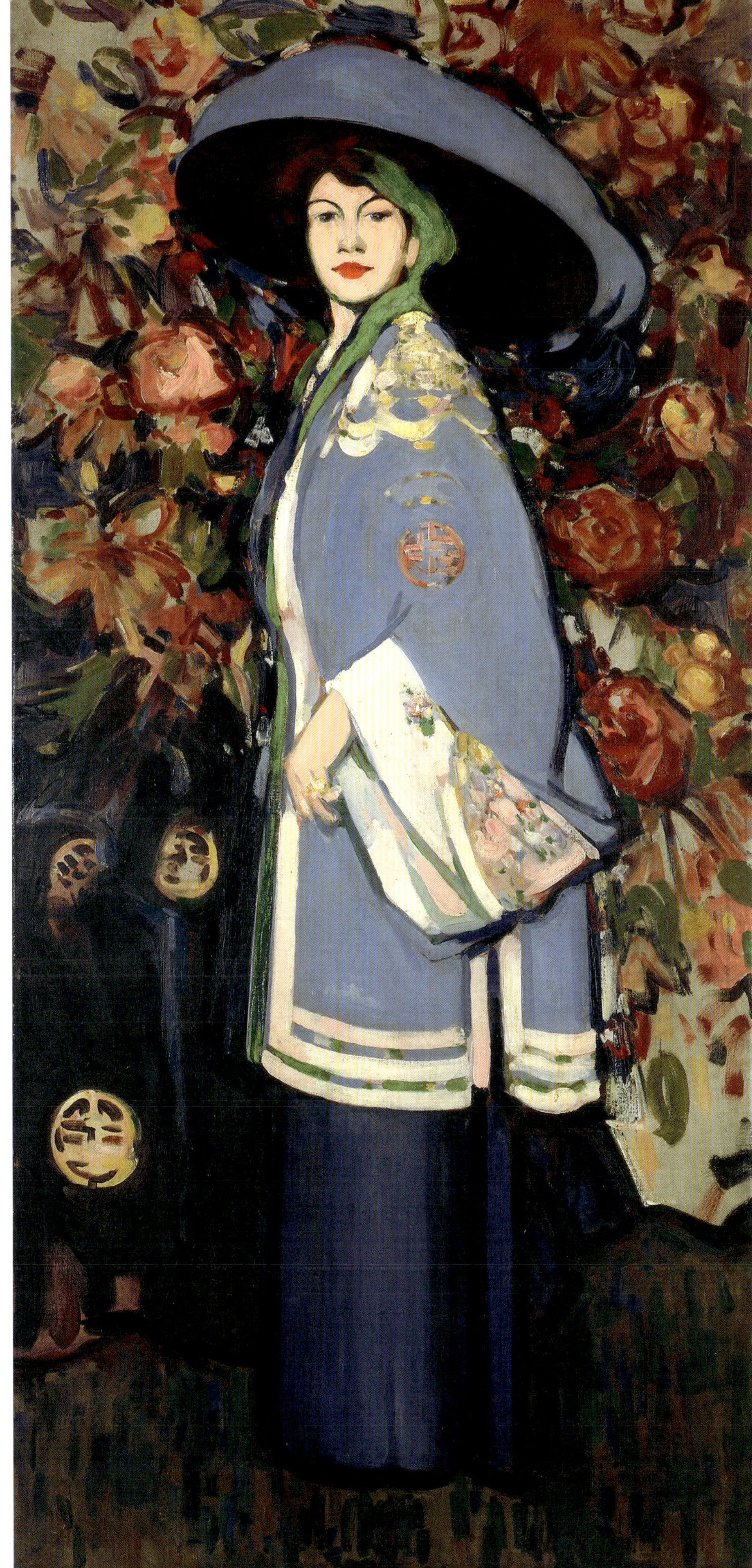

[64]

Le Manteau Chinois, 1909

Oil on canvas, 199.5 × 97
The Fergusson Gallery, Perth & Kinross Council
presented by the J.D. Fergusson Art Foundation 1991

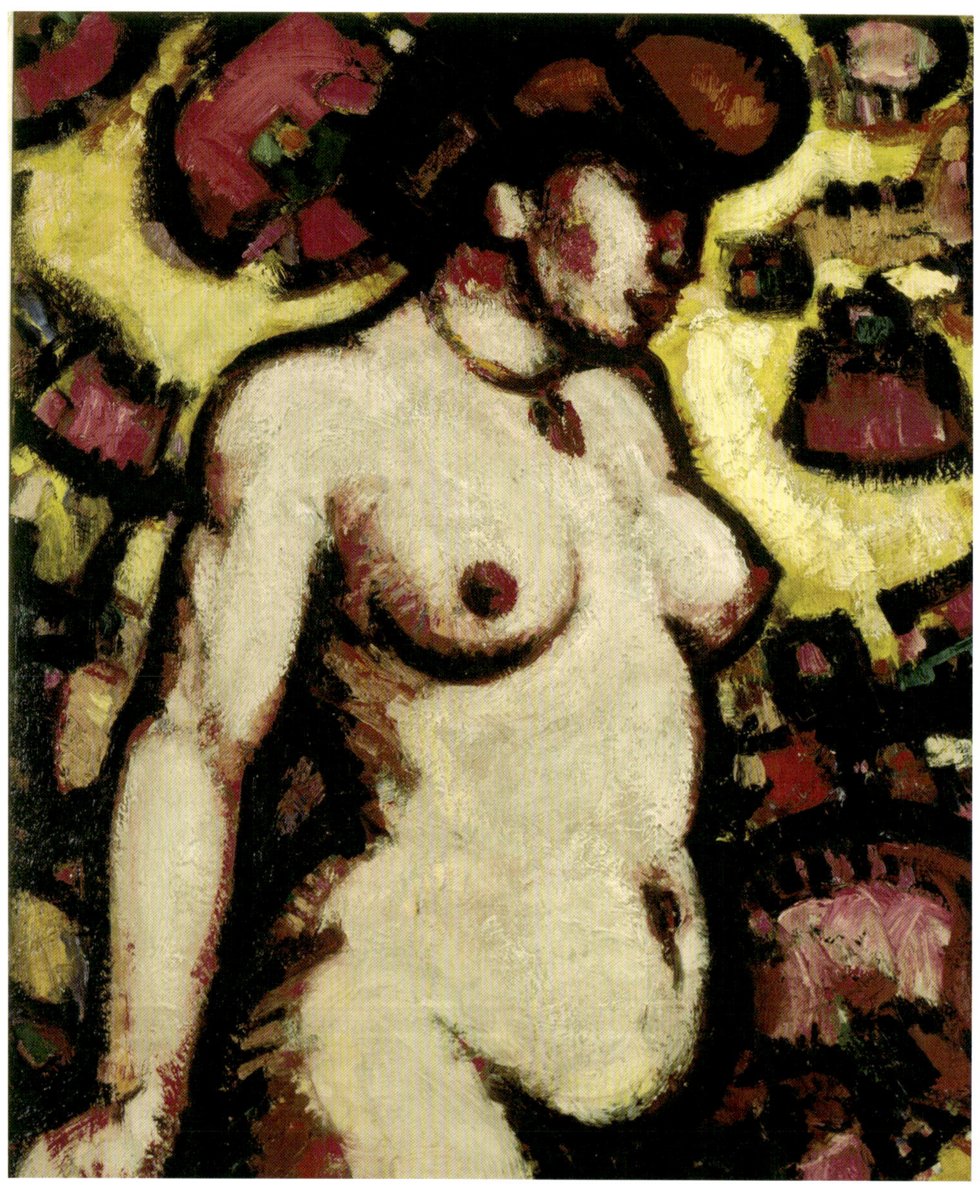

[67]

La Force, 1910

Oil on board, 67.5 × 57.5
Private collection, courtesy Duncan R. Miller Fine Arts, London

[68]

Les Eus, *c.*1913

Oil on canvas, 216 × 277
Hunterian Art Gallery, University of Glasgow
gift from the J.D. Fergusson Art Foundation 1990

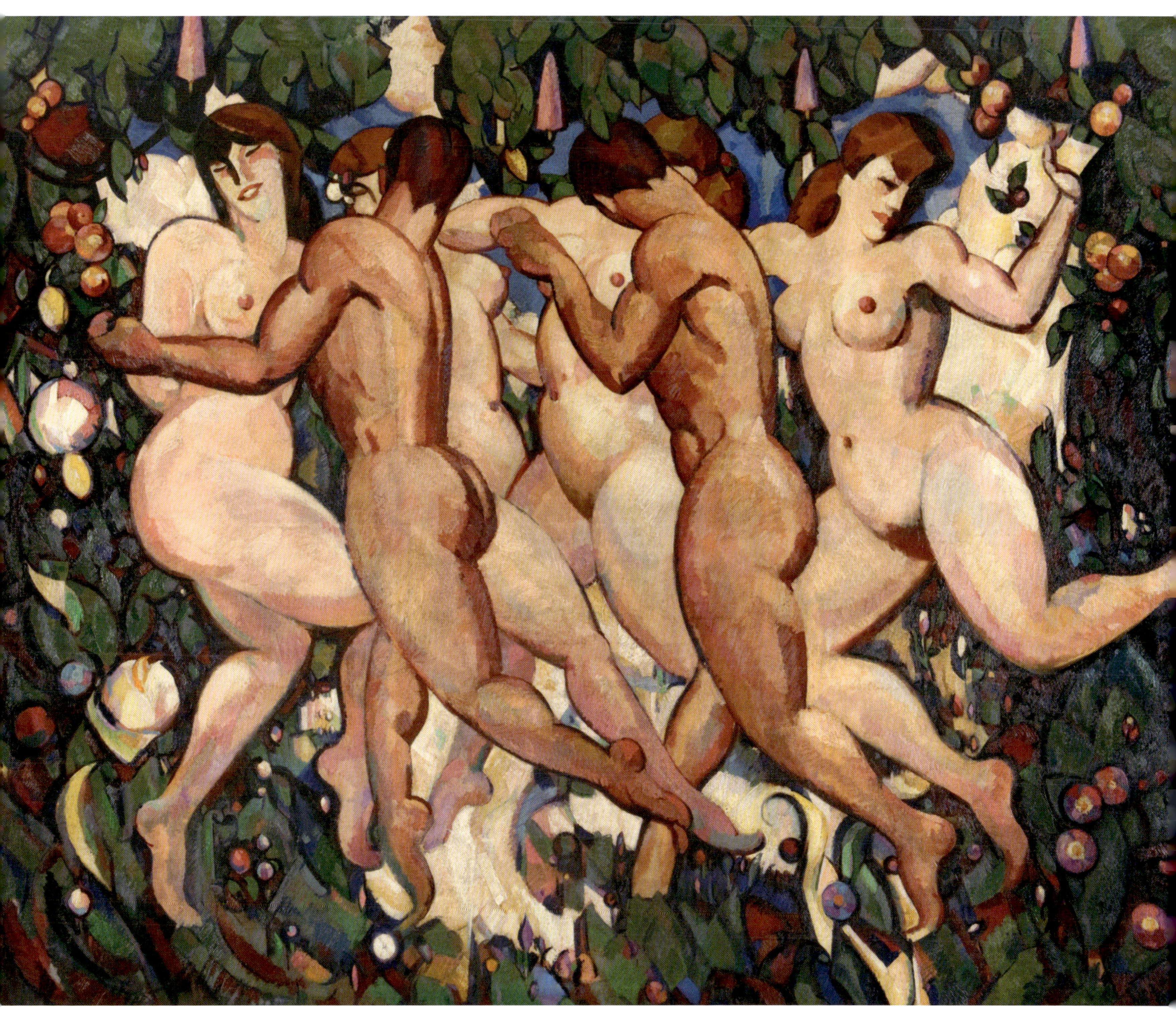

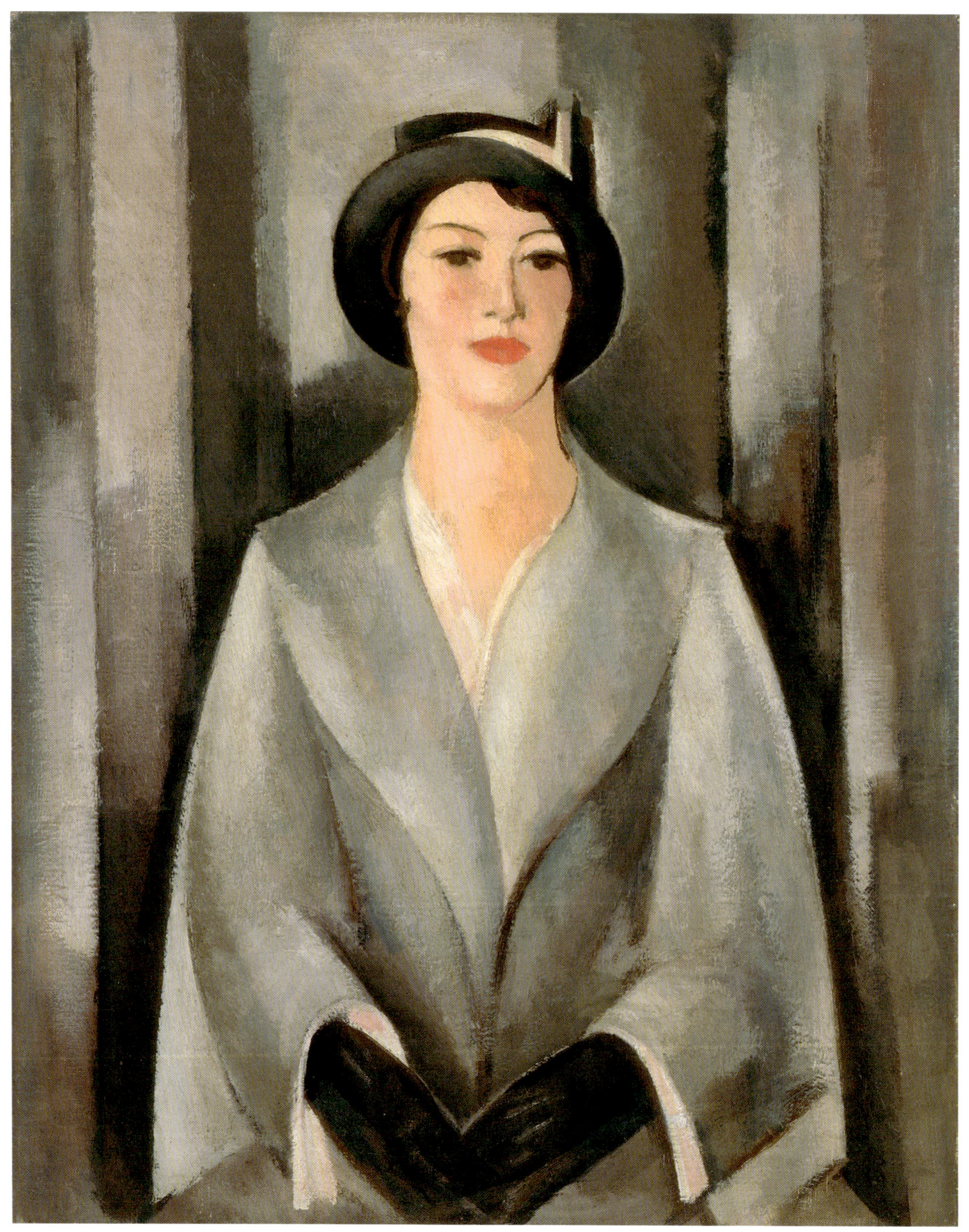

[69]
Souvenir de Jumièges, 1931
Oil on canvas, 92 × 74
The Fergusson Gallery, Perth & Kinross Council, presented by the J.D. Fergusson Art Foundation 1991

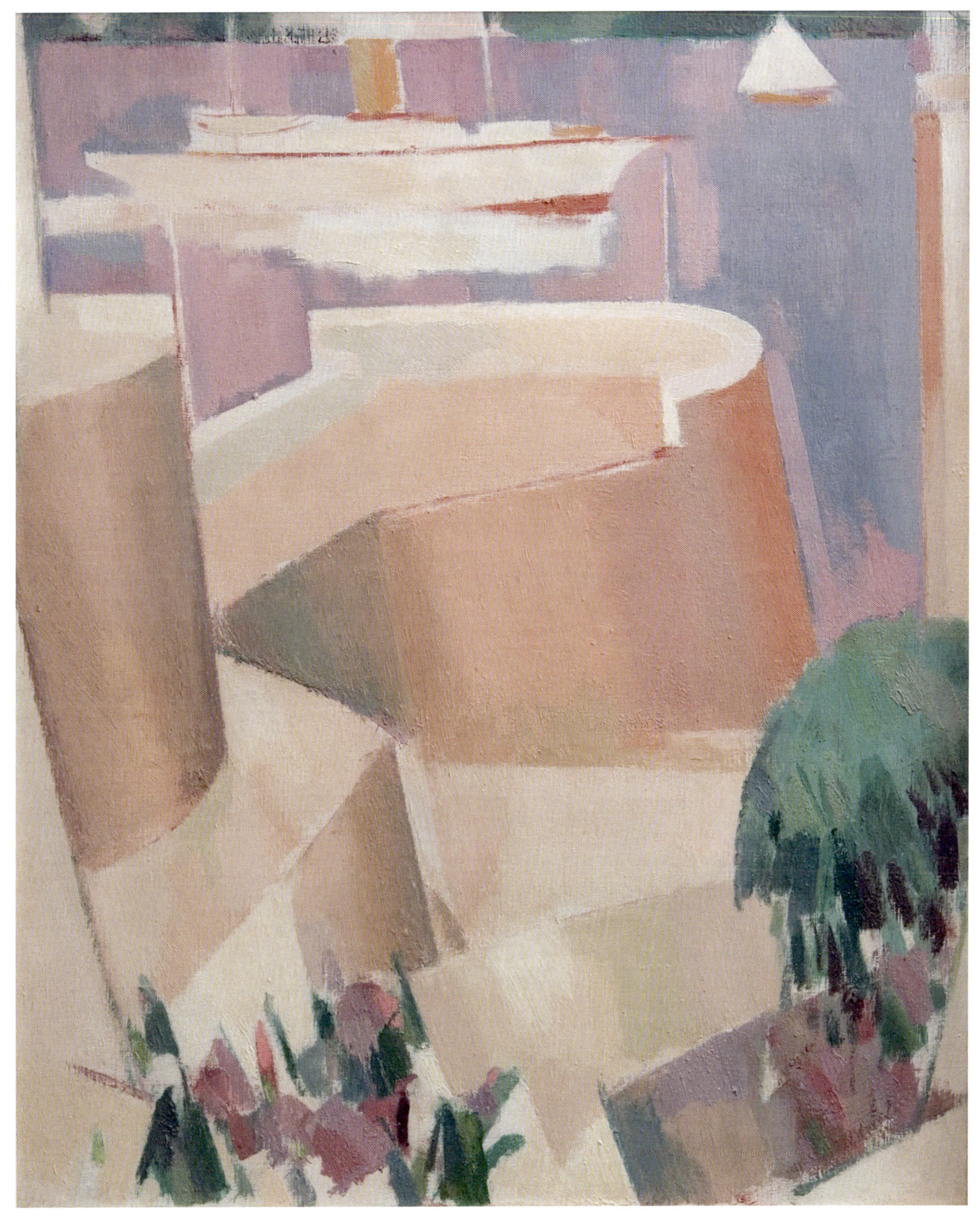

[70]

The Quay at Dinard, *c.*1930

Oil on canvas, 65 × 54

The Fine Art Society, London and Edinburgh

[71]

Christmas Time in the South of France, 1922

Oil on canvas, 61 × 55.8

The Fergusson Gallery, Perth & Kinross Council

purchased with the assistance of the Heritage Lottery Fund 1998

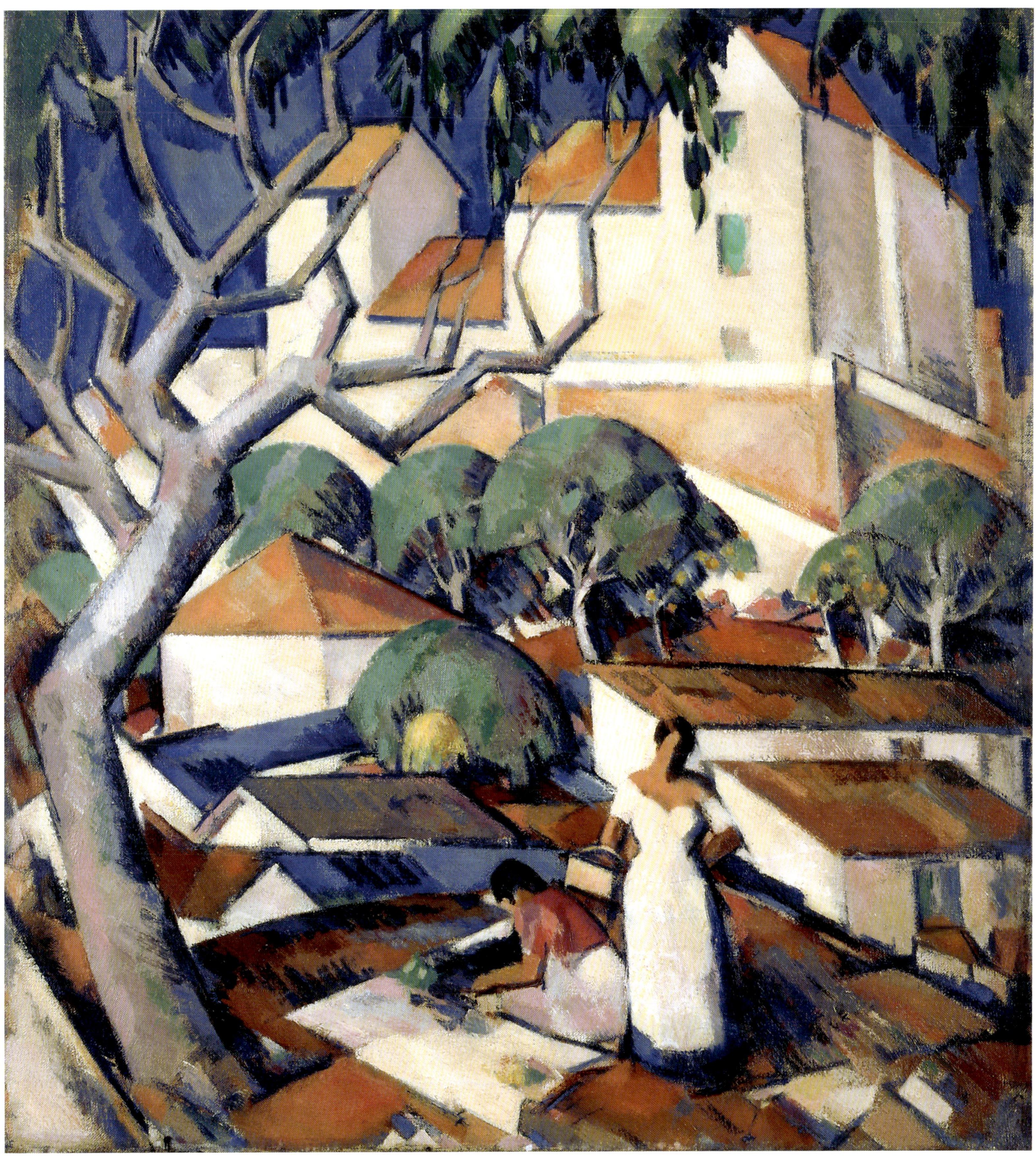

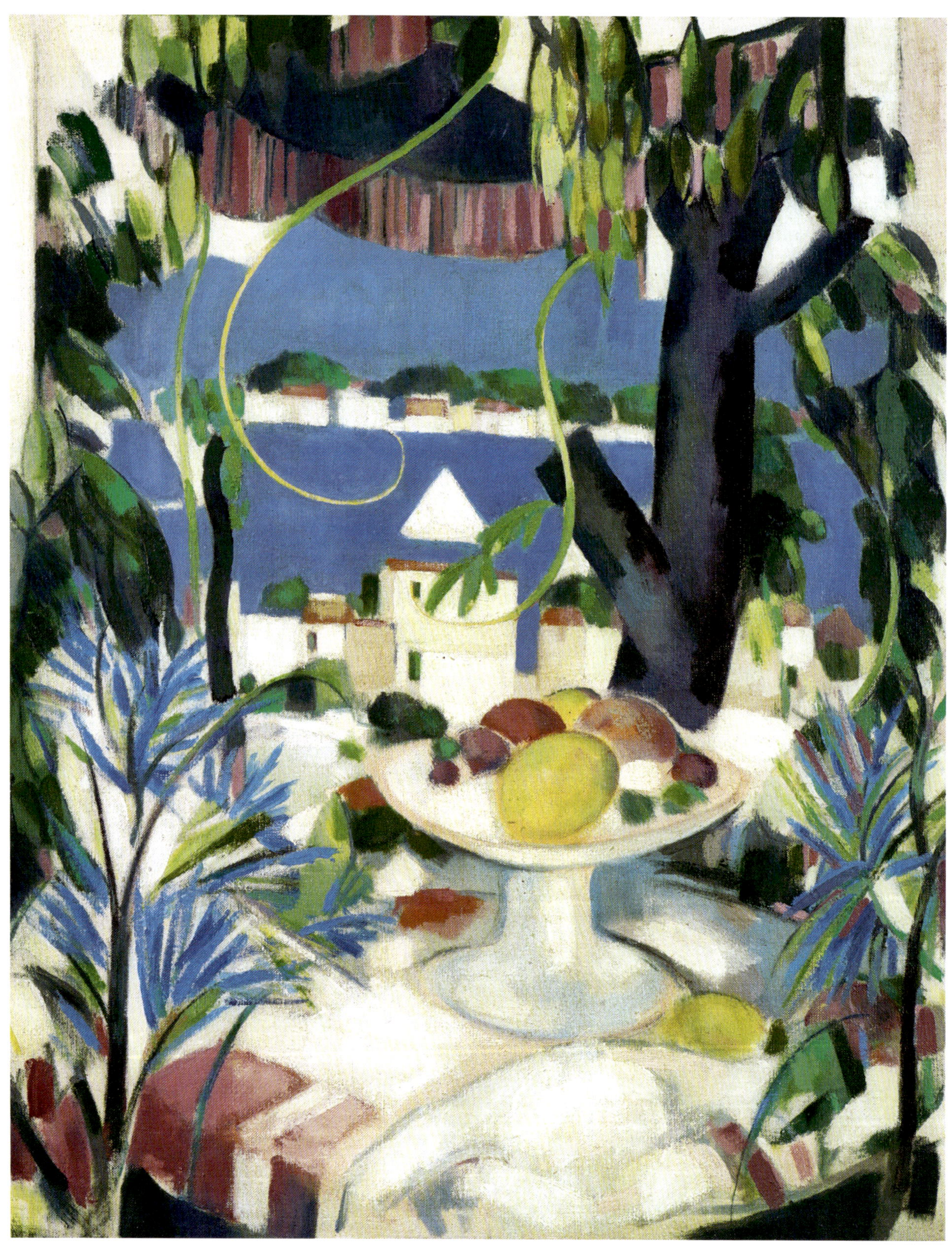

[72]

Wisteria, Villa Florentine, Golfe-Juan, 1957

Oil on canvas, 66 × 53.5

Private collection, courtesy Lyon & Turnbull

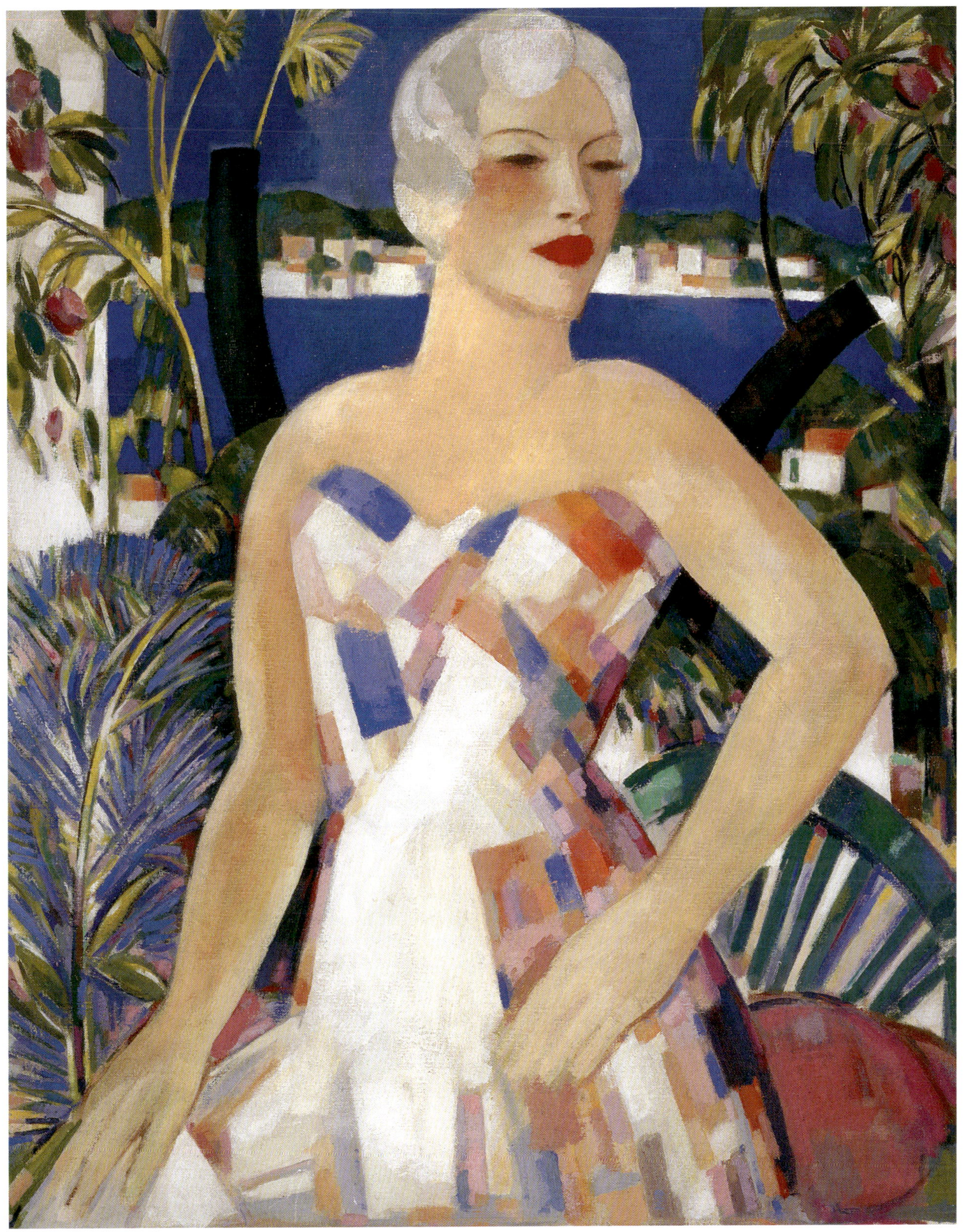

[73]

Blonde with Checked Sundress, 1958

Oil on canvas, 92 × 74

The Fergusson Gallery, Perth & Kinross Council, presented by the J.D. Fergusson Art Foundation 1991

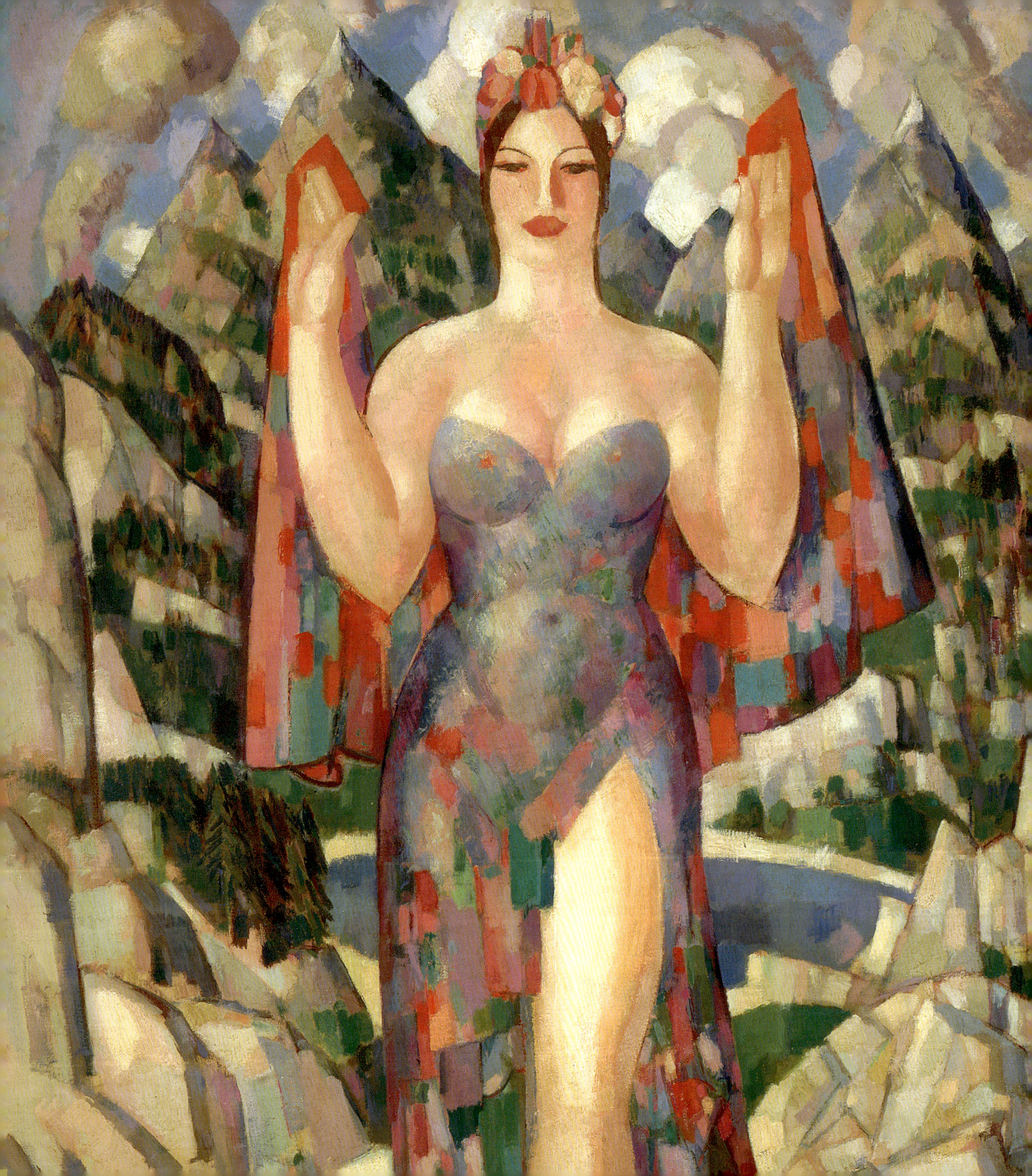

4 · L'esprit Gaulois: Fergusson's Celtic nationalism

SHEILA McGREGOR

When Fergusson and Morris returned to Scotland at the outbreak of war in 1939, they decided to settle in Glasgow [75], confident that it would provide a more sympathetic environment for their various creative endeavours than the artist's native Edinburgh. For Fergusson, now sixty-five years old, this was a moment to look back over the achievements of a lifetime and pass on his wisdom to a younger generation.

His book *Modern Scottish Painting* was conceived with this intention [76]. It was commissioned in 1939 by the publisher William MacLellan as part of a series of publications with an explicitly nationalist prospectus. As MacLellan announced in the flyleaf:

> *In Scotland we are today well served politically with two virile nationalist movements. In the cultural sphere we hope that our publishing organisation will become the focal centre for creative activity that recognises a Scottish tradition and way of life which is unique, distinct from surrounding cultures, has elements worth preserving and developing, and has a distinctive colour which can be harmoniously woven into the tartan of world culture.* [1]

Modern Scottish Painting is a meandering book, constructed with scant regard for logic or systematic historical analysis. As you turn its pages, you can almost hear Fergusson himself holding forth with the opinionated grandiloquence of the *éminence grise*. The book ranges widely across the ideas, experiences and influences that had informed Fergusson's creative outlook: the malign effect of academicism in art; the value of intuitive self-expression; the symbiotic relationship between art and science; the vital role of colour in Scottish culture; and the desire for independence that explains and unites the apparently contradictory cultural inheritance of John Knox and Robert Burns. Above all, *Modern Scottish Painting* champions the auld alliance between Scotland and France, two 'Celtic' peoples with a shared racial ancestry and aesthetic heritage:

> *French culture was founded by the Celts, and invasions have not changed the fundamental character of the French people. Every Celt feels at home in France. The 'esprit Gaulois' (the Celtic spirit) still exists and has not been submerged by Calvinism as it had been in Scotland.* [2]

Modern Scottish Painting rationalises Fergusson's French allegiances at a time when, as Keith Hartley has pointed out, a growing body of opinion was instead inclined to detect a northern European sensibility in Scottish painting.[3] It located his practice within a contemporary nationalist discourse and set the tone for his subsequent activities as instigator of the New Art Club, Art Editor of the periodical *Scottish Art and Letters*, President of the Dunedin Society and all-round elder statesman of the modern Scottish art scene.

In previous decades writers such as Lewis Spence, Edwin Muir, Lewis Grassic Gibbon, Neil Gunn and Hugh MacDiarmid had led a movement against the parochial, small-town mentality of 'Kailyard' literature, seeking instead to create an idiom that was both authentically vernacular in its linguistic expression and modernist in its general terms of reference. The Scottish National Party had come into being in 1934, and the cause of Home Rule was fiercely argued in a welter of nationalist periodicals over the next few years. As Fergusson's bookshelves attest, he was a subscriber to many of these publications in the 1940s and was also by now immersed in the study of ancient Celtic art and culture. There are even occasional indications in his correspondence during this period of a

[74] Detail from *Danu, Mother of the Gods*, 1952 [104]

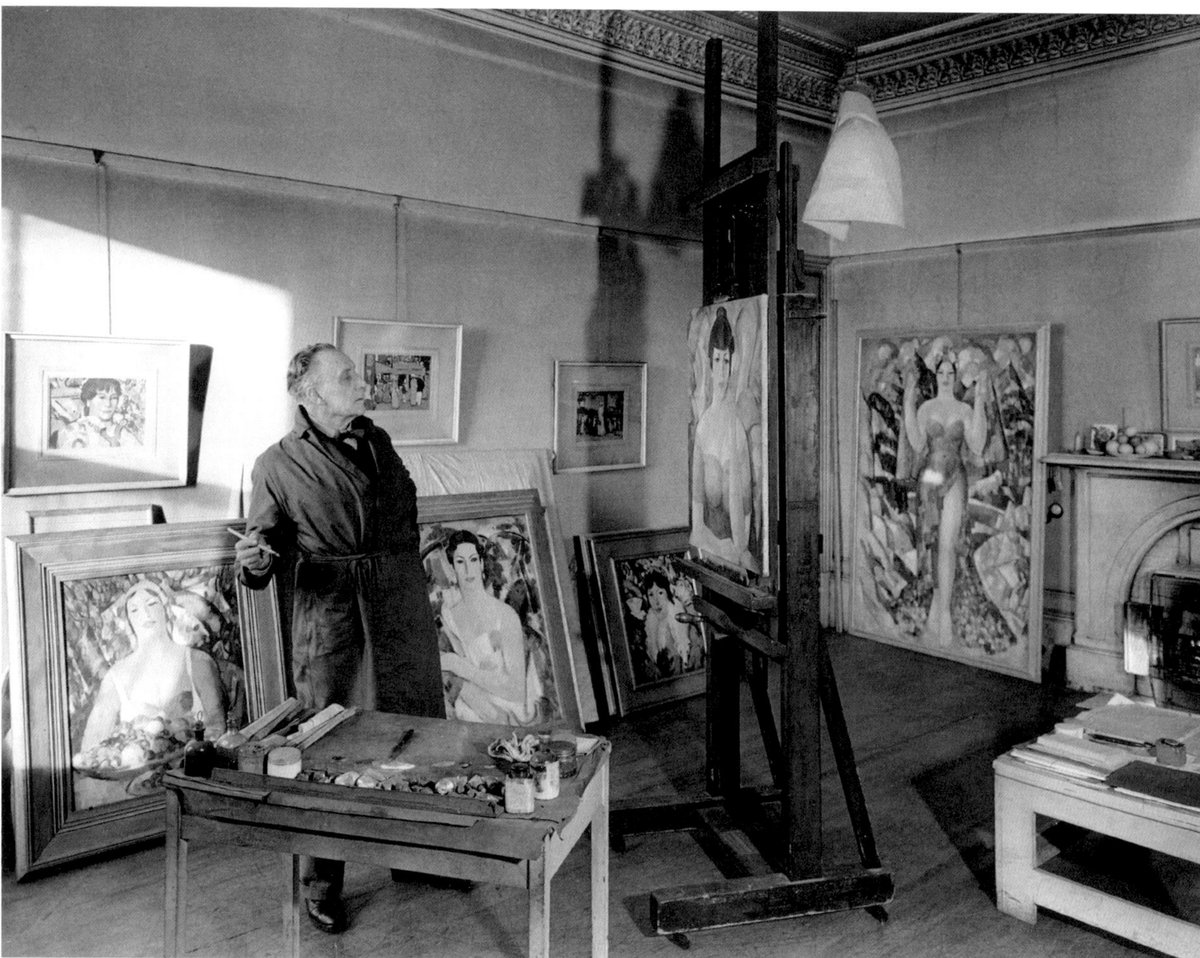

[75] J.D. Fergusson in his studio at 4 Clouston Street, Glasgow, *c.*1955

The Fergusson Gallery, Perth & Kinross Council

flirtation with such radical pro-Celtic organisations as the Celtic League and the Celtic Circle.[4]

Was this a defining aspect of his creative philosophy from the outset or primarily a response to the climate he found on his return to Scotland in 1939? Certainly his self-image was that of the Highland 'Gael', transplanted by family circumstance from Perthshire to Edinburgh and deprived of his Gaelic mother tongue – a linguistic loss he would always regret. Morris reports that he spelt his name with a double 's', in contrast to the spelling on his birth certificate, after an ancient Irish king called Fergus; and even on his death certificate she perpetuated the notion that Fergusson's father had been a farmer, when she must have known full well the less biographically convenient reality of his occupation as a spirit merchant in Leith.[5]

Commentators in pre-1914 Paris were invariably struck by the artist's thoroughgoing Scottishness. To the American novelist Theodore Dreiser, Fergusson appeared 'a solid, sandy, steady-eyed Scotchman who looked as though, had he not been an artist, he might have been a kilted soldier, swinging along with the enviable Scotch stride'.[6] And Fergusson would later feature, in fictional guise, as the 'glen and heather Scotchman' Keir McKail in one of Dreiser's short stories.[7] It is an image we can readily recognise in the piercing expression of Fergusson's self-portrait sketch of 1907 [77], which conveys an impression of unflinching modernist resolve while hinting through its calligraphic flourishes at his Celtic sympathies. Until comparatively recently, however, discussion of his early work has remained anchored within the formalist conventions of twentieth-century art history and has accordingly emphasised stylistic considerations over meaning – a characterisation which his own writings, including much of *Modern Scottish Painting*, only served to reinforce.

Yet the artist's formative years in Paris before the First World War were a period in which political and cultural debates about national identity were conducted with particular intensity, not least in Scotland. The Celtic Revival of the 1890s, originating distantly in the poetry of James 'Ossian' Macpherson and given a helping hand by Matthew Arnold's essays *On The Study of Celtic Literature*, found its principal exponent in the pioneering biologist and town planner Patrick Geddes, whose magazine *The Evergreen* [89], with its eclectic assortment of literary, scientific and artistic contributions, proclaimed the enduring relevance of Celtic art and culture to Scotland's future and implicitly asserted common cause with the other Celtic peoples of Europe.[8]

In France, Ernest Renan's seminal essay *La Poésie des Races Celtiques* of 1854 had prepared the intellectual ground for a resurgence of interest in the nation's Celtic heritage. Several figures loosely associated with Fergusson's Parisian circle, including the poets Francis Carco and Tristan Derème, had affiliations with the Celtic League, established in 1911 by the poet Robert Pelletier as a vehicle for asserting the Gallic, pre-Latin origins of French identity and character. On the political right, by contrast, the nationalist and monarchist movement Action Française, led by Charles Maurras, insisted on the classical foundations of French culture.[9] It is perhaps significant for our understanding of artistic practice that these ideological polarities were often expressed in terms of gender difference, as an opposition between the rational masculinity of Greco-Latin culture versus a more intuitive and feminine Celtic spirit. For Renan himself the Celts were '*une race essentiellement féminine*', their psychic world being fundamentally female in character.[10]

Against this background, Fergusson's large-scale 'rhythmist' nudes of 1910–13 take on a new resonance. Much has rightly been made of their connection with contemporary dance movements and, rather more speculatively, with the vitalist philosophy of Henri Bergson. But they also reflect a general avant-garde preoccupation with the idea of regression to a more natural and harmonious state of being. In Fergusson's case this coincided with personal convictions about the importance of lifestyle, to use a twenty-first-century word. He believed in the correlation between physical and emotional wellbeing, the pleasures of nudity and a new openness in sexual relations between men and women. This 'back to nature' credo was intimately linked in his thinking with his

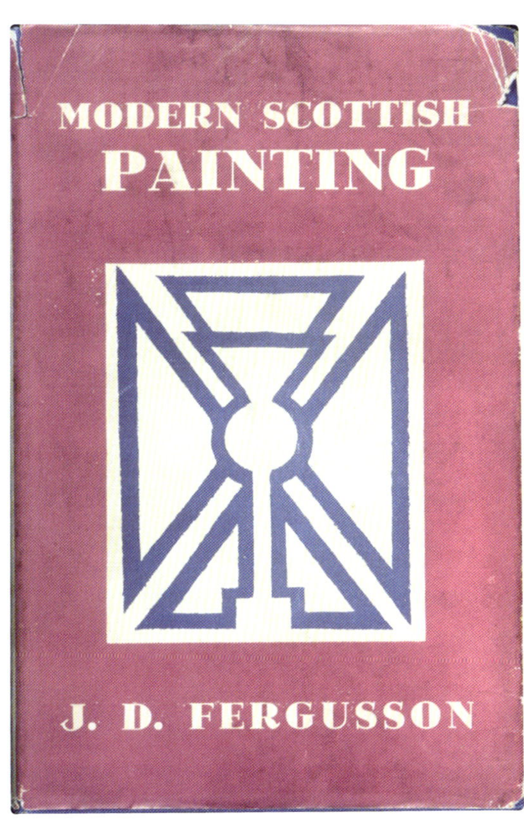

[76] Cover of *Modern Scottish Painting* by J.D. Fergusson, published 1943
The Fergusson Gallery, Perth & Kinross Council

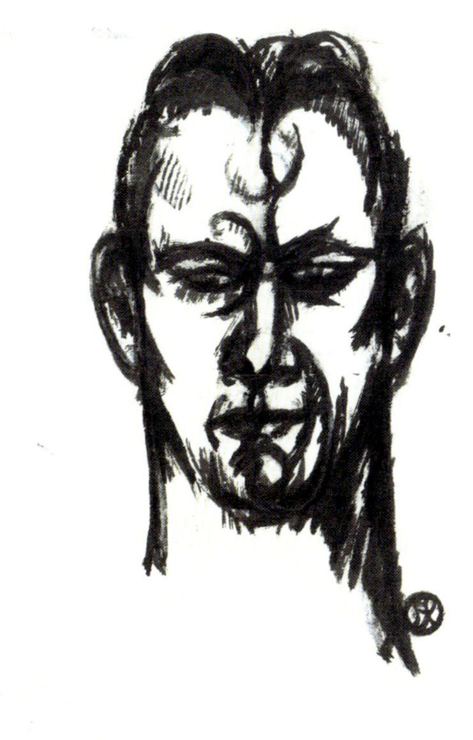

[77] *Self-portrait, c.*1907
Scottish National Portrait Gallery, Edinburgh, purchased 1992

sense of belonging to a Celtic nation. If we compare Fergusson's vision of Arcadia in *Les Eus* [68], for example, with the languid imagery of Matisse's *Le Bonheur de vivre* (*The Joy of Living*) [78], replete with Pan pipes and classical drapery, we can immediately see that the Scottish artist's iconography belongs to an altogether different cosmology.

The stylised setting in which the dancers in *Les Eus* disport themselves seems designed to signal Fergusson's connection with a Celtic past. Perhaps, indeed, this is his vision of a Celtic otherworld, which in Celtic mythology was seen as a place of unlimited happiness, feasting, music and lovemaking. In a similar way, the nude in *Rhythm* [66] is a pagan personification of beauty and fertility, a goddess borrowed from the Celtic pantheon of nature deities and brought up to date. Where her ancient counterparts might have been pictured holding a horn of plenty, she is portrayed with a modern-day fruit bowl, against a backdrop of heavily stylised shapes and motifs suggestive of Celtic decoration.

The presence of a well-established and programmatic Celticism in Fergusson's work at this time is corroborated by the account he gave in later life of the evolution of the painting *Rose Rhythm* [79], a portrait of Margaret Morris's dance pupil Kathleen Dillon. According to Fergusson's retrospective explanation, this was the culmination of a project already underway – his achievement of a 'thing thoroughly Celtic' that had been long in gestation.[11] The use of the word 'rhythm' in the title indicates that it was an attempt to apply the principles of his Parisian nudes to portraiture and to indicate through the wave-like undulations of the composition the sitter's closeness to a Bergsonian *élan vital*. The rose-like shape of the sitter's hat becomes the starting point for an intricate arrangement of curlicues and arabesques, whose curvilinear rhythms are a response to the Irish connotations of Kathleen's name and the grace of her dancing.

Only one month after completing this picture, Fergusson set to work on *Summer: Head of Woman* [81], a portrait of Kathleen Dillon in red sandstone and the first of a series of stone carvings in which his interest in dance and Celtic decoration converge. His enthusiasm for sculpture was by no means a new departure. In his article 'Memories of Peploe' he remembered the impact of seeing the Benin bronzes seized by the British in 1897 and subsequently brought to Edinburgh.[12] His sketchbooks from the early 1900s reveal a lively appreciation of the great 'ethnographic' collections of the Trocadéro in Paris, above all the Cambodian and Indian pieces he saw there. Like other artists at that time, he admired in non-Western sculpture a vigour, sensitivity to materials and formal inventiveness that seemed lacking in the conventions of the classical European canon. Today, of course, such appropriation from other cultures is widely viewed as essentially colonial in character, the by-product of imperialist impulses that reductively relegate non-Western peoples to the realm of instinct, sexuality and elemental religion.

In this respect, however, Fergusson was entirely a man of his time. *Ténèbres* [94] and *Female Head and Foliage* [95] share with the work of such pioneering sculptors as Brancusi, Epstein, Henri Gaudier-Brzeska (1891–1915) and Amedeo Modigliani (1884–1920) the desire to attain a new directness of expression through distortion and simplification. Other pieces, including *Dancing Nude: Effulgence* [98], *Female Dancer* [80] and *Gloxinia* [97], reflect the exuberant sexual and spiritual energy of Hindu sculpture. It is important to note that for Fergusson this stylistic reliance on non-European sources was by no means incompatible with his Celtic loyalties, since the very act of carving asserted his atavistic connection with a Celtic sculptural tradition and he saw the peoples of India as sharing a common racial ancestry with the Celts of Western Europe. His use of Indian prototypes was thus less a question of

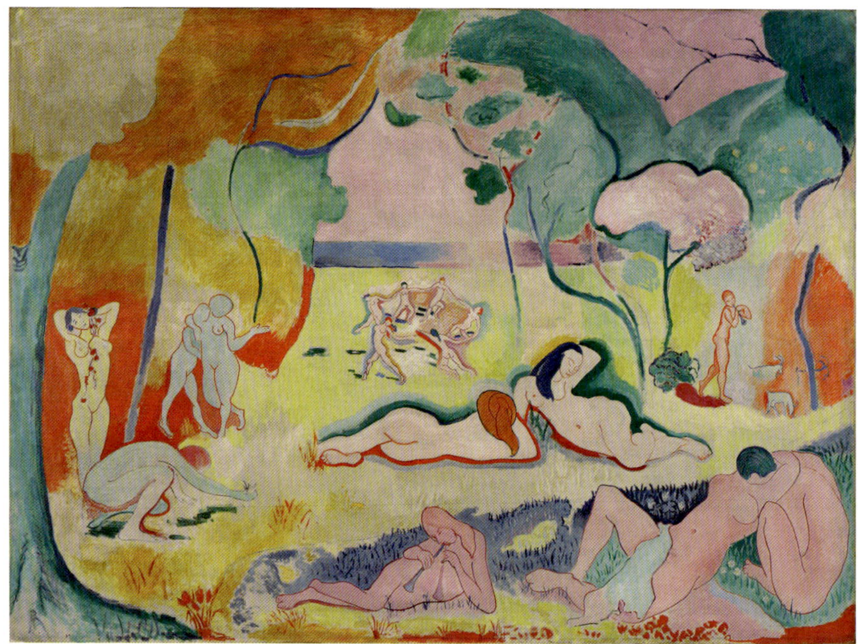

[78] Henri Matisse, *Le Bonheur de vivre*, 1905–6
Barnes Foundation, Philadelphia

borrowing than of acknowledging a shared aesthetic provenance. Fergusson's notion of what constituted 'the Celtic' could be very flexible indeed.

Fergusson's partnership with Margaret Morris was by now the defining factor in his personal and professional life. He encouraged her to broaden the classical basis of her teaching and embrace the dance traditions of other cultures, while she in turn provided a repertoire of choreographic ideas that kept him endlessly supplied with subjects for his painting and sculpture. Her Summer Schools in Wales and France were occasions of intense creative activity. At Wern Fawr near Harlech, home of their friend and philanthropic patron George Davison and setting for the Summer School of 1919, Fergusson carved an elaborate triple portrait of Davison, Morris and himself which shows the three companions in a state of trance-like, almost mystical accord. Only photographs of it, including an atmospheric study by the American photographer Alvin Langdon Coburn [82], now survive. During the same stay, Fergusson was captivated by Davison's newly acquired herd of mountain goats, which would inspire him to create a splendidly modernist and Celtic 'take' on the nineteenth-century tradition of small-scale *animalier* sculpture [96].

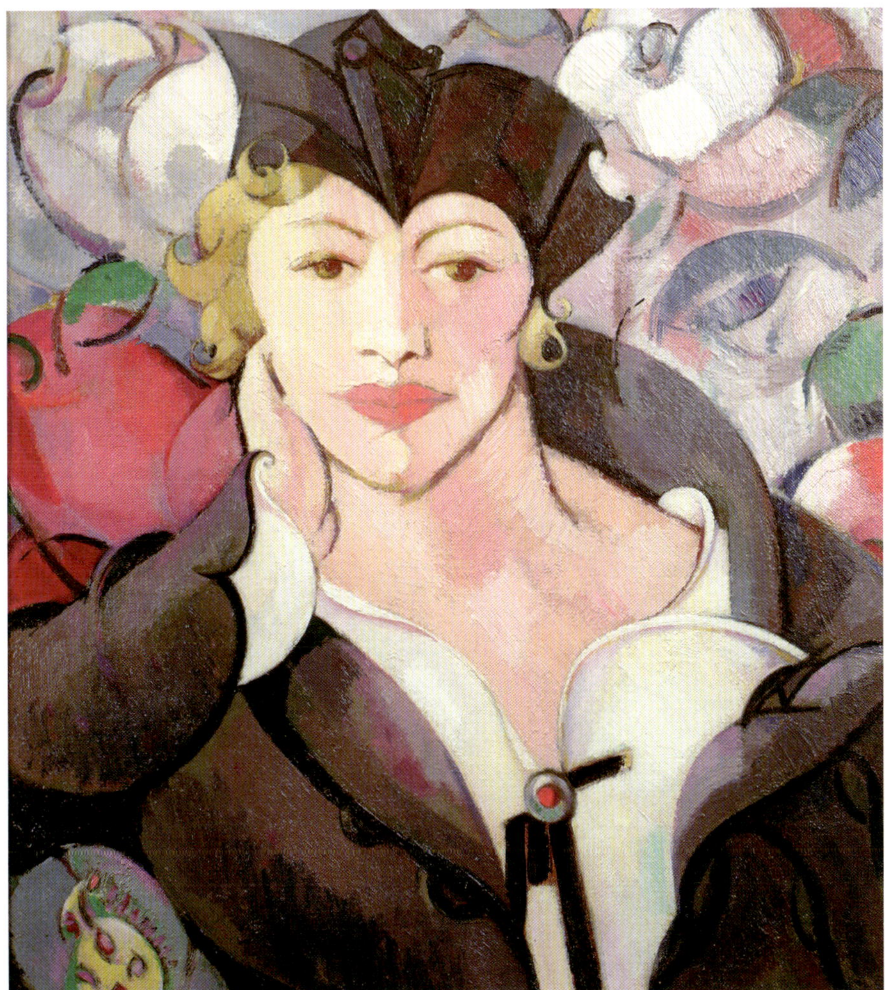

[79] *Rose Rhythm: Kathleen Dillon*, 1916
Private collection

In the 1920s Davison's homes in the south of France, Villa Gotte and Château des Enfants, became the idyllic backdrop for Margaret's Summer Schools. Fergusson's sculpture now embodied an increasingly pantheistic and overtly Celtic vision of man's relationship with the natural world. *Eástre* (*Hymn to the Sun*) [93] is a tribute to the life-giving power of the sun and, almost certainly, a portrait of Margaret, whose ballet of the same title [83] took its inspiration from the music of Rimsky-Korsakov. Fergusson would later describe this piece as the work of 'a pure Highland Scotsman, definitely a Celt. He still has a great sympathy with Celtic sculpture, and on the Celtic crosses there are "bosses" – round shapes, half-spheres which express for him "Suns", fullness, open eyes, women's breasts, apples, peaches, health and overflow – something to give, and depending on the Sun for its ripeness and usefulness.'[13] Yet although the title and to some extent the appearance of this piece invoke age-old pagan ritual, Fergusson chooses to express his sun-worship in shining brass, a material much favoured by other sculptors of the avant-garde to signify modernity. This is the language of Modernism with, in the words of Jonathan Blackwood, a distinctly 'Scots brogue'.[14]

Fergusson continued this vein of Celtic symbolism in his sculptures *Dryad* [99] and *Oak Rhythm* [100], both carvings in which the female figure becomes synonymous with the tree from which the piece is made. His article 'Art and Atavism' describes how *Dryad* began with observation of an ancient plantain tree in the south of France and evolved, via the gift of a potted plant from his friend Charles Rennie Mackintosh and his recollection of hand-carved bagpipes in Kelvingrove Art Gallery, into a more personal exploration of his ancestral relationship with trees.[15] In a similar way, *Oak Rhythm* was later said by Margaret Morris to have represented the 'soul of the oak' from which it was carved.[16]

It is easy to see the formal affinity between these sculptures and the swaying and twisting of Margaret's dancers as they pranced through the forests of Harlech and the palm trees of the Cap d'Antibes [84]. Ana Carden-Coyne's recent appraisal of conceptions

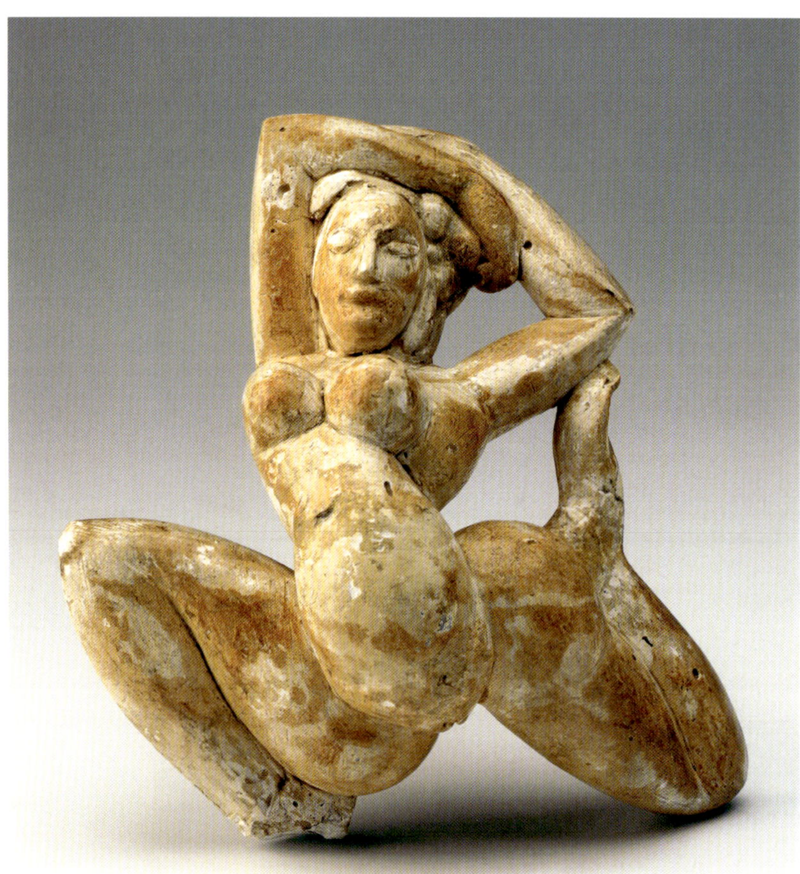

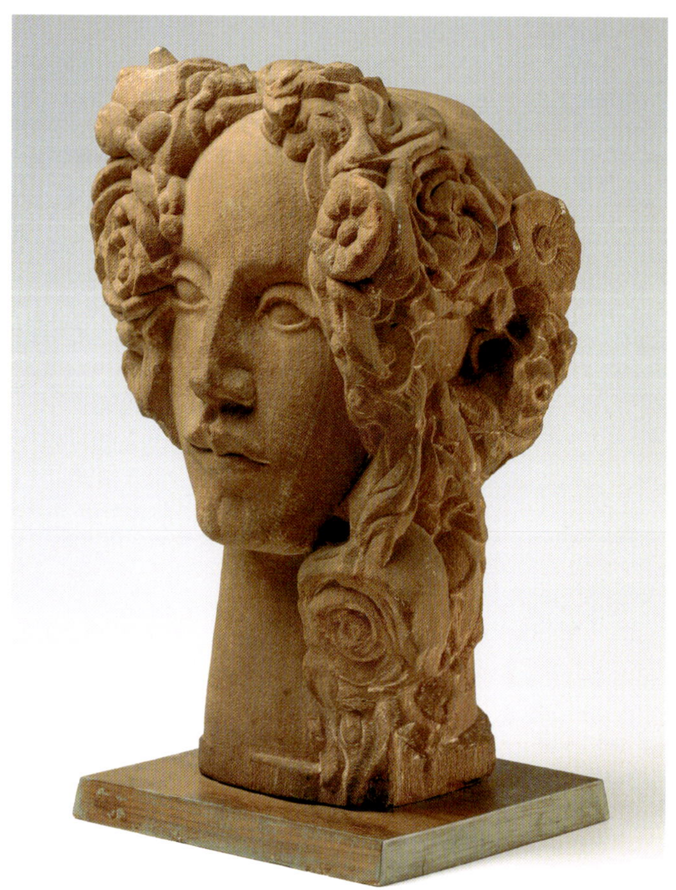

[80] *Female Dancer*, *c.*1920

The Fergusson Gallery, Perth & Kinross Council

[81] *Summer: Head of Woman*, 1916

The Fergusson Gallery, Perth & Kinross Council

of the body during and after the First World War points to the ubiquity of this particular trope among the many alternative dance movements of the period: nymphs and dryads were 'models of nubile sexuality' whose closeness to nature intimated their liberation from the prudish sexual mores of the day.[17]

The overt eroticism of Fergusson's work troubled many contemporary observers, even at a time when the tradition of representing the female nude was not itself at issue. The art critic of the Observer, P.G. Konody, described the 'pink-fleshed nude' in *Rhythm* as the ultimate 'pneumatic woman' and noted how 'every part of her anatomy is inflated to globular roundness'.[18] Katherine Mansfield, one of the artist's closest friends, was similarly disconcerted by the mannequin-like imperturbability of his female portraits, mischievously accusing him in private correspondence of fitting women with mouths 'as a dentist might fit them with teeth'.[19]

An interview given by Fergusson to the *New York Sun* on the occasion of his second American exhibition in 1928 echoes the gendered rhetoric which surrounded turn-of-the-century debates about philosophy, nationality and race and reveals the extent to which his sexual politics were intertwined with notions of a Celtic zeitgeist.[20] To a faintly bemused journalist, he explained the similarity between New York skyscrapers and women and acknowledged in passing the influence on his thinking of his friend, the writer and journalist John Ressich:

> *They are as simple, as sweeping as the modern woman, who is efficiently artistic in everything she does. I must say they have given me a tremendous surprise. I hadn't expected anything like this.*

Apparently he was still talking about the skyscrapers.

> *You see, there are two distinct forces at work in the world. My friend Ressich has all this worked out and is going to lecture about it. One is the Celtic spirit, the other the Roman. I prefer to call one the masculine spirit; the other the feminine or universal.*[21]

[82] George Davison, Margaret Morris and J.D. Fergusson with Fergusson's sculpture *Harlech, c.*1920

Photograph by Alvin Langdon Coburn
The Fergusson Gallery, Perth & Kinross Council

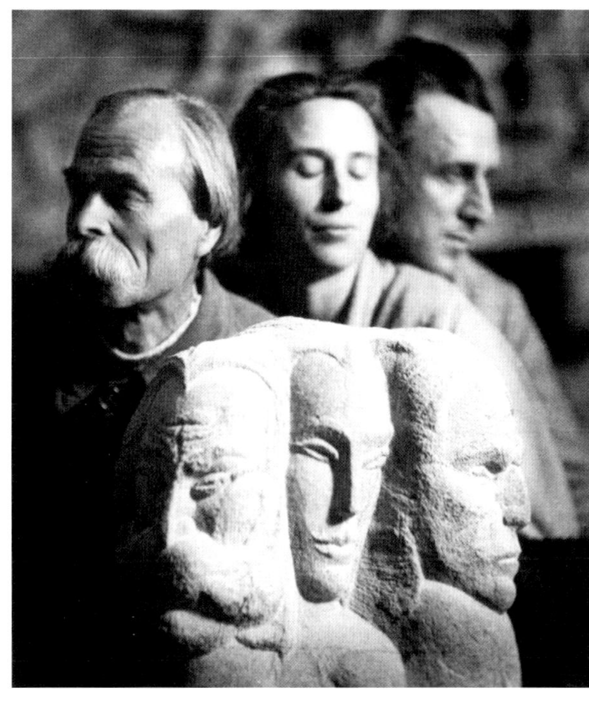

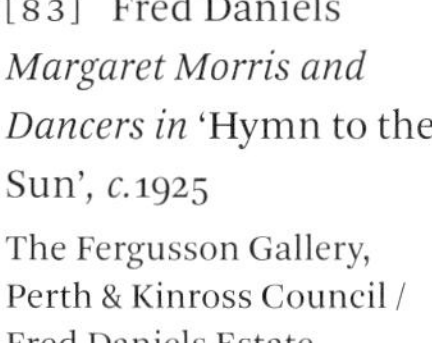

[83] Fred Daniels *Margaret Morris and Dancers in* 'Hymn to the Sun', *c.*1925

The Fergusson Gallery, Perth & Kinross Council / Fred Daniels Estate

[84] Fred Daniels *Frieze Silhouette*, *c.*1925

The Fergusson Gallery, Perth & Kinross Council / Fred Daniels Estate

Whereas the Roman spirit that imbued Rome, Napoleon and the Kaiser is doomed to fail, the Celtic and Gaelic spirit lives on as a 'sympathetic, imaginative spiritual force' in which women are the governing influence. Women, says Fergusson, do not need to accomplish anything themselves in order to dominate a civilisation. But they must inspire and express beauty, just like the modern skyscraper.[22] Here, in his own words, is the central paradigm and paradox of Fergusson's art: women are the agents of a creative energy that is linked in the artist's thinking with the possibility of a Celtic renascence. Yet in his painting and sculpture they remain impassive and inert, all individuality and capacity for action suppressed in accordance with their author's idiosyncratic world-view.

In this, of course, Fergusson was also influenced by the conflicted visual vocabulary of Art Deco, which promoted an ideal of athletic, emancipated womanhood while simultaneously reducing the female form to decorative motif or functional prop. Paintings such as *Souvenir de Jumièges* [69] and *Grace McColl* [37] employ the svelte simplifications of Art Deco to fashionable effect, and the presence of Fergusson's own sculpture in several compositions of this period adds a note of 'primitive chic'. This decorative impulse found its most extreme expression in a portrait of Margaret Morris entitled *Megalithic* [103], in which the statuesque Meg, as the punning title suggests, becomes the twentieth-century personification of some ancient, no doubt Celtic, civilisation. Thus the Bergsonian cult of rhythm re-emerges in the 1920s and 1930s in a suitably rectilinear guise.

Fergusson's friend John Ressich was not only one of

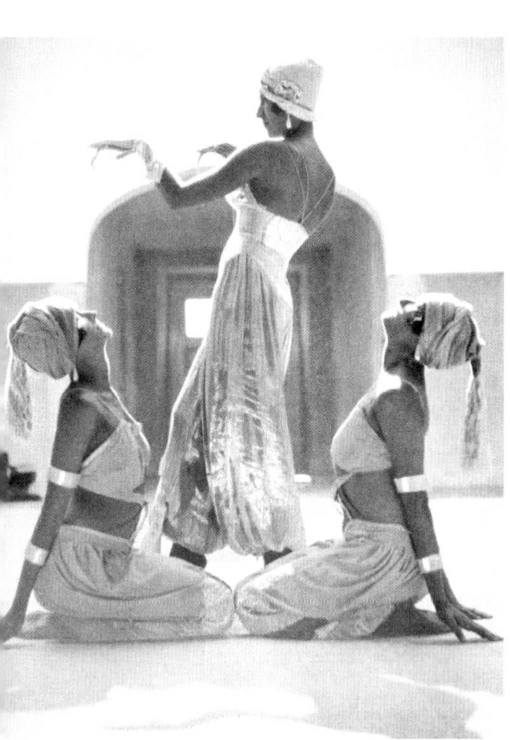

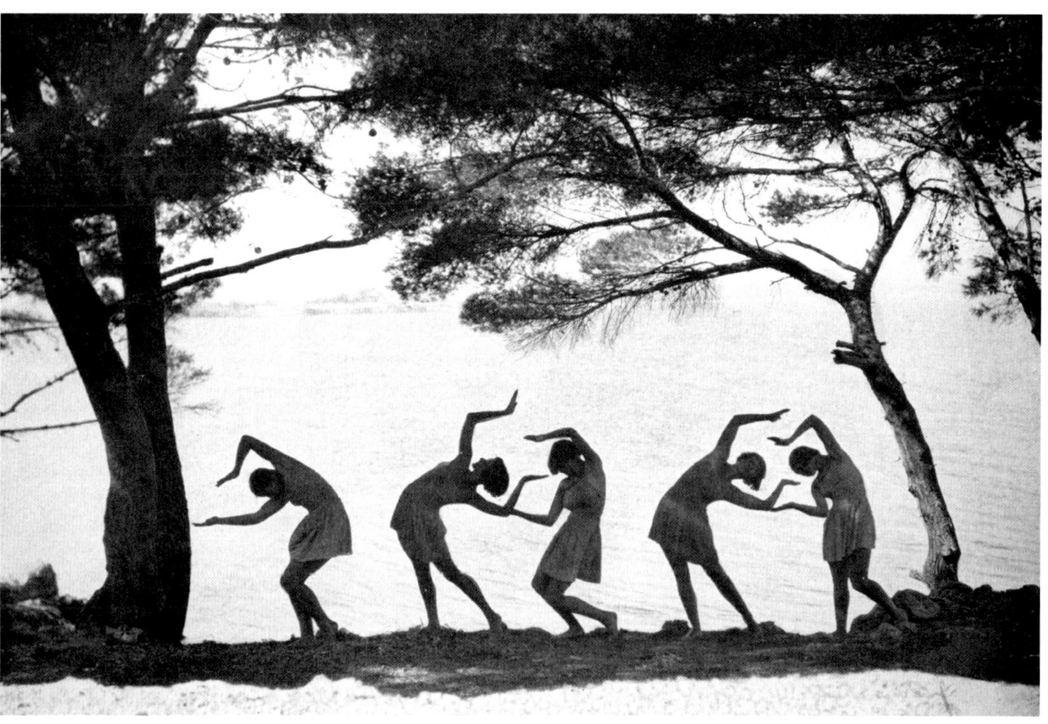

his closest intellectual allies, but also a reliable source of companionship and professional support. The car tours of the Scottish Highlands on which he accompanied Fergusson in 1922 and 1928 rekindled the artist's interest in the Scottish landscape and precipitated periods of concentrated productivity.[23] It is curious, given Fergusson's self-image as a Highlander, that he had so far remained impervious to the pictorial possibilities of this subject matter. But that was to change with his Highland tours, which resulted in a flurry of paintings, watercolours and sketches. The grandeur and variety of the vistas that confronted Fergusson on his travels brought out a Cézanne-like concern for pictorial structure and a richly hued palette. Paintings such as *Storm around Ben Ledi* [102], *The Rocky Glen* and *A Puff of Smoke near Milngavie* [101] vividly register his response to the ever-changing drama of the Scottish scene.

Landscape, however, was never more than an interlude. The human figure continued to dominate Fergusson's art, even after his return to Scotland in 1939. Undeterred by the admonitions of his dealer, who pleaded with him not to 'overdo' the nudes, he produced a steady stream of bather compositions set on the sun-drenched French Mediterranean coast where, during the 1950s, he and Margaret spent the summer months.[24] From time to time he also made portraits of his (female) friends, pressing them all, whatever their appearance, into the mould of an identikit physique.

The real interest of Fergusson's Glasgow years lies not so much in his painting as in his activities as a champion of Scottish culture and contributor to debates about Scottish nationalism. His arrival in Glasgow in 1939 had an immediate practical effect, as he and Margaret set about establishing a meeting-place for people who shared their commitment to artistic experimentation outside the straitjacket of academies and institutions. The first outcome of their campaign was Margaret's Celtic Ballet Club on West George Street, followed soon after by the New Art Club, whose members would eventually launch themselves as the New Scottish Group [85].

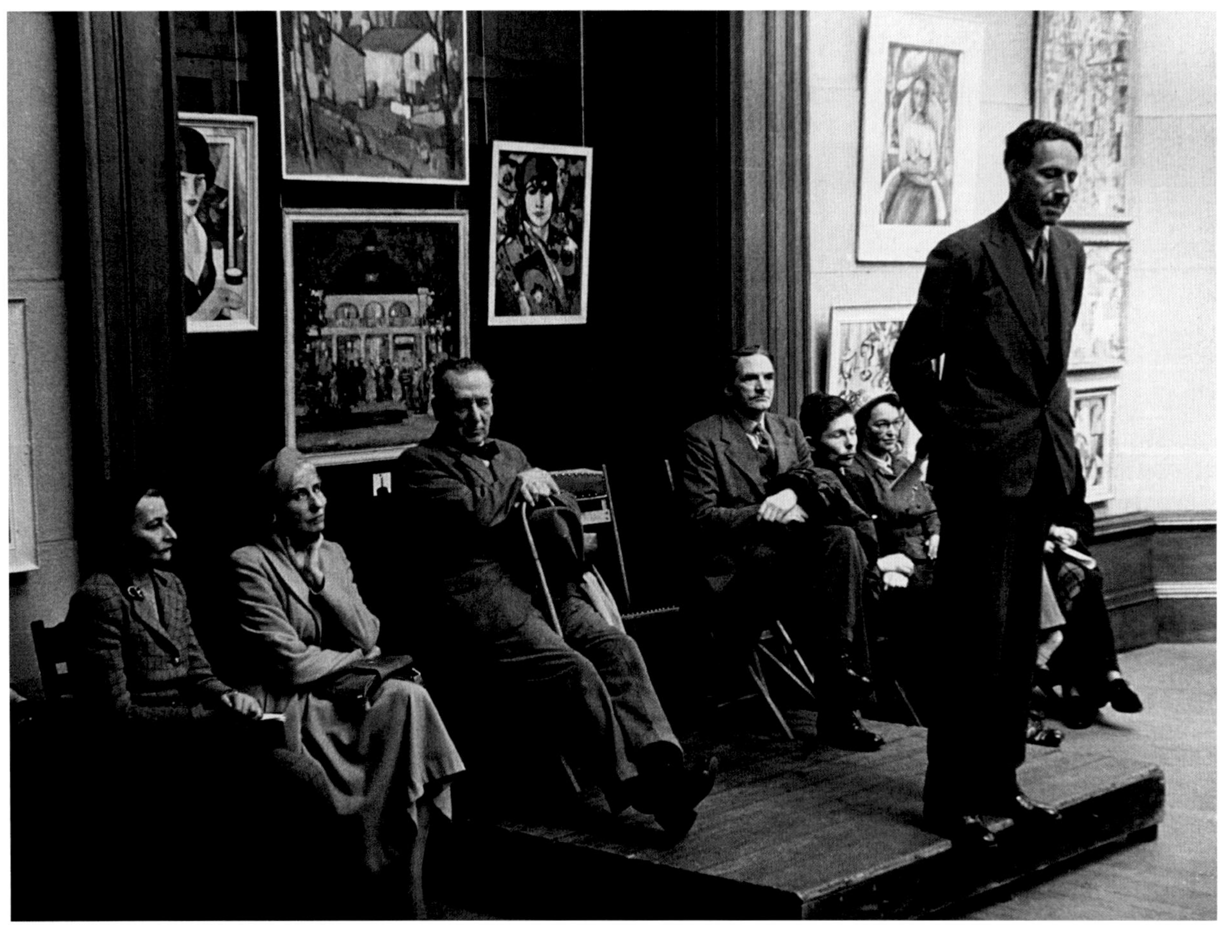

[85] The Earl of Selkirk opening the *First Retrospective Exhibition of the New Scottish Group* at the McLellan Galleries, Glasgow, 1951. Margaret Morris and J.D. Fergusson are second and third from left.

Private collection, courtesy Lyon & Turnbull

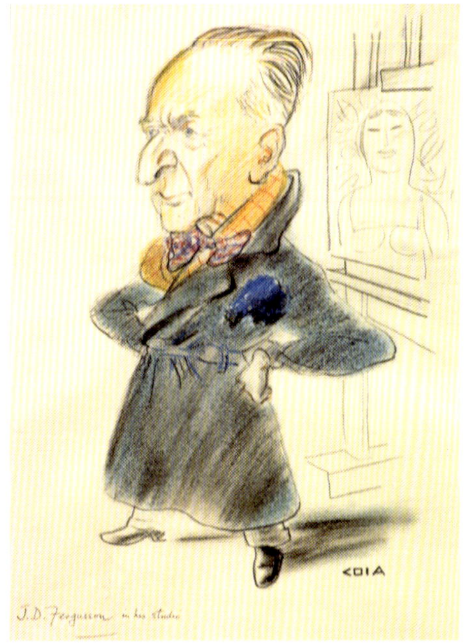

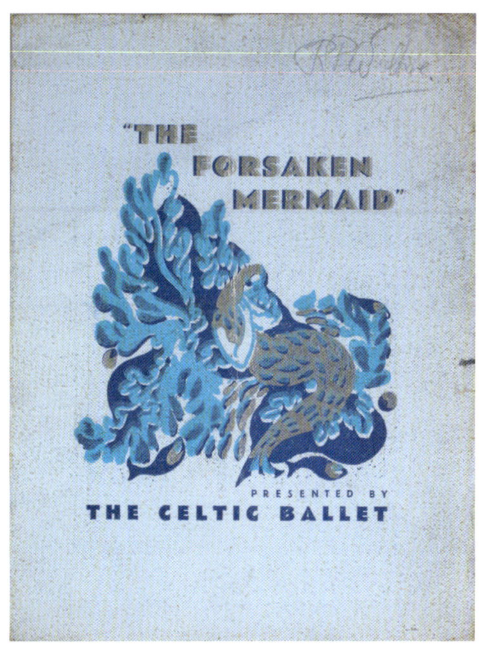

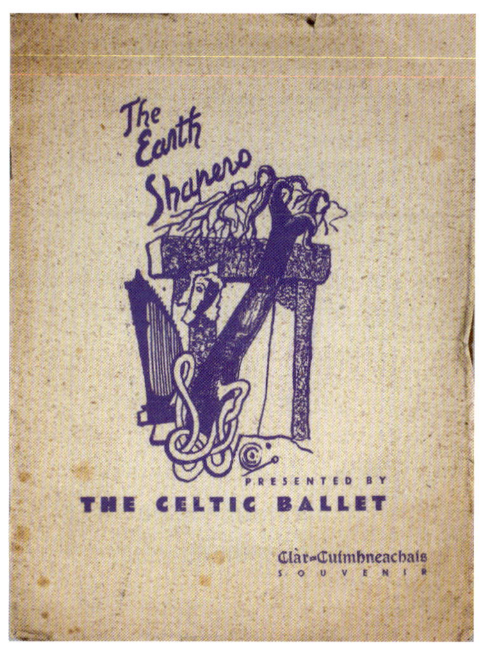

[86] Emilio Coia
J.D. Fergusson
Private collection

[87] *Mermaid* (Celtic Ballet programme)
The Fergusson Gallery, Perth & Kinross Council

[88] *Earth Shapers* (Celtic Ballet programme)
The Fergusson Gallery, Perth & Kinross Council

For young artists Fergusson was the most encouraging of mentors and a link with the events and personalities that had shaped the Modern Movement. The New Art Club became a magnet for semi-professional and established artists alike, including the notable refugees Josef Herman and Jankel Adler (1895–1949). Members enjoyed a diverse programme of educational talks and performance, from Gaelic song recitals to political discussions about the prospects for Scottish independence. Many of those who were involved remember Fergusson's missionary zeal and his at times misplaced indulgence towards artists of lesser talent – a consequence perhaps of his own self-taught status. As Emilio Coia (1911–1997) observed, there was 'no shortage of rank bad art to attest, among other things, to the wonderful magnanimity of that Grand Old Man "J.D.", who was sublimely uncritical of those around him' [86].[25]

It could be said that Margaret's Celtic Ballet Club, with its explicitly nationalist repertoire, and broadly based curriculum, ultimately had the greater impact [87, 88]. Through her indefatigable efforts she nurtured many a successful theatrical career and set the scene for the emergence of Scotland's national ballet company some years later. The New Art Club, on the other hand, had run its course by 1947. And although the New Scottish Group continued to exhibit intermittently until 1956, its self-consciously anti-establishment stance and espousal of an epigonic Post-Impressionism were already behind the times. Fergusson's refusal to select or censure became, in the end, a limitation.

The artist's activities did nonetheless contribute to an atmosphere in which ideas about state support for the arts, cultural self-determination and the value of indigenous tradition could flourish. It was typical of the man that he should chide his friend Tom Honeyman, Director of Glasgow Art Gallery (Kelvingrove), for spending so much money on a painting by Salvador Dalí (1904–1989) – *Christ of St John of the Cross* – in 1952, at a time when, so Fergusson claimed, young Scottish artists had little opportunity to exhibit their work.[26] With his protégé Donald Bain he also petitioned the Scottish Arts Council to set up a 'materials' fund for young painters, even going so far as to prescribe exactly what equipment he thought a young artist might need.[27]

His writings, as we have seen, followed a more or less nationalist line, often explicitly linking the possibility of artistic progress with the attainment of political autonomy. 'Art, as I understand it, cannot be produced by a nation lacking the spirit of freedom,' he wrote in an article of 1946 entitled 'The Scotland I'd Like to See'.[28] 'Let's have freedom in Scotland and art may appear. I mean really Scottish Art, at present I think Scotland is producing British Imperial Art, that is Art that is doing its best to fit in with the Imperial control.'[29] But Fergusson's support for nationalism aspects of contemporary Scottish painting and instead modelled their practice, to varying degrees, on Cubism, German Expressionism, Abstract Expressionism and European abstraction. Gear and Davie lived much of their lives outside Scotland, and at a slightly later stage Eduardo Paolozzi (1924–2005), John Bellany (1942–2013) and Bruce McLean (b.1944) all abandoned Edinburgh and Glasgow for the more stimulating atmosphere of London, just as Fergusson himself had done on the occasion of his first one-person show at the Baillie Gallery in 1905.

Over time these patterns began to change. Political devolution and civic investment, in tandem with Lottery and European funding, have transformed the cultural infrastructure in Scotland, especially in the city that Fergusson made his home in 1939. Fergusson might have been baffled by the more conceptual aspects of artistic practice today, for his art was grounded in observation of the real world. But he would have been gratified to witness Glasgow's re-housing of the Burrell Collection, the proliferation of galleries and project spaces across the city, the emergence of discerning commercial dealers and the pre-eminence of Glasgow School of Art. Although he might have been less pleased about the commercialisation of the legacy of his good friend Charles Rennie Mackintosh, he would nevertheless have welcomed the restoration of his reputation as a presiding genius of twentieth-century architecture. We can only assume, too, that Fergusson would have taken satisfaction in the election of a majority SNP administration to Holyrood in 2011 and rejoiced in the visibility now given to the Gaelic language. [105]

Today Glasgow has the most international artists' community of any British city outside London and offers an atmosphere of confidence and opportunity not unlike that which sustained Fergusson in pre-1914 Paris. Of the three Glasgow-based artists representing Scotland at the Venice Biennale in 2013, not one was actually born in Scotland. But if artists can remain in Scotland or migrate here, it is because they participate in a culture of exhibiting and curating that transcends national boundaries. An artist resident in Scotland is just as likely to exhibit in Berlin, Istanbul, São Paulo or Gwangju as in Edinburgh or London; their work can be disseminated and consumed online by anyone with an internet connection; their thematic concerns and means of expression have international currency. The relativistic climate of this globalised art economy may seem far removed from the essentialist theories about national identity that exercised Fergusson sixty years ago. But the process of globalisation raises questions about the relationship between local and international, difference and homogeneity, oppression and power, which he would have recognised. Such political and cultural negotiations remain a continual work in progress.

[93]
Eástre (*Hymn to the Sun*), 1924 (cast 1971)
Brass, 41.8 × 22 × 22.5
Scottish National Gallery of Modern Art, Edinburgh, purchased 1972

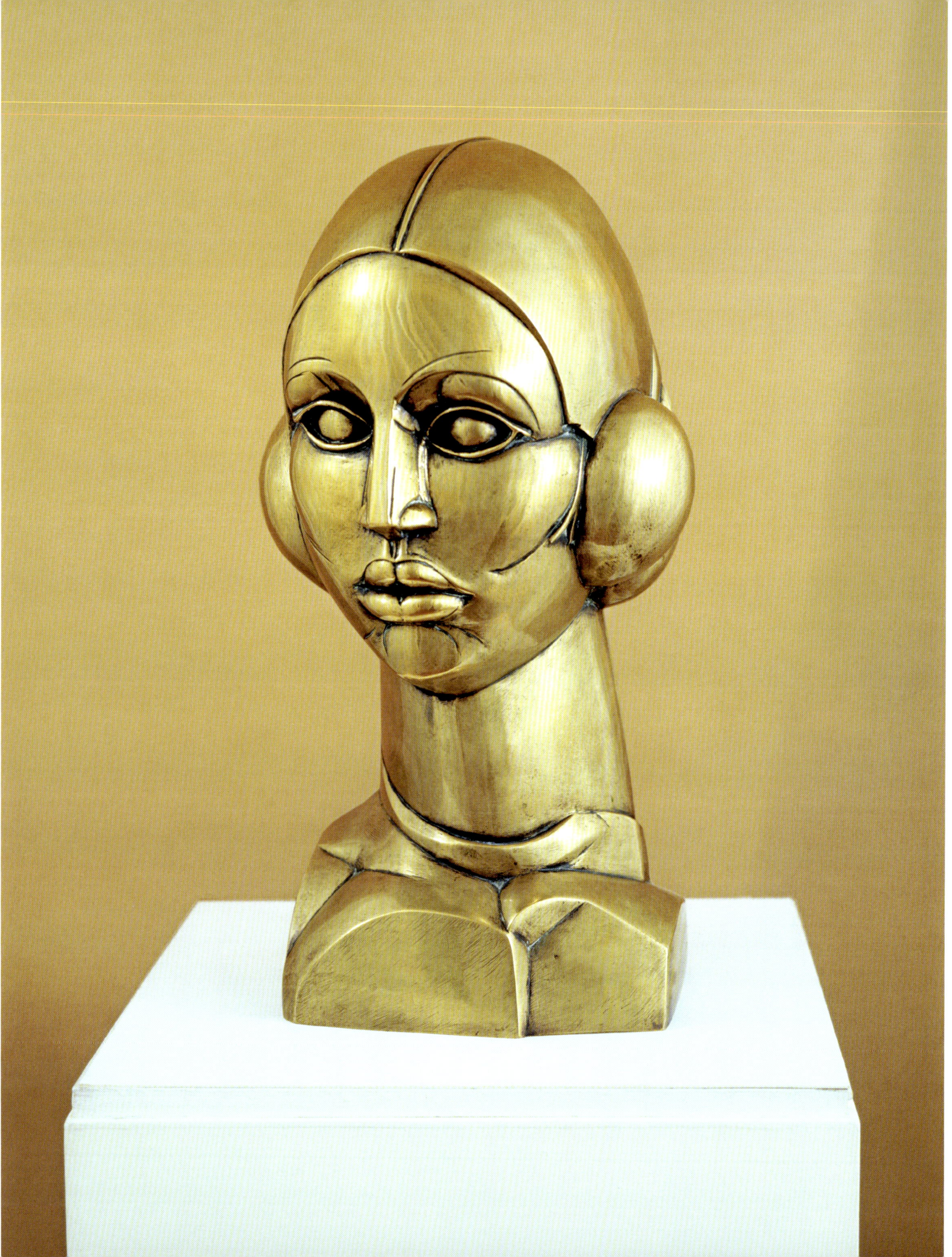

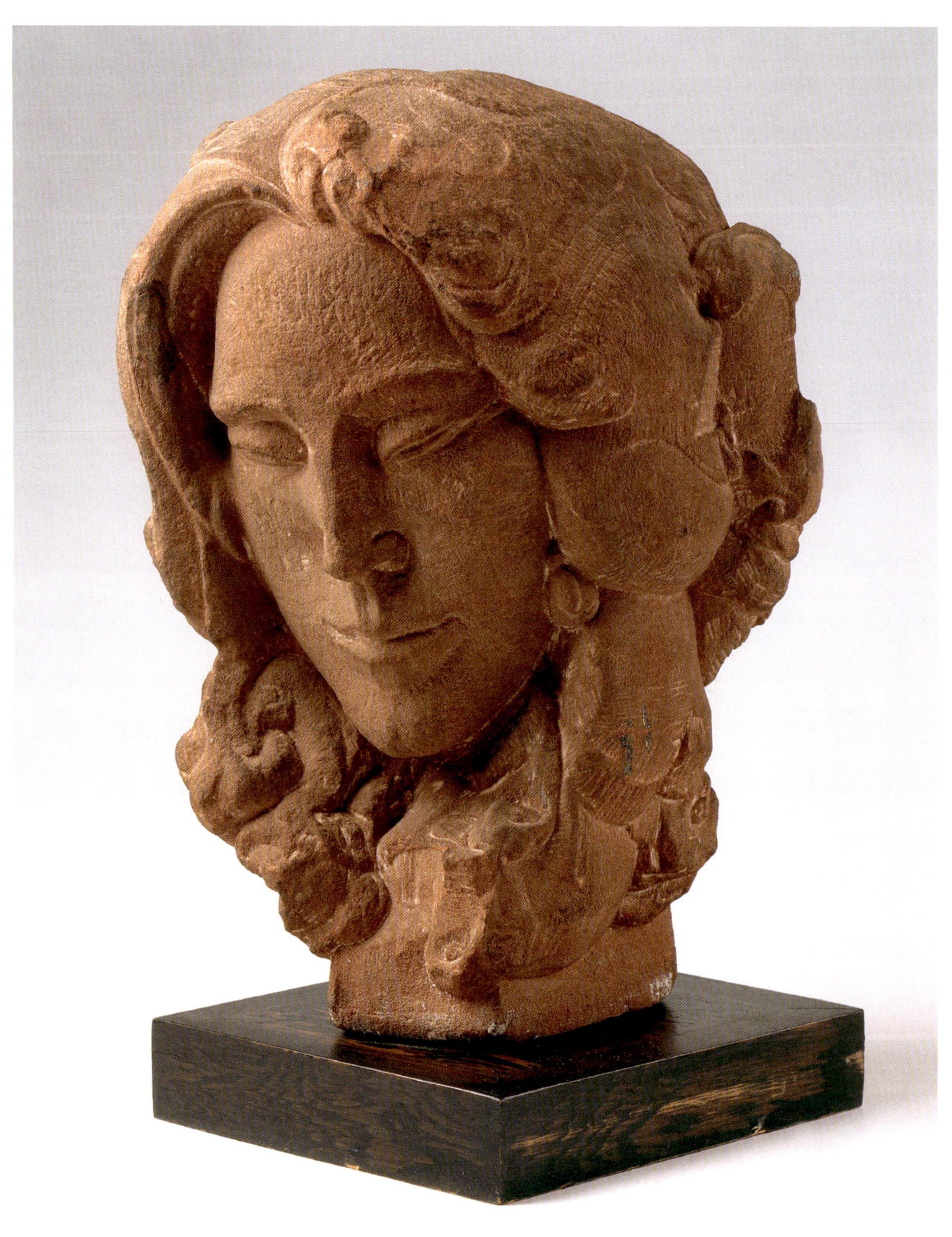

[94]

Ténèbres, 1915

Dumfries stone, 38 × 20 × 24
The Fergusson Gallery, Perth & Kinross Council
presented by the J.D. Fergusson Art Foundation 1991

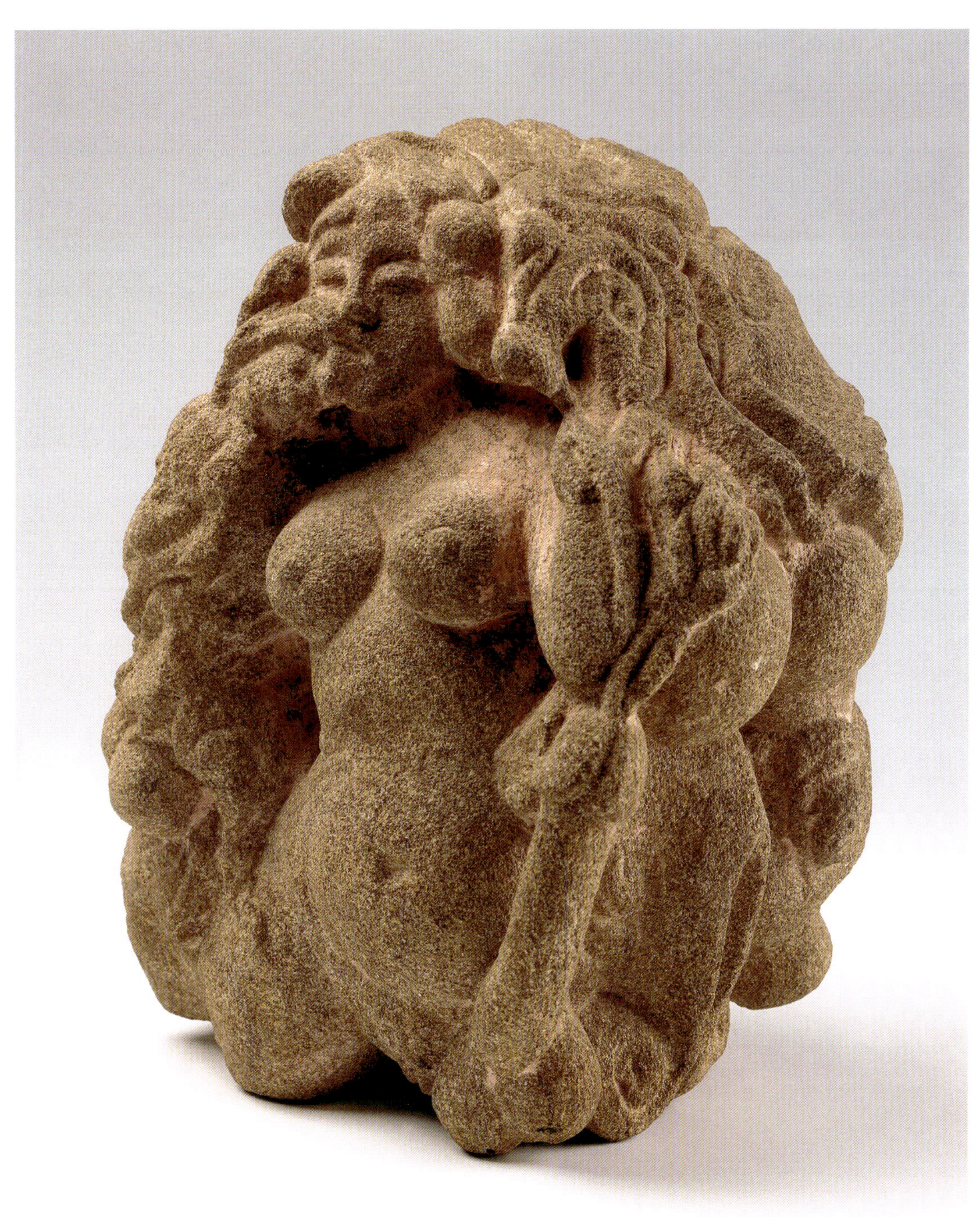

[95]

Female Head and Foliage, 1916

Sandstone, 28 × 22 × 16
The Fergusson Gallery, Perth & Kinross Council
presented by the J.D. Fergusson Art Foundation 1991

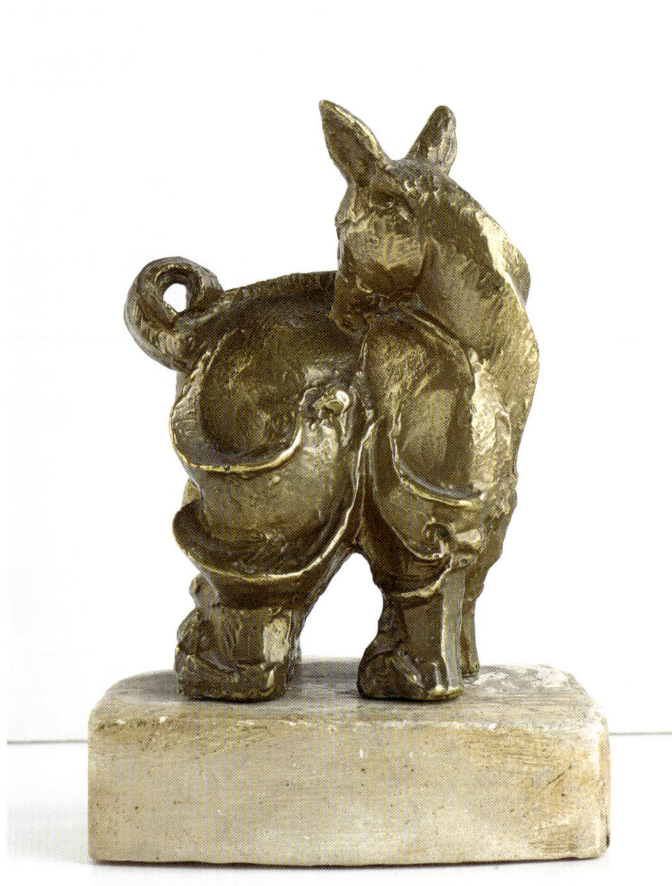

[96]

Goat, 1921, (cast at a later date)

Brass on plaster base made by the artist,
11 × 8 × 6 exc. base 14 × 19.5 × 6.5 inc. base
Private collection

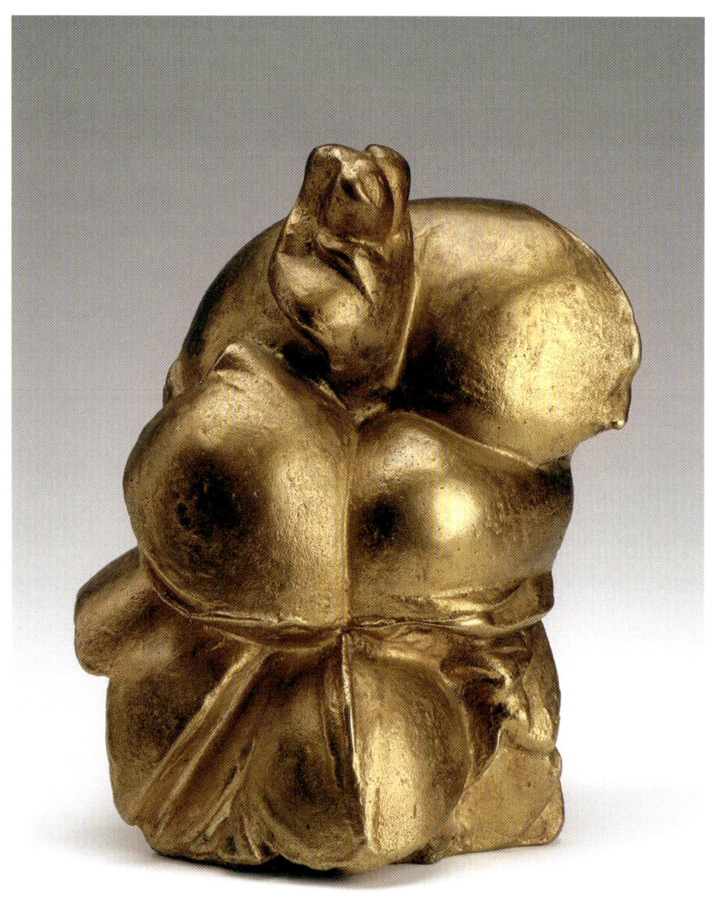

[97]

Gloxinia, 1919

Brass, 18 × 12 × 14
The Fergusson Gallery, Perth & Kinross Council
presented by the J.D. Fergusson Art Foundation 1991

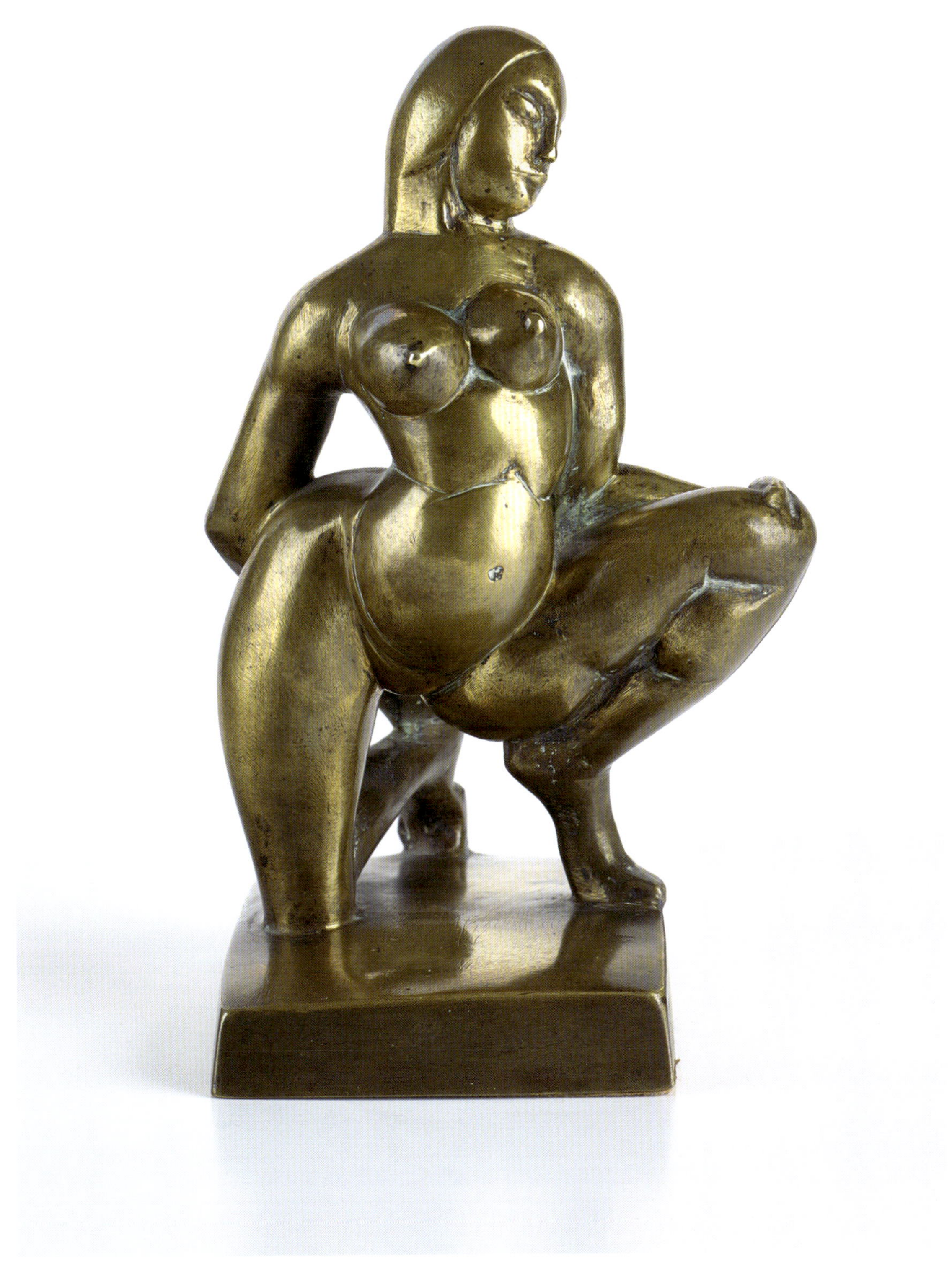

[98]

Dancing Nude: Effulgence, *c.*1920 (cast date unknown)

Bronze, 22 × 13 × 13.5

Private collection

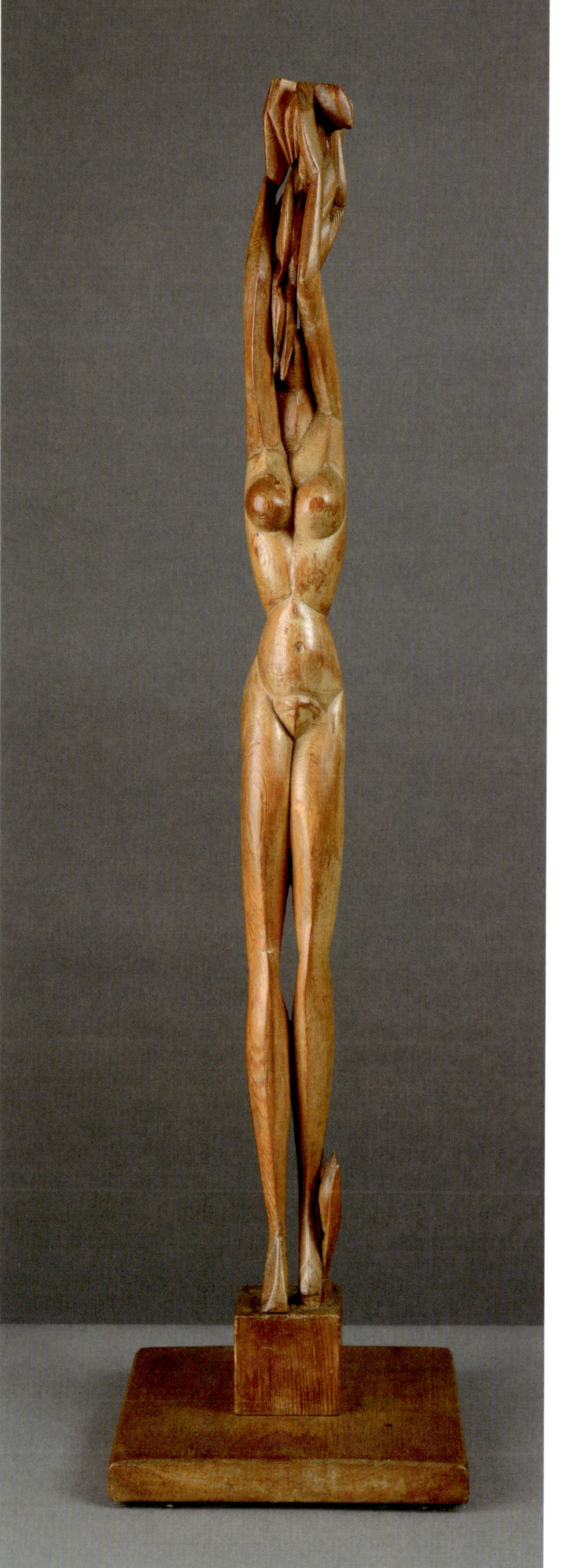

[99]

Dryad, 1924

Pine, 84.5 × 23.5 × 21.5 inc. base
Hunterian Art Gallery, University of Glasgow, purchased 1966

[100]

Oak Rhythm, 1925

Oak, 42.5 × 12.7 × 7.6 exc. base
Tate: presented by the Friends of the Tate Gallery 1964

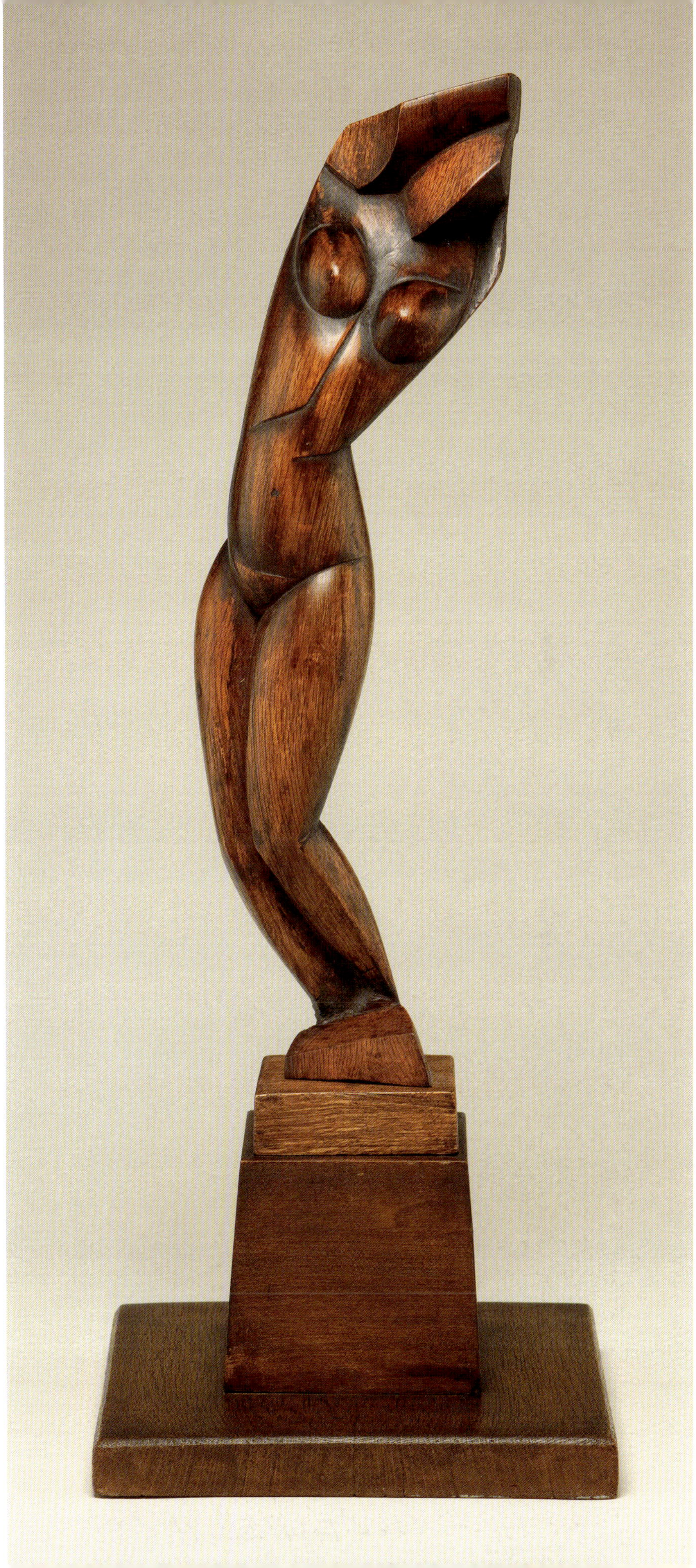

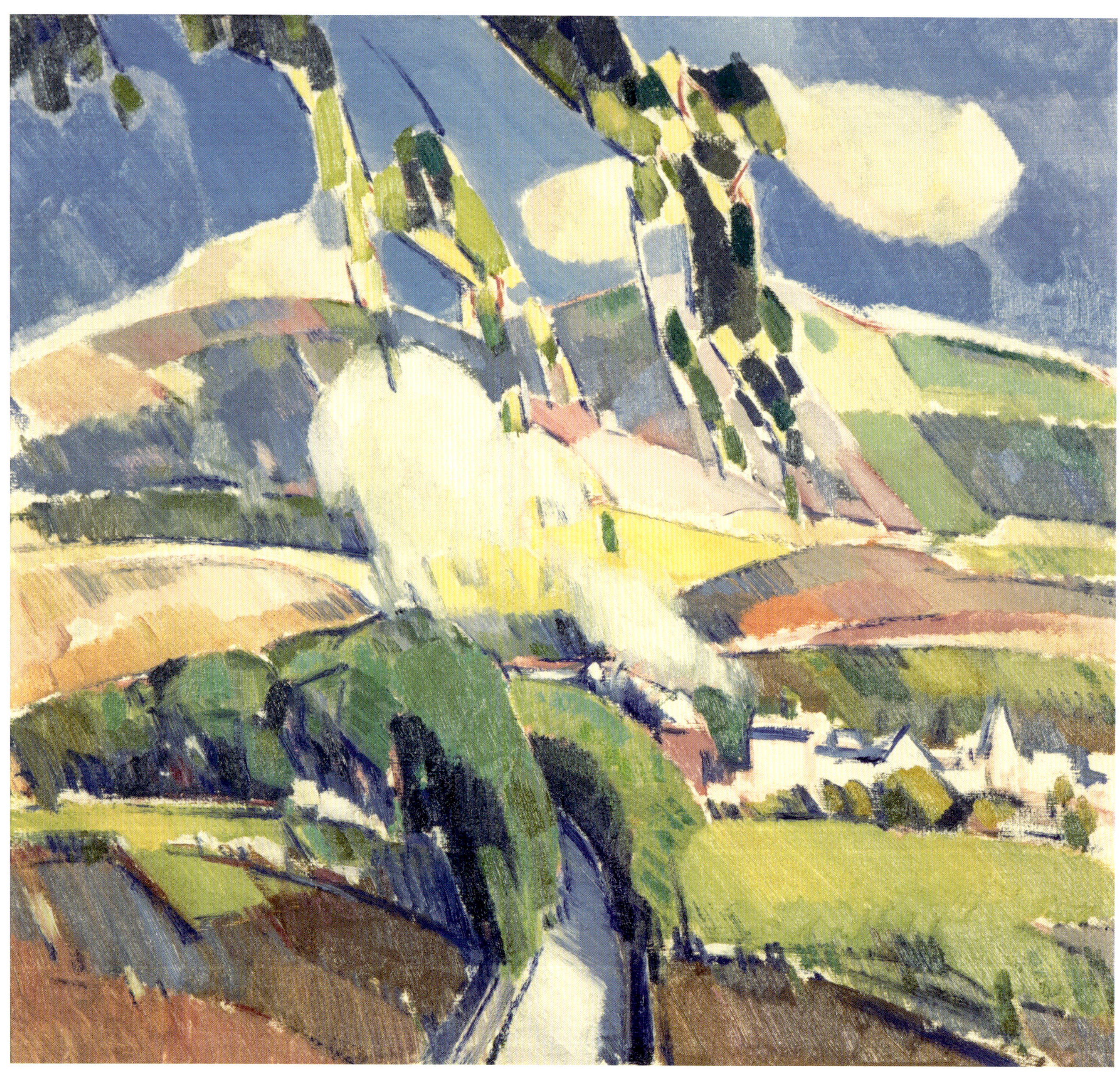

[101]
A Puff of Smoke near Milngavie, 1922
Oil on canvas, 56 × 61
Private collection

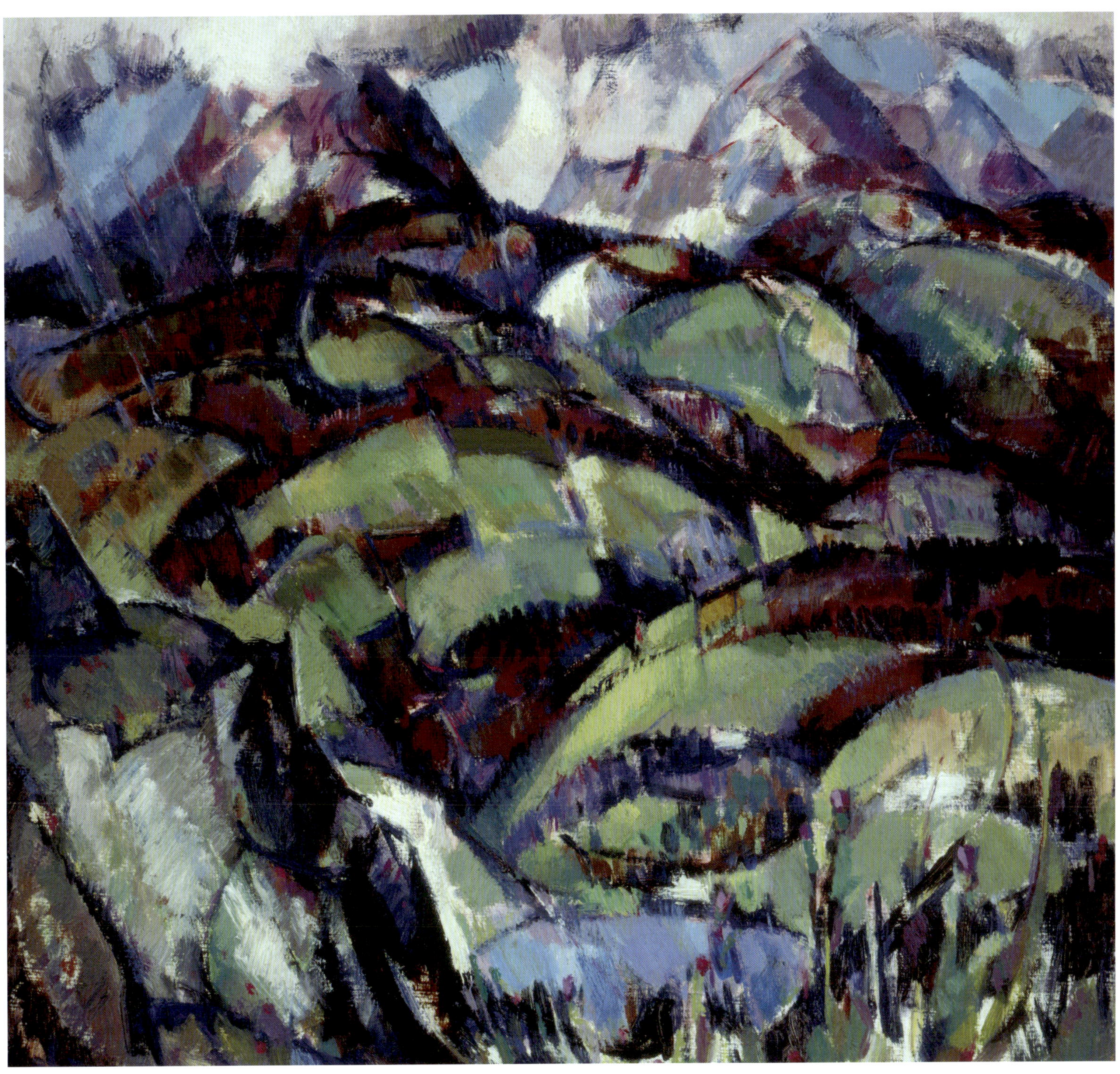

[102]

Storm around Ben Ledi, 1922

Oil on canvas, 54.5 × 55.8

Private collection, courtesy Duncan R. Miller Fine Arts, London

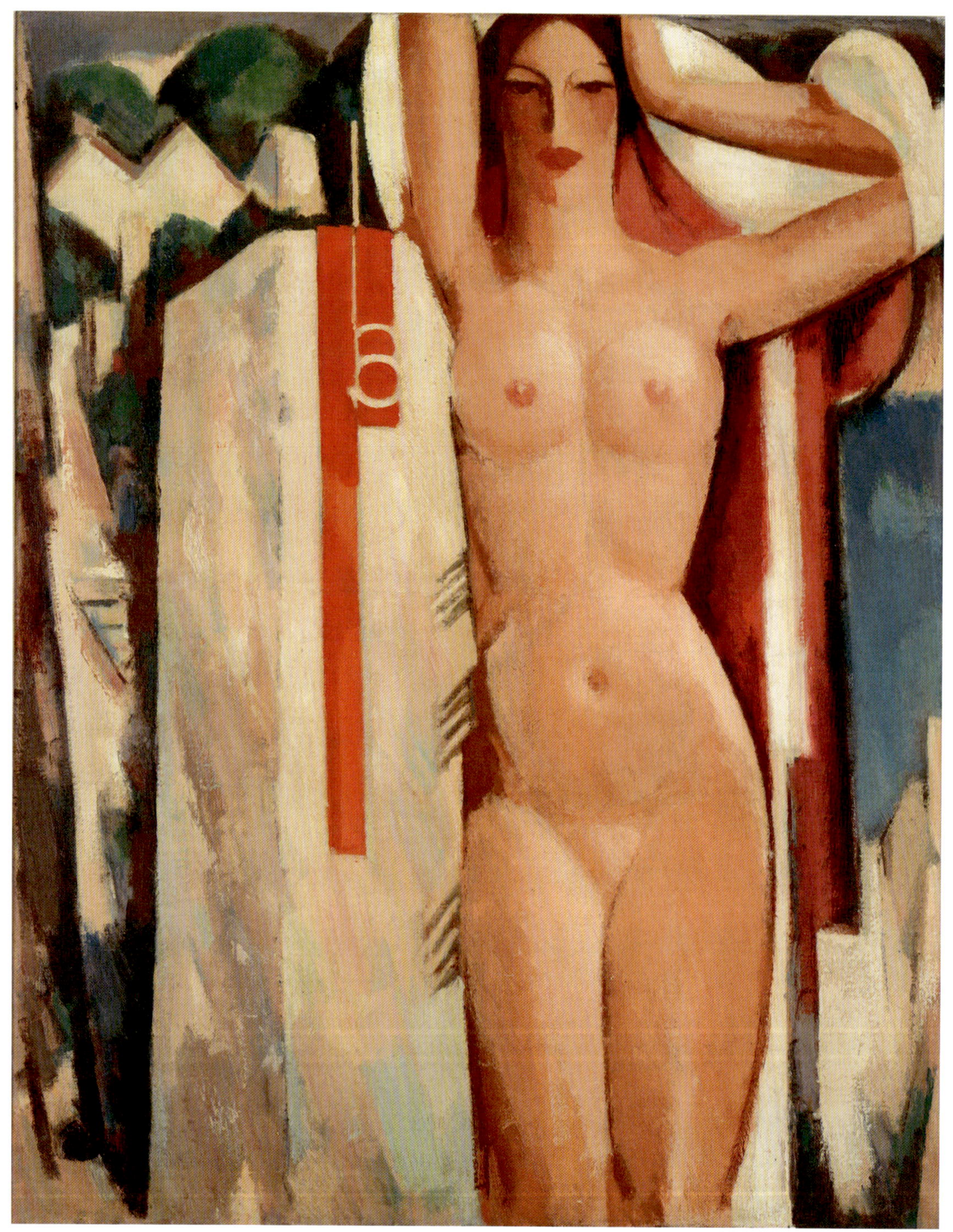

[103]
Megalithic, 1931
Oil on canvas, 92 × 73
Private collection

[104]
Danu, Mother of the Gods, 1952
Oil on canvas, 184 × 123
On loan to the Scottish National Portrait Gallery, Edinburgh
from The Fergusson Gallery, Perth & Kinross Council

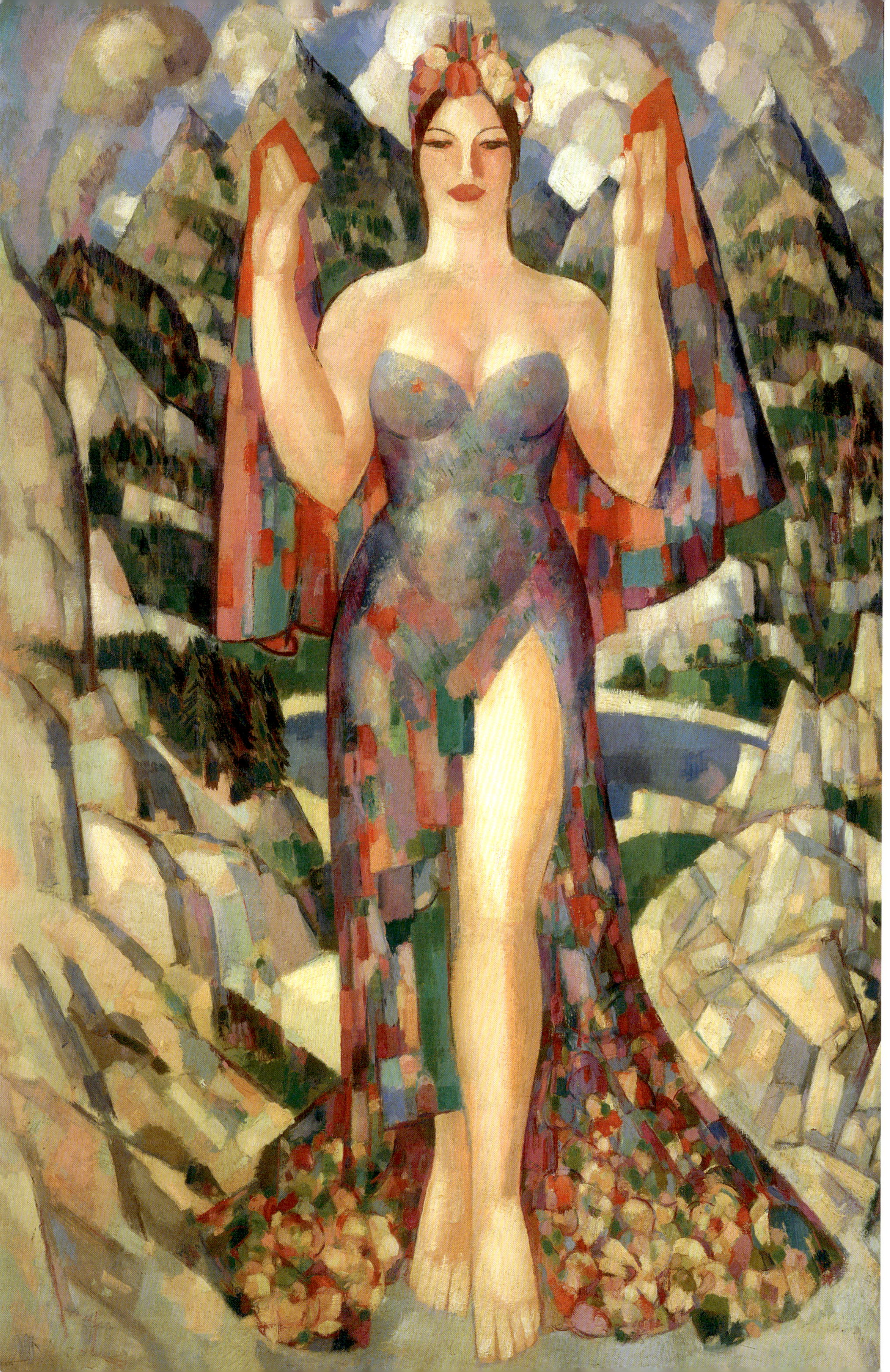

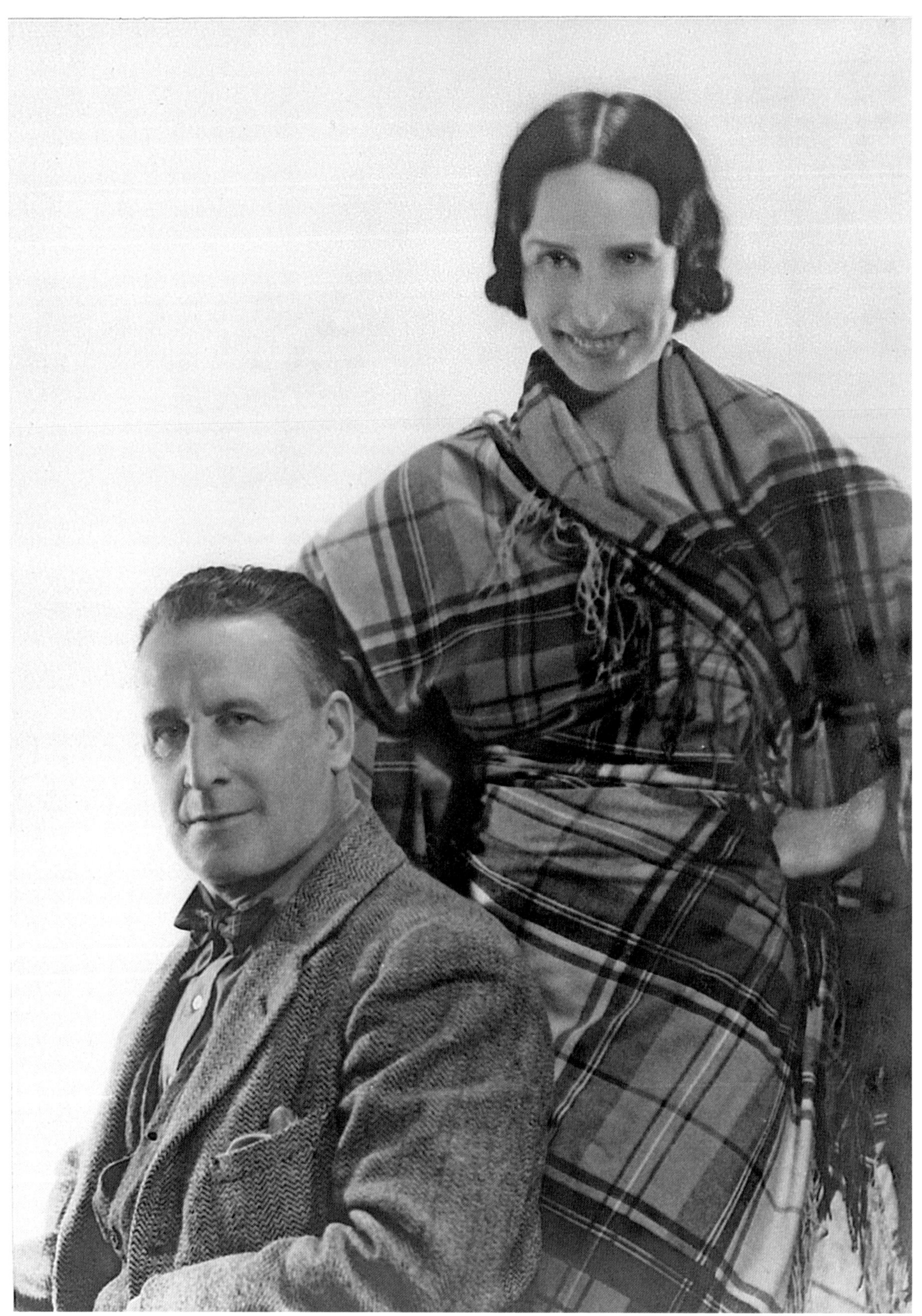

CHRONOLOGY

[105] J.D. Fergusson and Margaret Morris, 1940s
Photograph by Madame Yevonde
The Fergusson Gallery, Perth & Kinross Council

1871
Birth of Samuel John Peploe.

1874
Birth of John Duncan Fergusson on 9 March at 7 Crown Street, Leith. Grows up in Leith and Edinburgh.

1877
Birth of George Leslie Hunter.

1883
Birth of Francis Campbell Boileau Cadell.

1891
Birth of Margaret Morris.

*c.*1897
Begins extended visits to France, in particular to Paris. Sporadic attendance at the Académies Colarossi and Julian.

1897
Exhibits for the first time, in the RGI annual exhibition (and continues to do so every year until 1902, then 1904–6).

1898
Exhibits for the first time in the RSA annual exhibition (also in 1900–02, 1904, 1923 and 1933).

Exhibits for the first time in the SSA annual exhibition (also in 1900, every year 1902–5, 1913 and 1933).

1899
Travels to Morocco.

*c.*1900
Friendship with Peploe begins.

1901
Travels to Spain.

Exhibits in London for the first time, at the RBA biannual exhibitions (and continues to do so every year until 1908).

*c.*1902
Begins relationship with Jean Maconochie.

1902
Establishes himself in his first studio, at 16 Picardy Place, Edinburgh.

1904
Summer painting trips to France with Peploe from now until 1907.

1905
First solo exhibition, held at the Baillie Gallery, London.

1906
Death of father John.

1907
Begins relationship with Anne Estelle Rice.

Moves to Paris and establishes himself in a studio at 18 boulevard Edgar Quinet.

Begins teaching at the Académie de la Palette.

Exhibits for the first time in the Salon d'Automne (and continues to do so every year until 1912).

Exhibits for the first time in the Salon de la Société Nationale des Beaux-Arts (and also in 1908).

1908
Makes his first sculpture; last one thought to date from *c.*1955, with most made *c.*1918–*c.*1922.

Exhibits in the first AAA annual exhibition, London (and continues to do so every year until 1912).

1909
Elected a *sociétaire* of the Salon d'Automne.

Exhibits for the first time at the Venice Biennale (also in 1912, 1928 and 1930).

1910
Paints with Peploe in Royan.

Peploe moves to Paris where he remains until 1912.

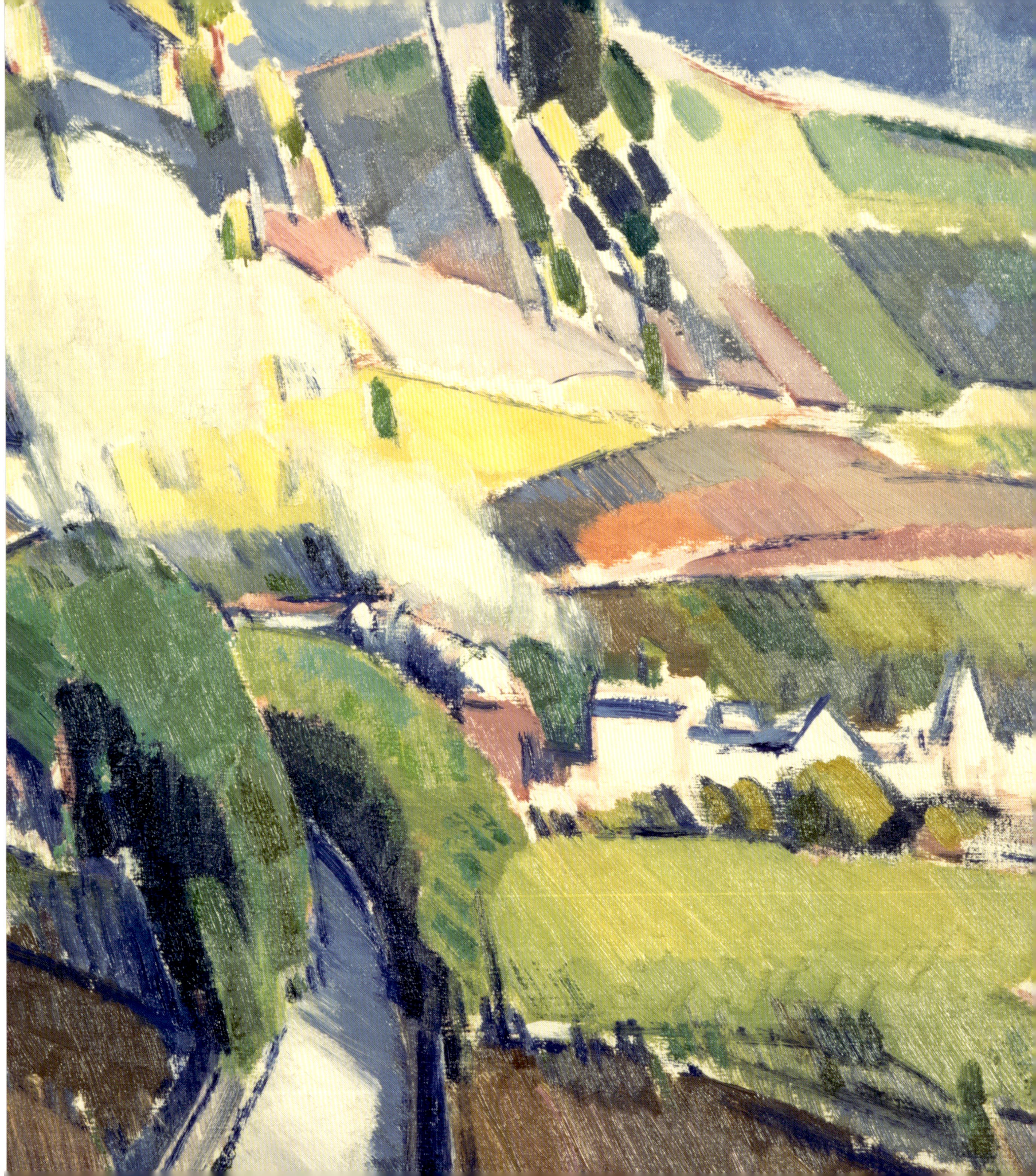

NOTES AND REFERENCES

KEY TO ABBREVIATIONS

AAA
Allied Artists' Association

MMM
Margaret Morris Movement

RBA
Royal Society of British Artists

RGI
Royal Glasgow Institute of the Fine Arts

RSA
Royal Scottish Academy

SNGMA
Scottish National Gallery of Modern Art

SSA
Society of Scottish Artists

[106] Detail from *A Puff of Smoke near Milngavie*, 1922 [101]

1 · INTRODUCTION · PAGES 11–13

1. Fergusson 1943, p.22.
2. At the Galerie Barbazanges, Paris in 1924; Leicester Galleries, London in 1925; and Galerie Georges Petit, Paris in 1931.
3. P.G. Konody, 'Art and Artists: The Leicester Galleries', *The Times*, 12 January 1925.
4. Fergusson's *Le Cocher* [59], which he consigned to the gallery on 16 August 1948, was also shown; see Annans 1929–57 ledger in a private collection.
5. Honeyman 1950.
6. Simister 2001, p.23.
7. Fergusson 1962, p.32.
8. Email from Bill Smith, Hunter's biographer, to the author 8 July 2013; see also Long and Cumming 2000, p.42.
9. Honeyman 1950, p.105.
10. Letter from Hunter to Matthew Justice of late 1923 quoted in Smith and Marriner, 2012, p.115.
11. Letter from F.C.B. Cadell to Ion Harrison of 18 September 1936, private collection on loan to the SNGMA Archive, GMA AL/21/48.
12. Fergusson 1943.
13. He sent work to the RBA in London in 1901.

2 · A LIFE · PAGES 15–25

1. Prologue in catalogue for *Paintings by J.D. Fergusson*, Baillie Gallery, London, 1905.
2. Despite maintaining in public that they were husband and wife, Fergusson and Morris never married.
3. MMM is still taught today, see www.margaret-morrismovement.com.
4. 'Obituary: Mr John Duncan Fergusson', *The Times*, 31 January 1961.
5. The family appears to have alternated between spelling their surname with a single and double 's', with the artist settling on 'Fergusson' by about 1897–8; see endnote 5 of Sheila McGregor's essay in this publication.
6. As explained by Sheila McGregor in an email to Rachel Smith of 23 April 2013; see also McGregor 2000, p.11 and note xxiii, p.14. The author is grateful to Sheila McGregor for making this available.
7. As explained by the daughter of Marshall (1879–1949) in an interview with the author on 1 May 2013. The portrait is reproduced on p.182 of Morris 2010.
8. Fergusson 1960, p.28.
9. See Fergusson 1960, p.29. The Académie Colarossi Archive has not survived. See register in the Archives de l'Académie Julian, Archives Nationales, Paris, 63AS1, Box 63A39. The author is grateful to Jane MacAvock for establishing this fact.
10. See Valuation Roll for the Burgh of Edinburgh for the Year 1905–6, Census of 1901 and Edinburgh and Leith Post Office Directories 1900–1 to 1905–6.
11. S.J. Peploe, *Man Laughing (Portrait of Tom Morris)*, early 1900s, Scottish National Gallery of Modern Art, GMA 33. The work was later owned by the painter Anne Estelle Rice, who was Fergusson's partner between 1907 and 1913: see Cumming 1985, no.5, p.25 and acquisition file for Fergusson's self-portrait, Scottish National Portrait Gallery, PG 2515.
12. Frank Rutter, 'John Duncan Fergusson' in the catalogue for *Pictures by John Duncan Fergusson*, The Doré Galleries, London, February 1914.
13. Information supplied to the author by Jean Maconochie's great-niece in April 2013.
14. *Painting and Sculpture by J.D. Fergusson*, The Scottish Gallery, Edinburgh, 1923.
15. Fergusson 1943, p.70.

16. See rental agreements, The Fergusson Gallery Archive, acc.no.1994.2795.L2290.

17. Rutter 1922, pp.160–1.

18. Ibid., p.162.

19. The accounts book is in a private collection.

20. Fergusson 1962, pp.31–2.

21. Rutter 1911, p.207.

22. Morris 2010, p.15.

23. Fergusson 1962, p.31.

24. Morris 2010, pp.89–90.

25. Morris 2010, p.115.

26. Charles Rennie Mackintosh, *Theatre for Margaret Morris* (*front elevation and sections and plans*), pencil, ink and watercolour, 1920, The Hunterian, University of Glasgow, acc.no.GLAHA 52590.

27. See catalogue for *Arts League of Service Exhibition of Practical Arts*, Twenty-One Gallery, London, 17 November – 6 December 1919. See also Elizabeth Cumming's essay in this publication.

28. Letter of 5 June [1927] quoted in Pamela Robertson (ed.), *Chronycle: The Letters of Charles Rennie Mackintosh to Margaret Macdonald Mackintosh*, Glasgow, 2001, p.81.

29. As quoted in Morris 2010, p.98.

30. Elizabeth Dryden, *Paris in Herrick Days*, Paris, 1915, p.16. The author is grateful to Carol A. Nathanson for drawing this quote to her attention.

31. Morris 2010, p.120.

32. Letter from Commodore Sir Douglas Brownrigg to J.D. Fergusson of 9 July 1918, Imperial War Museum Archive, file ref.216/6, no.27.

33. Letter from Fergusson to Alfred Yockney of the British War Memorials Committee of 4 August 1918, Imperial War Museum Archive, file ref.216/6, no.35.

34. *Dockyard, Portsmouth* was purchased by the Imperial War Museum, London in 1975.

35. McGregor 2000, p.8.

36. Exhibited in brass in *J.D. Fergusson*, The Fine Art Society Ltd, London, 10 September – 4 October 1974, no.104.

37. In conversation with the author on 7 May 2013. The author is grateful to Dr Blackwood and to Dr Patrick Elliott for sharing their expertise in this field.

38. Morris 2010, p.137.

39. Duncan Macmillan, 'A Very Scottish Colourist' in Tom Hewlett and Duncan Macmillan, *F.C.B. Cadell*, London, 2011, p.169.

40. Glasgow Life (Glasgow Museums) on behalf of Glasgow City Council, acc.no.1571.

41. *Exhibition of Paintings by S.J. Peploe, Leslie Hunter, F.C.B. Cadell and J.D. Fergusson*, exh. cat., Leicester Galleries, London, 1925.

42. Royal Cortissoz, 'Random Impressions in Current Exhibitions', *New York Herald Tribune*, 5 December 1926 and see Berman 1999, p.14.

43. Invoice from C.W. Kraushaar Art Galleries, New York, account with Mr John Duncan Fergusson, 27 November 1928, in a private collection.

44. The Fergusson Gallery, Perth and Kinross Council, acc.no.1992.425. See Long and Cumming 2000, p.147, note 23.

45. Letter from A.J. McNeill Reid of 27 March 1928, The Fergusson Gallery, Perth & Kinross Council, acc.no.1994.2011.12 L 158.1–2.

46. Both in Eric de Banzie, 'A Gallery of Fergusson', *Scotland's Magazine*, July 1962, p.35.

47. The author is indebted to Richard Emerson for clarification of the dates and locations of the Summer Schools, based on the Summer School programmes held in The Fergusson Gallery Archive (not yet accessioned).

48. Collection of the Musée national d'art moderne, acc.no.JP 525 P.

49. Letter from Fergusson to M. Valland of 12 February 1934 in the Archives des Musées Nationaux, ref: P30 FERGUSSON (John Duncan) peintre écossais. The author is grateful to Jane MacAvock for drawing this to her attention.

50. Maximilien Gauthier, 'Expositions', *L'art vivant*, April 1931. Quote found and translated by Jane MacAvock.

51. Letter from Fergusson to Morris of 6 December 1913, quoted in Morris 2010, p.74.

52. They all participated in the group's third exhibition, held at the Galerie de Paris, Paris, 8–22 June 1936; Winifred Nicholson showed under the name 'Winifred Dacre' to avoid confusion with her estranged husband.

53. Invitation to the first exhibition of the Groupe d'Artistes Anglo-Américains, held at the Renaissance Gallery, 11 rue Royale, 14–26 June 1935, The Fergusson Gallery Archive, ref.no.L2720, acc.no.1994.2984.1–2, as quoted in McGregor 2000, p.23.

54. 'London Art Reviews', Manchester Guardian, 8 March 1932.

55. As explained by Robin Anderson in an interview with the author on 26 February 2013.

56. As recalled by Fiona Hepworth (née Riach), who trained with Morris from 1955 until 1957, in an interview with the author on 29 March 2013.

57. Fergusson 1946b.

58. Annand 2003, p.13.

59. Letter from Fergusson to Pablo Picasso of 10 September 1950; draft in SNGMA Archive, John Duncan Fergusson / Donald Bain Collection, GMA A02/21/2.

60. Fergusson 1947 and Fergusson 1943.

61. It appears MacLellan revived a journal of this name which is recorded in the listing of The Mitchell Library, Glasgow as running from 1901 to 1904. The author is grateful to Patricia Grant, Principal Librarian at The Mitchell Library, for pointing this out.

62. Herman 1972, p.4.

63. '"Scots Colourist's" Show in Glasgow', *The Scotsman*, 5 May 1948.

64. See Annans ledgers of 1929–57 and 1945–66 in a private collection and catalogue for *Exhibition of Pictures by J.D. Fergusson*, Stafford Gallery, March 1912.

65. The author is grateful to Sir Jack Baer, who organised the exhibition, for sharing this information with her.

66. Information about the pension provided in McGregor 2000, p.14.

67. All published on 31 January 1961.

68. John Duncan Fergusson Inventory and Will registered on 11 July 1961, National Archives of Scotland, NAS02024 SC36/48/943–00112 and SC36–51–459–00249.

69. Fergusson's will, op.cit.

70. Letter from Morris to John Milner Ross of 14 June 1972 in a private collection.

71. *The Toreador* was the first work to enter the national collection when it was presented to the SNGMA by Miss Violet Couper in 1962, GMA 793.

72. See Cameron 2011 and Morris 2010.

73. From undated pamphlet entitled 'J.D. Fergusson Art Foundation', SNGMA Archive.

74. See www.pkc.gov.uk.

75. André Dunoyer de Segonzac, 'John Duncan Fergusson' in *J.D. Fergusson 1874–1961, Memorial Exhibition of Paintings and Sculpture*, 1961–62.

3 · FERGUSSON IN FRANCE PAGES 53–63

My particular thanks go to Richard Emerson, Jenny Kinnear and Sheila McGregor for generously sharing their research with me.

1. De Segonzac 1961, p.3.

2. Simister 2001, p.22; McGregor 2000, chapter 1, p.6.

3. McGregor notes that from 'his first visit, and possibly on subsequent visits, he stayed in the Haute Loire Hotel in Montparnasse, which he found through a little magazine called the *Quartier Latin*'.

4. Fergusson 1960, p.31.

5. Fergusson's credo of 1905 would heavily influence his sculptor friend Jo Davidson when he came to compile his own catalogue for his 1911 New York exhibition. See Davidson 1951, p.64.

6. Louis Vauxcelles's review of the Salon d'Automne in *Gil Blas*, 17 October 1905, had described the artists as thrown to the lions, with the public as the 'wild beasts', but this term was soon applied to the painters by other critics. See Hilary Spurling, *The Unknown Matisse – Man of the North: 1869–1908*, London, 1998, p.332.

7. M. Nicolle, 'Le Salon d'Automne', *Journal de Rouen*, 20 November 1905; quoted in Judi Freeman, *The Fauve Landscape*, London, 1990, p.81.

8. Maurice Denis, 'De Gauguin, de Whistler, et de l'excès des théories', *L'Ermitage*, November 1905; quoted in Freeman, p.81.

9. Nathanson 1992/1993, p.4.

10. Ibid.

11. Fergusson's review of 'The Autumn Salon' appeared in Frank Rutter's *Art News*, 21 October 1909.

12. Another painting called simply *Au Café d'Harcourt* was shown there following its inclusion in the London shows of the RBA and the AAA in 1908.

13. Notes on the painting I myself made about 1983 record the artist's inscription 'J D Fergusson The Café 1907' on the back of the canvas, but as the painting was relined a few years later it is impossible to check the date.

14. Murry 1935, p.131.

15. Fergusson's 1912 group exhibition (with Peploe and others) at the Stafford Gallery, London, included *The Red Shawl* [27] and *Le Manteau Chinois* [64] and was captured in watercolour by Douglas Fox Pitt [12].

16. These sketches are now with the Fergusson Gallery. See Helen Beale, '"Mingling with the torrent of post-impressionism": Toulouse-Lautrec, Auguste Chabaud and John Duncan Fergusson as outsiders in Paris', *Outsiders in Paris: John Duncan Fergusson, Katherine Mansfield and their Circles*, University of Stirling, 2000, p.7.

17. Nathanson 1992/1993, p.5.

18. Fergusson 1909: 'Probably M. Van Dongen, next to Matisse is the painter who annoys the bourgeois most ....'

19. McGregor 2000, chapter 1, p.7.

20. Davidson 1951, p.60.

21. Fergusson completed the painting too quickly. With the creamy underpainting still wet, the paint surface soon cracked open to expose it.

22. If the accounts of others are credible, Fergusson started teaching at La Palette only in 1910. Emily Carr, a Fergusson pupil, started at the Académie Colarossi but transferred to Fergusson's studio within weeks, moving with him and other pupils to Blanche's atelier. Maria Tippett, *Emily Carr: A Biography*, Toronto and Oxford, 1994, p.88; quoted in Angela Smith, 'Tigers in Paris: Katherine Mansfield, Emily Carr, John Duncan Fergusson and Fauvism', *Outsiders in Paris: John Duncan Fergusson, Katherine Mansfield and their Circles*, University of Stirling, 2000, p.38.

23. After the war, Fergusson's woodcut cover designs were used for a few early copies of Katherine Mansfield's *Prelude*, published by Leonard Woolf's Hogarth Press in 1918.

24. In his article on Rice in the first issue Sadler referred to the 'one fundamental desire with which all start – the desire for rhythm. Be it of line or colour, be it simple or intricate, in every true product of Fauvism it will be present. And this rhythm is of a piece with the use of strong flowing line, of strong massed colour, of continuity. The work must be strong, must be alive, and must be rhythmical.' Michael T.H. Sadler, 'Fauvism and a Fauve', *Rhythm*, Summer 1911, vol.1, no.1, p.17. Fergusson, writing in 1914 to Margaret Morris, expressed his distaste for the 'bloody Burne-Jonesey' London set whom he hoped she might avoid.

25. John Middleton Murry, 'Art and Philosophy', *Rhythm*, Summer 1911, vol.1, no.1, p.9.

26. Tippett, p.88; quoted in Smith, p.38. Fergusson's other students included Jessica Dismorr from England and Marguerite Thompson and William Zorach from the United States of America.

27. Card dated 27 August 1984 to the author from Sir Anthony Lousada, son of Fergusson's London lawyer, in reference to a still life of *c.*1914 in his possession: 'the apples [were] actually painted by JDF blue etc. before he painted his picture!'.

28. Margaret Scott (ed.), *The Katherine Mansfield Notebooks*, Lincoln University Press and Daphne Brasell Associates, New Zealand, 1997, vol.2, p.133; quoted in Smith, p.37.

29. Fergusson took his new partner Margaret Morris to Stein's salon, probably in 1913, but afterwards said he had no wish to return lest he be considered one of Stein's protégés. Morris 2010, p.65.

30. Handwritten notes by Fergusson, The Fergusson Gallery Archive, ref.no.L300, acc. no.1993.1650.3.

31. The term *artiste-peintre* was commonly used to differentiate a painter from an artist-designer (*artiste-décorateur*). It was used by both Fergusson and later Glasgow associates such as Donald Bain.

32. Ada Leverson, *Tenterhooks*, subsequently published in her trilogy *The Little Ottleys*, London, 1962, pp.264–5.

33. Ibid., p.266.

34. Rice was elected a *sociétaire* in 1910.

35. Letter from Fergusson to Margaret Morris in London of 20 June 1913, The Fergusson Gallery Archive, acc.no.2010.718.1.3036.2: 'I am going to the Ballets Russes again tonight'. For details of the performances in June 1913, see Richard Buckle, *Diaghilev*, London, 1979, p.256.

36. Morris 2010, p.84.

37. Quoted in Modris Eksteins, *Rites of Spring*, London, 1990, p.72.

38. *I Stravinsky: Publitsist I sobesednik*, Moscow, 1988, p.10; quoted in Irina Vershinina, 'Diaghilev and the Music of the Saisons Russes', Ann Kodicek (ed.), *Diaghilev, Creator of the Ballets Russes*, London, 1996, p.85.

39. Quoted in Eksteins, p.31.

40. Letter from Rice to Dreiser of 31 August 1913, Dreiser Archive, University of Pennsylvania Library Special Collections; quoted in Nathanson 1997, p.19.

41. Fergusson's original notes for the article 'Art and Atavism: The Dryad', The Fergusson Gallery Archive, acc.no.1993.1649.2, L299.

42. Morris 2010, p.76.

43. Fergusson's pamphlet was published in his *Modern Scottish Painting*, 1943, pp.95–7.

44. McGregor 2000, chapter 4, p.8.

45. See also Morris 2010, pp.183–5.

46. Fergusson and Morris stayed with her at the Château des Enfants in 1950 and also possibly in other post-war years. Correspondence in the SNGMA Archive records that they spent many summers in the Antibes area, staying for a month or two for example at the Hôtel Grand Valse, Cap d'Antibes in 1947; La Petite Florentine, Golfe-Juan in 1955; the Villa la Fauvette, chemin de l'Ermitage in Cap d'Antibes in 1956; and the Villa la Folette in Antibes in 1960. The dating on other paintings such as *Wisteria, Villa Florentine, Golfe-Juan* (1957) adds more information on the French visits.

47. Richard Emerson has noted that Picasso was staying at the Hôtel du Cap in 1923 when they met again after the war, and that in 1924 Picasso was staying in nearby Juan-les-Pins.

48. Letter from A.J. McNeill Reid to Fergusson of 30 November 1939, Tate Archive: TGA 200211, Alex Reid & Lefevre Ltd papers.

49. *The Scotsman*, 3 March 1931.

50. *Glasgow Record*, 15 March 1928.

51. *Manchester Guardian*, 12 February 1936.

52. Drey 1962, pp.622–4.

53. Fergusson 1943, p.22.

4 · Fergusson's Celtic Nationalism · pages 91–102

1. Fergusson 1943.

2. Ibid., p.69.

3. Keith Hartley, *Scottish Art since 1900*, London, 1989, pp.19–20. Herbert Read, Professor of Fine Art at the University of Edinburgh from 1931 to 1933, championed the historic connection between Scotland and northern Europe. Exhibitions by German and Scandinavian artists in Edinburgh and Glasgow in the 1930s were also influential.

4. What remains of Fergusson's library at The Fergusson Gallery in Perth includes a number of books and periodicals relating to Scottish nationalism and the Celtic revival. A prospectus for the Celtic Circle states: 'The Circle is open to all who sympathise with its aim, the restoration of Celtic civilisation in the West.' (The Fergusson Gallery Archive, ref.no.L2358, acc.no.1994.2984.1–2.)

5. Fergusson began to adopt this spelling in exhibition catalogues in 1897–8. His mother's maiden name was also Fergusson, with a double 's'. Fergusson's parents had moved to Leith before his birth. Although his father came from a farming family near Perth, he appears in local trade directories as a spirit merchant.

6. Dreiser 1913, p.233; Fergusson appears as Mr McG and Anne Estelle Rice as Miss N.

7. 'Ellen Adams Wrynn', in Dreiser 1929, pp.106–7; Ellen Adams Wrynn herself was based on Anne Estelle Rice.

8. Macpherson's Ossianic publications – *Fragments of Ancient Poetry, collected in the Highlands of Scotland* (Edinburgh, 1760), *Fingal, an Ancient Epic Poem ... composed by Ossian the son of Fingal* (London [December 1761], 1762) and *Temora, an Ancient Epic Poem* (London, 1763) (titles abridged) – were published in a 'carefully corrected, and greatly improved' form in 1773 as *The Poems of Ossian* (London), a 1914 edition of which is among Fergusson's books at The Fergusson Gallery in Perth. Matthew Arnold's collection of essays *On The Study of Celtic Literature* was published in 1867 and exerted a powerful influence on the Irish authors of the 'Celtic Twilight'. Patrick Geddes's *The Evergreen: A Northern Seasonal* appeared in four volumes between spring 1895 and winter 1896–7.

9. For a detailed discussion of these issues, see Antliff, 1993, especially chapter 4.

10. Ernest Renan, *La Poésie des Races Celtiques*, Paris, 1854, p.8.

11. Fergusson's notes on Celtic design, quoted in Morris 2010, p.99, and held in The Fergusson Gallery Archive, acc.no.1994.1964.3, L3334.3.

12. Fergusson 1962, pp.10–11.

13. Quoted in Morris 2010, p.185.

14. Blackwood 2004.

15. Fergusson 1944.

16. Letter from Margaret Morris addressed to Miss Charnot at the Tate, dated 25 July 1964, Tate Catalogue files: Artists: British: Fergusson, J.D.

17. Ana Carden-Coyne, *Reconstructing the Body: Classicism, Modernism, and the First World War*, Oxford, 2009, p.293.

18. P.G. Konody, 'Post-Impressionism at Doré Galleries', *The Observer*, 26 October 1913. Reviewing Fergusson's one-person exhibition at The Doré Galleries the following year, he observed in a similar vein how 'His nudes are very nude indeed – obtrusively nude in their accentuated roundness of form. The breasts seem to be drawn with compasses, and so do the shoulders, the knees, the thighs.' 'Mr Fergusson's Paintings', *The Observer*, 22 February 1914.

19. Katherine Mansfield to John Middleton Murry, 18 June 1918, in John Middleton Murry (ed.), *Katherine Mansfield's Letters to John Middelton Murry 1913–1922*, London, 1951, p.305.

20. Interview with Dorothy Dayton, *New York Sun*, 31 October 1928, The Fergusson Gallery Archive, ref.no.PC1/548, acc.no.1995.1213.6.

21. Ibid.

22. Ibid.

23. It would appear from the evidence that there were two Highland tours, in 1922 and 1928 respectively, although Margaret Morris only mentions one (1922) in her biography. The itinerary she reproduces in fact relates to the second tour, since the chronology of dates corresponds exactly with the calendar for 1928. However, Fergusson's exhibiting record in the 1920s suggests that the majority of his Highland pictures were painted in the aftermath of the first tour in 1922.

24. Letter from A.J. McNeill Reid to Fergusson of 19 October 1954, The Fergusson Gallery Archive, ref.no.L3113, acc.no.1994.3554.

25. Emilio Coia, review of 'New Painting in Glasgow, 1940–46', *The Scotsman*, 16 September 1968.

26. 'Cost of Dalí better spent on Scots', undated press cutting, The Fergusson Gallery Archive, acc. no.1995.1074.

27. Letter from J.D. Fergusson and Donald Bain to the Scottish Arts Council of 20 April 1950, The Fergusson Gallery Archive, ref.no.2445, acc. no.1994.1683.

28. Fergusson 1946b, p.26.

29. Ibid.

30. Fergusson's position can be inferred from a letter to him from R.E. Muirhead, first Chairman and Secretary of The National Party, of 26 January 1943, The Fergusson Gallery Archive, ref.no.586, acc.no.1994.417.

31. Honeyman 1955.

32. Proofs for Hugh MacDiarmid's *In Memoriam James Joyce*, 1955, The Fergusson Gallery Archive, ref.no.L3318.1, acc.no.1994.1948.1.

33. Roderick Watson, 'Celtic Modernism', in Cameron 2011, pp.28–33.

34. Ibid.

35. Tom Normand, 'J.D. Fergusson and the Culture of Nationalism in Scotland', *Etudes Ecossaises*, no.5, 1998, p.160.

36. Ibid.

SELECT BIBLIOGRAPHY

PUBLISHED WRITING BY J.D. FERGUSSON

FERGUSSON 1905
J.D. Fergusson, 'Prologue', *Paintings by J.D. Fergusson*, exh. cat., Baillie Gallery, London, 1905

FERGUSSON 1909
J.D. Fergusson, Review, 'The Autumn Salon', *The Art News*, 21 October 1909

FERGUSSON 1911
J.D. Fergusson, 'Contribution to an International Symposium on the Theatre', *The New Age*, 2 March 1911

FERGUSSON 1943
J.D. Fergusson, *Modern Scottish Painting,* Glasgow, 1943

FERGUSSON 1944
J.D. Fergusson, 'Art and Atavism: The Dryad', *Scottish Art and Letters*, no.1, 1944, pp.47–9

FERGUSSON 1946a
J.D. Fergusson, 'Art and the People', *Chapbook*, no.6, August 1946, p.98

FERGUSSON 1946b
J.D. Fergusson, 'The Scotland I'd Like to See', *The New Scot*, October 1946

FERGUSSON 1947
J.D. Fergusson, 'Foreword', *Modern Scottish Painters: The New Scottish Group*, Glasgow, 1947, pp.5–7

FERGUSSON 1960
J.D. Fergusson, 'Chapter from an Autobiography', *Saltire Art Review*, vol.vi, no.21, 1960, pp.27–32

FERGUSSON 1962
J.D. Fergusson, 'Memories of Peploe', *Scottish Art Review*, vol.viii, no.3, 1962, pp.8–12, 31–2

BOOKS AND JOURNALS

ANNAND 2003
Louise Annand, *J.D. Fergusson in Glasgow 1939–1961*, Kelso, 2003

ANTLIFF 1993
Mark Antliff, *Inventing Bergson: Cultural Politics and the Parisian Avant-Garde,* Princeton, 1993

BERMAN 1999
Avis Berman, 'J.D. Fergusson's American Exhibitions: Background and Context', *Archives of American Art Journal*, vol.39, no.1/2, 1999, pp.12–16

BEALE AND SMITH 2000
Helen Beale and Angela Smith, *Outsiders in Paris: John Duncan Fergusson, Katherine Mansfield and their Circles*, Stirling, 2000

BILLCLIFFE 1974
Roger Billcliffe, 'Introduction', *J.D. Fergusson 1874–1961, A Centenary Exhibition*, exh. cat., The Fine Art Society Ltd, London, 1974

BILLCLIFFE 1996
Roger Billcliffe, *The Scottish Colourists*, London, 1989 (1996 edition)

BINCKES 2010
Faith Binckes, *Modernism, Magazines, and the British Avant-Garde: Reading* Rhythm, *1910–1914*, Oxford, 2010

BLACKWOOD 2004
Jonathan Blackwood, 'Sculpture with a Scots brogue: John Duncan Fergusson, *c.*1916–24', in David J. Getsy (ed), *Sculpture and the Pursuit of a Modern Ideal in Britain, c.1880–1930*, Aldershot, 2004, pp.245–61

CAMERON 2011
Jane Cameron et al., *Fergusson at Stirling: Colour, Light, Freedom – The J.D. Fergusson Memorial Collection at the University of Stirling*, Stirling, 2011

CASSAVETTI
Eileen Cassavetti, 'Remembering Fergus', *Scottish Art News*, Autumn 2005, pp.20–25

CRAWFORD 1994
Alan Crawford, *C.R. Mackintosh, The Chelsea Years*, exh. cat., Hunterian Art Gallery, University of Glasgow, 1994

CUMMING 1985
Elizabeth Cumming et al., *Colour, Rhythm and Dance: Paintings and Drawings by J.D. Fergusson and his circle in Paris*, exh. cat., Scottish Arts Council, Edinburgh, 1985

DAVIDSON 1951
Jo Davidson, *Between Sittings: An Informal Autobiography of Jo Davidson*, New York, 1951

DREY 1962
Raymond Drey, 'Some Memories of John Duncan Fergusson', *Apollo*, vol.lxxvi, no.8, October 1962, pp.622–4

DREISER 1913
Theodore Dreiser, *A Traveler at Forty*, New York, 1913

DREISER 1929
Theodore Dreiser, *A Gallery of Women*, New York, 1929

DULAU AND SKIPWITH
Anne Dulau and Selina Skipwith, *Intimate Friends: Scottish Colourists from the Hunterian Art Gallery and The Fleming Collection*, London, 2003

EMERSON 2013
Richard Emerson, 'The Architect and the Dancer', *Charles Rennie Mackintosh Journal*, to be published 2013

FOWLE 2010
Frances Fowle, *Van Gogh's Twin: The Scottish Art Dealer Alexander Reid 1854–1928*, Edinburgh, 2010

GRUETZNER ROBINS 1997
Anna Gruetzner Robins, *Modern Art in Britain 1910–1914*, exh. cat., Barbican Art Gallery, London, 1997

GUARDIAN
Obituary of J.D. Fergusson, *The Guardian*, 31 January 1961

HERMAN 1972
Josef Herman, 'Notes from a Glasgow Diary 1940–43', *Scottish Art Review*, vol.xiii, no.3, 1972, pp.1–6

HOLBROOK 1918
Holbrook Jackson, 'J.D. Fergusson and his Pictures', *Today*, vol.iii, 1918, pp.108–11

HONEYMAN 1950
T.J. Honeyman, *Three Scottish Colourists*, London, 1950

HONEYMAN 1955
T.J. Honeyman, 'J.D. Fergusson', *Scottish Field*, vol. ciii, no.627, March 1955, pp.44–6

HOPKINSON 1999
Martin Hopkinson, 'The Prints of J.D. Fergusson', *Print Quarterly*, vol.xvi, no.2, June 1999, pp.163–7

HOPKINSON 2013
Martin Hopkinson, 'The Arts League of Service in London, 1919–28', *Print Quarterly*, vol.xxx, no.2, June 2013, pp.179–82

LONG AND CUMMING 2000
Philip Long and Elizabeth Cumming, *The Scottish Colourists 1900–1930*, exh. cat., Scottish National Gallery of Modern Art, Edinburgh, 2000

MACARTHUR 1928
Charles MacArthur, 'Foreword', *Paintings and Sculpture by J.D. Fergusson*, exh. cat., C.W. Kraushaar Art Galleries, New York, 1928

MACDIARMID AND FERGUSSON 1955
Hugh MacDiarmid, *In Memoriam James Joyce*, Glasgow, 1955, with 'decorations' [sic] by J.D. Fergusson

MACFALL 1907
Haldane MacFall, 'The Paintings of John D. Fergusson R.B.A.', *The Studio*, vol.xl, no.169, April 1907, pp.202–105

MACMILLAN 1994
Duncan Macmillan, *Scottish Art in the Twentieth Century*, Edinburgh, 1994

MANSFIELD AND FERGUSSON 1918
Katherine Mansfield, *Prelude*, London, 1918, with illustrations by J.D. Fergusson

MARRIOTT 1918
Charles Marriott, 'Building in Paint', *Land and Water*, May 1918, p.20

MARRIOTT 1920
Charles Marriott, 'The Work of J.D. Fergusson', *Shama'a*, vol.i, no.2, July 1920, pp.91–5

MCGREGOR 2000
Sheila McGregor, *A Colourist Abroad: The Art and Life of J.D. Fergusson*, unpublished manuscript, completed 2000

MORRIS 1969
Margaret Morris, *My Life in Movement*, London, 1969

MORRIS 2010
Margaret Morris, *The Art of J.D. Fergusson: A Biased Biography*, Glasgow, 1974 (2010 edition)

MORRIS AND DANIELS 1925
Margaret Morris and Fred Daniels, *Margaret Morris Dancing*, London, 1925

MORRIS AND GEDDES 1974
Margaret Morris and Jean Geddes, *Café Drawings in Edwardian Paris from the Sketchbooks of J.D. Fergusson 1874–1961,* Glasgow, 1974

MURRY 1918
John Middleton Murry, 'Introduction', *Painting and Sculpture by J.D. Fergusson*, exh. cat., The Connell Gallery, London, 1918

MURRY 1935
John Middleton Murry, *Between Two Worlds: An Autobiography*, London, 1935

NATHANSON 1992/1993
Carol A. Nathanson, 'Anne Estelle Rice: Theodore Dreiser's "Ellen Adams Wrynn"', *Woman's Art Journal*, vol.13, no.2, Fall 1992 / Winter 1993, pp.3–11

NATHANSON 1997
Carol A. Nathanson, *The Expressive Fauvism of Anne Estelle Rice*, exh. cat., Hollis Taggart Galleries, New York, 1997

NEW YORK TIMES
Obituary of J.D. Fergusson, *New York Times*, 31 January 1961

NORMAND 2000
Tom Normand, *The Modern Scot: Modernism and Nationalism in Scottish Arts, 1928–1955*, Aldershot, 2000

PEPLOE 2012
Guy Peploe, *S.J. Peploe*, Edinburgh, 2000 (2012 edition)

RHYTHM
Rhythm, J.D. Fergusson Art Editor Summer 1911–November 1912, with illustrations in vol.1, nos 1–4, 1911–1912 and vol.2, nos 5–11 and 13–14, 1911–1912

RUTTER 1911
Frank Rutter, 'The Portrait Paintings of John Duncan Fergusson', *The Studio*, vol.liv, no.225, 15 December 1911, pp.203–7

RUTTER 1922
Frank Rutter, *Some Contemporary Artists,* London, 1922

SCOTSMAN
Obituary of J.D. Fergusson, *The Scotsman*, 31 January 1961

SCOTTISH ART AND LETTERS, 1944–1950
J.D. Fergusson Art Editor of all these volumes

DE SEGONZAC AND MCLAREN YOUNG 1961
André de Segonzac, 'John Duncan Fergusson' and Andrew McLaren Young, 'Introduction', *J.D. Fergusson 1874–1961: Memorial Exhibition of Paintings and Sculpture*, exh. cat., Arts Council of Great Britain, Scottish Committee, 1961

SICKERT 1925
Walter Sickert, 'Preface', *Paintings by S.J. Peploe, Leslie Hunter, F.C.B. Cadell and J.D. Fergusson*, exh. cat., The Leicester Galleries, London, 1925

SIMISTER 2001
Kirsten Simister, *Living Paint: J.D. Fergusson 1874–1961*, Edinburgh, 2001

SMITH 2000
Angela Smith, *Katherine Mansfield: A Literary Life*, Hampshire, 2000

SMITH AND MARRINER 2012
Bill Smith and Jill Marriner, *Hunter Revisited: The Life and Art of Leslie Hunter*, Edinburgh, 2012

STRANG 2012
Alice Strang et al., *S.J. Peploe*, exh. cat., Scottish National Gallery of Modern Art, Edinburgh, 2012

TIMES
Obituary of J.D. Fergusson, *The Times*, 31 January 1961

TIS 1918
"TIS", 'J.D. Fergusson: His Place in Art', *Colour Magazine*, vol.8, no.5, June 1918, pp.98–103

WATT 1937
Alexander Watt, 'Artists of Note, No.27: J.D. Fergusson', *The Artist*, vol.xiii, May 1937, pp.86–9

ARCHIVES

Archives of American Art, Smithsonian Institution, Washington: Kraushaar Galleries Records 1885–2006

Whitney Museum of American Art Archives, New York

The Fergusson Gallery Archive, Perth

Glasgow University Special Collections: Jessie M. King and E.A. Taylor Papers, MS Gen 1654

Imperial War Museum Archive: First World War Artists Archive / Fergusson, J.D., file ref. 216/6

National Library of Scotland, Edinburgh: T.J. Honeyman Papers, acc.no.9787/37; Bet Low Papers, acc.no.12177/5; F. Marian McNeill Papers, Letters MS.26195 & MS.26196; Poems and short stories by David Morrison, acc.no.6329/5; MacDiarmid/Grieve Papers, MS.27152, MS.27059, MS.27067 and MS.27074

National Records of Scotland, Edinburgh: Will and Inventory of J.D. Fergusson, NAS02024 SC36/48/943-00112 and SC36-51-459-00249

The Scottish Gallery Archive, Edinburgh

The Stewartry Museum Archive, Kirkcudbright: E.A. Taylor Papers, ref.1995/74

Scottish National Gallery of Modern Art Archive, Edinburgh: John Duncan Fergusson / Donald Bain Collection, GMA A02; Anonymous donation of J.D. Fergusson Solo and Group Exhibition Catalogues 1905–1974, GMA A112/3; F.C.B. Cadell Archive on loan from a private collection, GMA AL/21

Tate Archive, London: Alex Reid & Lefèvre Ltd Papers, TGA 200211 and Anne Estelle Rice Archive, TGA 200920

TELEVISION AND FILM

Post-Impressions: The Story of J.D. Fergusson, BBC Scotland, 1976

Portrait of John Duncan Fergusson: The Artist 1874–1961, The Fergusson Gallery, Perth & Kinross Council, 1992 (remastered 2006)

ACKNOWLEDGEMENTS

For their help with this project we are grateful to: Tom Bell; Roger Billcliffe; Athina Athanasiadou and Emily Walsh of Bourne Fine Art; Patrick and Cordelia Bourne and Simon Edsor of The Fine Art Society; Andrew Benns and Selina Skipwith of The Fleming Collection; Jill Gerber; Matthew and Richard Green of the Richard Green Gallery; Calum Milne of Llangoed Hall Hotel; Alexander Meddowes; Duncan Miller; Ewan and Carol Mundy; Guy Peploe of The Scottish Gallery; and Peyton Skipwith.

We are also grateful to: Bernard Williams and André Zlattinger of Christie's; Anita Manning of Great Western Auctions; Campbell Armour, Nick Curnow and Gavin Strang of Lyon & Turnbull; and Simon Toll and Anthony Weld Forester of Sotheby's.

Our research has been aided by: Robin Anderson; Sir Jack Baer; Dr Jonathan Blackwood; Richard Emerson; Philip R. Freiensener and Michael Gaskin of The Art Bronze Foundry (London) Ltd; Bill and Fiona Hepworth of The Alyth Art Foundry; Jane MacAvock; Lisa Mason, National Museums Scotland; David Mitchell, Royal Botanic Garden, Edinburgh; Anthony d'Offay; Carol A. Nathanson, Professor Emeritus, Wright State University; and Peter Shaw.

We are also grateful to the following people who have helped with this publication and the exhibition and displays which it accompanies: Faith and Josh Archer; Richard Bapty, University of Glasgow; Sara Bevan, Imperial War Museum, London; Dr Chris Brickley, Bonhams; Sarah Bromage, Jane Cameron and Professor Angela Smith, University of Stirling; Sharon Bromberger; Rosina Buckland and Dr Geoffrey N. Swinney, National Museums Scotland; Grant E.L. Buttars, Cecily Hughes, Joseph Marshall and Mary Stevens, University of Edinburgh; Griffin Coe, Aberdeen Art Gallery; Jennifer Cooper; Alexander D.M. Corcoran, Lefevre Fine Art, London; Tim Craven, Southampton City Art Gallery; Jenny Cutts, National Records of Scotland; Sarah Demb, Museum of London; David Devereux and Anne Ramsbottom, The Stewartry Museum, Kirkcudbright; Angela Doane and Janet Snowman, Royal Academy of Music, London; Arielle Dorlester and Suz Massen, The Frick Collection, New York; Emily Down and Adrian Glew, Tate, London; Alistair Drennan; Anne Dulau, Hunterian Art Gallery, University of Glasgow; Shona Elliott, University of Aberdeen; Jane Freel, Kirkcaldy Museum and Art Gallery; Anne Galastro; Andrew Gifford, Courtauld Institute of Art, London; Abigail Grater; Alastair Gray; Douglas Hall; Sally Harrower and Alison Metcalfe, National Library of Scotland; Elspeth J. Hector, The National Gallery, London; Tom Hewlett, Portland Gallery, London; Jimmy Hogg, Central Library, Edinburgh; Rachel Hosker, Edinburgh College of Art; Richard Hunter, Edinburgh City Archives; Bill Jackson; Cat MacEachen; Isobel MacLellan and Kirsten McCormick, Mitchell Library, Glasgow; Dr Ian McKenzie Smith; Anita Manning, Great Western Auctions; Amy Marletta, Royal Glasgow Institute of the Fine Arts; Stephen Marquardt, Doughty Hanson & Co.; Dr Joanna Meacock, Glasgow Life; Colin and Lorna Meier; Matilda Mitchell; Susan Morris, Richard Green Gallery, London; Ian O'Riordan, City Art Centre, Edinburgh; Anne Orr, National Museums Northern Ireland; Fiona Pearson; Margaret Pirnie, Pitlochry Festival Theatre; Yamuna Ravindran, Royal Academy of Arts, London; David Roberts, Studio SP Ltd; Anna Robertson, The McManus: Dundee's Art Gallery and Museum; Kirsten Simister, Ferens Art Gallery, Hull; Inge and Peter Sloan; Alastair G. Smith, National Trust for Scotland; Bill Smith; Rob and Patsy Strang; Christine and Rod Tipple; Elizabeth Wemyss, The Scottish Gallery, Edinburgh; George Woods, McLean Museum and Art Gallery, Greenock. We are also grateful to all those who have contributed to the Fergusson project who wish to remain anonymous.

COPYRIGHT AND PHOTOGRAPHIC CREDITS

1, 3, 6, 7, 8, 9, 10, 17, 19, 21, 26, 39, 38, 42, 44, 49, 51, 64, 65, 69, 71, 73, 75, 76, 80, 81, 82, 87, 88, 90, 91, 92, 94, 95, 97, 101, 104, 105 images courtesy of The Fergusson Gallery, Perth & Kinross Council; 15, 34, 55, 56, 72, 77, 85, 96, 98 photography by John McKenzie; 47 © National Galleries of Scotland, photography John McKenzie; 36 courtesy of Sotheby's Picture Library; 31 Dundee Art Galleries and Museums Collection (Dundee City Council); 20, 24 photograph © Fleming – Wyfold Art Foundation; 28, 32, 52 images © CSG CIC Glasgow Museums Collection; 25 courtesy Roger Billcliffe Gallery, Glasgow; 37 photograph courtesy The Richard Green Gallery, London; 18, 22, 23, 46, 58, 93 photography by Antonia Reeve; 5 © The National Galleries of Scotland, Photography by Antonia Reeve; 27, 29, 33, 40, 66 Photo © The Art Collection, University of Stirling; 35 photography by Jim Pattison; 16 © Stuart Wallace Pictures; 14, 43, 68, 99 image © Huntarian Museum and Art Gallery, University of Glasgow; 12 © Tate, London 2013; 13, 83, 84 © Fred Daniels Estate, images courtesy of The Fergusson Gallery, Perth & Kinross Council; 57 image courtesy of the University of Aberdeen Museums; 63 photograph courtesy of the City Art Gallery, Edinburgh; 50 photograph courtesy of Bonhams; 30, 70 Photo © The Fine Art Society, London, UK; 61 © The Fine Art Society, London, UK / The Bridgeman Art Library; 62 photography Prudence Cumming Associates Ltd; 53, 59, 60, 67, 102 photography courtesy Duncan R. Miller Fine Arts, London; 54 photography courtesy of Christies; 45 courtesy Alexander Meddowes Fine Art Broker, Edinburgh; 48 © Anne Estelle Rice; 103 photography by Marcus Leith; 100 © Tate, London 2013; 89 © Estate of John Duncan. All rights reserved, DACS 2013; 78 © 2013 The Barnes Foundation; 79 Photo © Lefevre Fine Art Ltd., London / The Bridgeman Art Library; 86 © Estate of the Artist.